H.M.S.
RICHARDS

H.M.S.
RICHARDS

ROBERT E. EDWARDS

REVIEW AND HERALD® PUBLISHING ASSOCIATION
HAGERSTOWN, MD 21740

This book was
Edited by Gerald Wheeler
Designed by Willie Duke
Cover photo supplied by Voice of Prophecy
Typeset: 12/15 Bembo

PRINTED IN U.S.A.

02 01 00 99 98   5 4 3 2 1

R&H Cataloging Service
Edwards, Robert Elden, 1924-
    H.M.S. Richards.

    1. Richards, Harold Marshall Sylvester, 1894-1985.   I. Title.

        922.6   [92]   [B]

To order additional copies of H.M.S. Richards, call **1-800-765-6955.**
Visit our Web site at http://www.rhpa.org for information on other Review
and Herald products.

ISBN 0-8280-1332-2

CONTENTS

THE CHIEF

I have often heard H.M.S. Richards say—
and I think he was quoting Gladstone—"We
are an omnibus in which all our ancestors ride."

Richards was the unique product of the
gene pool of generations of ancestors. I have
known some great preachers and some accomplished poets, men with great command of the
English language, men with a marvelous sense
of humor, men with keen memories, men with
a grasp of the importance and drama of history,
men with the great gift of telling stories, and
men with sincere and unalloyed dedication to
God, but only in H.M.S. Richards have I found
all these gifts wrapped up in one package.

Oops! When I began to write this story of
the life of H.M.S. Richards, I determined that it
would be objective—that it wouldn't be just another book of hero worship. In fact, when I
wrote this chapter, I hadn't begun the main
body of the book yet. In place of this paragraph
I wrote, "But don't worry, this will not be a
book of cloying hero worship." Now that I've
almost completed the story of his life and re-
read this chapter, I can see that I failed. Why?

Because as I look back on it, I can see that he was a hero to me. He was a role model.

Oh, it's true I knew him on a day-to-day basis. He and I ate together. We traveled together, sometimes for days on end, 16 hours a day with six men in a car. You don't live that closely without seeing the clay as well as the stars. Sometimes when it was late and he was tired, he'd slump down in the right front seat of the car (that was always his special place to sit), pull a scarf up over his head, and grumble because the last five motels we had tried all had "No Vacancy" signs lit up in bright orange neon. But in spite of all that, he was still my hero—our hero—the hero of all the men and women who worked with him.

The first time I remember seeing him I was a freshman at Union College. It was October 19, 1942, and the Voice of Prophecy had only been on a coast-to-coast network for a few months. H.M.S. Richards, Fordyce Detamore, and the quartet came to the college from Denver by train. (In those days during the war it was almost impossible to get gasoline ration tickets or tires for traveling by car.) They had been on a tour of the country, and we were fortunate enough to be one of their itinerary stops.

Jerry Pettis, my Bible doctrines teacher (and later a U.S. congressman) introduced the Voice of Prophecy team to a packed church in the evening, and the next day they put on our chapel program. How I loved listening to the quartet. The voice of George Casebeer (who sang my quartet part) with his lyric first tenor especially attracted me. The first seeds of longing to sing in that quartet began to germinate in my heart that day.

I had a great interest in history, and that morning when H.M.S. Richards filled his sermon with stories about Moses and Hatshepsut, the queen whom some believe to be his Egyptian foster mother, I was hooked.

I would encounter them again a couple years later at Emmanuel Missionary College (now Andrews University), this time with Ben Glanzer singing first tenor in the quartet. I thought to myself then (sorry, Ben), "Hey, I can sing first tenor as good as that guy." But my next real thrill in seeing H.M.S. Richards and the quartet was when I was a young minister in Florida.

I was a 22-year-old singing evangelist in the Florida conference, and we were all looking forward to the visit of the Voice of Prophecy at our camp meeting. It was Friday afternoon, and I had started out for Apopka to get some groceries and supplies to carry us over Sabbath when I saw a big black Cadillac limousine drive by going east. I recognized Richards with five other men crowded into the car, some of whom I guessed to be the King's Heralds quartet. Quickly flipping a U-turn, I followed them back to the campground.

Sabbath morning Richards preached on "Four Reasons Never to Be Worried." (It was a sermon I would enjoy hearing again and again in succeeding years, though I didn't know that at the time.) The place was packed. That afternoon he assisted in the ordination of young pastors Bob Spangler and Bill Hatch. At the afternoon youth meeting he preached on the vision of Isaiah 6, then left the campground for a couple hours of rest. And, of course, we all were amused when Wayne Hooper blew the pitchpipe for one of their songs, and two of the quartet started on one song while the other two started another.

I was thankful the quartet stayed at the campground. After I had hounded their steps all that weekend they finally let me sing a song with them. I had heard that two of the members were leaving the quartet, and that they were looking for a first tenor.

On Sunday morning I was right there on their heels again when they put on their regular Sunday morning broadcast from the steaming radio studio of station WLOH in Orlando.

They must have thought I was a pestiferous brat, but it paid off. Later that summer I received an invitation to audition for the first tenor spot in the quartet. When they got me there, they couldn't get rid of me. I stayed until I retired 44 years later.

I cherish my years with H.M.S. Richards. He became a second father to me, as well as to the other men who sang in the quartet through the years. Richards knew our weaknesses, yet he loved us all just the same. I don't think he ever had favorites, though I know he had a special affection for Bob Seamount and Ray Turner. And he never took sides in the personality battles that inevitably crop up when people live together side by side hours and days and weeks at a time.

In the car on the road every summer he had his own little nest with his box of books and sometimes with a food sack (we each had what we called a "crud sack" from which we snacked when we had to travel long distances and didn't have time to stop for meals). During those tedious hours in the car together he would often share with us some choice passage from the latest book he was reading. I can still see him pushing his glasses up and pulling the book close to his good right eye as he would read aloud some poem or a verse from the Bible.

We heard some of his sermons hundreds of times, yet none of us were ever bored, because none of them were ever exactly the same. It would always have something fresh injected into it from his reading in the car that day.

Often he would quote us poetry he had memorized as a boy. One of his favorites (and mine) was *The Rubaiyat* by Omar Khayyam. At some time in his early life he had learned all 101 stanzas of Edward Fitzgerald's translation. As we rolled along Highway 66 he would begin:

"The Moving Finger writes; and, having writ,
Moves on: nor all your Piety nor Wit
Shall lure it back to cancel half a Line,
Nor all your Tears wash out a Word of it."

Or it might be the lines:

"Into this Universe, and Why not knowing,
Nor Whence, like Water willy-nilly flowing;

And out of it, as Wind along the Waste,
  I know not Whither, willy-nilly blowing."

Or if he was in a romantic mood it might bring forth these lines:

"A Book of Verses underneath the Bough,
  A Jug of Wine, a Loaf of Bread—and Thou
Beside me singing in the Wilderness—
  Oh, Wilderness were Paradise enow!"

He would always end that stanza with a chuckle, no doubt thinking of his wife Mabel whom he hadn't seen for weeks, and wouldn't see for yet still more weeks.

His love and taste for poetry gave great strength and rhythmic balance to even the prose of his sermons. And right in the midst of his poetic prose, some poignant stanza lurking in the darkness of his subconscious would come bubbling out at just the right time.

This book is about him—"the Chief," that's what we called him. We will never forget him, and I hope his story will cause you to cherish his memory and never forget either.

"I BEGAN TO HATE THAT MAN"

A biography always begins with a history of the family—where the family started out, and how they contributed to the life of the individual and what he or she became. But in this story I want to let H.M.S. Richards tell about something that happened to him in early life that could have driven him from the ministry. But it didn't. The episode forged for him a special suit of armor that would protect him in future battles with both the devil and with good human beings.

I have often heard him say "You'll never do any great work without having to fight against the arguments of good men."

Young Harold Marshall Sylvester Richards was a senior in college. Someone—a high officer in the Columbia Union—did something that hurt his mother's feelings. But let him tell it in his own words, as nearly as I can remember.

"It was the fall of 1918. I would be graduating in the spring. Father was president of the East Pennsylvania Conference, and mother was educational superintendent and headed up several other departments.

"The president of that union was Elder B. G.

13

Wilkinson, one of the few men with a Ph.D. degree—maybe the only one—we had at that time. A highly educated man, he was supremely talented and gifted.

"I'm not going into the rightness or wrongness of the thing, but my parents felt and others felt and I felt that he had wronged my parents, especially my mother. You know, a man can stand a lot, but when a man—especially a young man— thinks his mother has been hurt, it's almost more than he can endure.

"That thing grew and grew in me. I'd had disappointments and sorrows before, but I'd never known what hatred was. It was just like a poison in me. Every time I would hear of this man or see him, this thing would grow up in me. I got to the place where it was killing my life, spiritually and in every other way. The more I thought about it, the angrier I became. You know hatred is a terrible thing. It's like a cancer and it is corrosive.

"Right at the crisis of this thing, when I couldn't stand the thoughts of this man and didn't even want to be near him, I heard he was coming to hold a revival at the church within a block of where I lived with 'Twomoms.' [Twomoms was his maternal grandmother. More about her later.]

"I was a senior in college, and about that time I found out the conference was going to ordain me. It doesn't happen like that often, but I'd held meetings and built up churches, and brought people to the Lord.

"Well, the thing grew on me as I sat in my little upper room where I studied. I realized I couldn't permit myself to be ordained with that in my heart. It would ruin my ministry and destroy my life. For a man with that feeling in his heart to be ordained would be like a death sentence to him.

"I realized that the man I hated would be putting his hands on my head in ordaining me to the ministry. God helped me as I fought this thing out for several days. Finally He gave me a complete victory over it, for which I praise His name.

"I went to that revival meeting where he was in charge—this man, the only person in all my life I have ever hated. At the close he made a call and I went forward in that call. I came up to him and took his hand and told him the whole story. I explained how I'd begun to hate him, but that God had given me the victory, and I wanted him to forgive me for my evil thoughts.

"You know, he broke down and began to weep himself. He told me he was sure he had done some things that had caused my pain. We forgave each other, and got our tears all mixed up together that day.

14

"We became special friends, special friends. I would always try to see him whenever he was nearby and go to hear him preach. I never have appreciated anyone preaching more than he. His command of English was absolutely superb.

"Many years later, just before he died, he was in a rest home on the edge of Washington, D.C. During one of my trips east I asked someone how he was and said I wanted to see him. 'Oh,' the other person said, 'he wouldn't know you at all. There's no use for you to go out there.'

"His wife had died and he was alone. Slipping physically, he was in very bad condition.

"I said, 'I want to see him anyway,' so I went out there and entered a room filled with old men. Everybody loves dear old grandma and other old women, but old men have a special place of need. If there's no mother or wife to look after them, we must pity them above all.

"There he sat on a straight chair, his eyes closed, barely breathing, almost dead, it seemed. He appeared to be aware of nothing.

"Finding a chair, I sat down by his side. Taking his hand in mine, I began to talk to his hand. I said, 'There's the hand that was laid on my head in ordination. When I was ordained that hand was on my head.'

"I continued to talk about his hand, where it had been, how it had been upraised in preaching the gospel. I spoke quite a while to his hand, about his hand. Suddenly his eyes opened and he saw me. 'Why, brother Richards,' he said, 'where did you come from?' He knew me, and we had a wonderful talk and a prayer together.

"Finally I kissed him goodbye, and he closed his eyes and resumed just like he had been before. He died a few days later without knowing anyone, but he knew me. I loved him and I love his memory still."

Often in his diary Richards would mention his friend B. G. Wilkinson. Once they were on the same campground together soon after the publication of B. G.'s book, *Truth Triumphant*. H.M.S. gave that book such a hearty promotion that the people swamped the camp meeting bookstand with requests. It sold more than 100 copies that night, and when the bookstand ran out of stock, it had to back order many more for others who were disappointed.

He settled his problems with B. G. as Jesus suggested that we should settle all differences between brothers and sisters in the faith. On the evening of September 21, 1918, B. G. Wilkinson was one of the elders of the church who laid his hands lovingly on the head of young H.M.S. Richards as the church set him aside by ordination to the ministry of the gospel.

The experience gave H.M.S. Richards a healthy balance between respect for people in duly constituted positions of authority, and a recognition that they were human beings, capable of errors of judgment and sometimes even of behavior. It was a lesson he often would have occasion to remember.

During various Voice of Prophecy crises H.M.S. Richards would in future years sometimes find himself in strong opposition to good, powerful leaders. Some of their decisions would cause him great sorrow and consternation, but even though he thought their decisions wrong, he never carried personal grudges, and he tried to make the best of what he thought was a mistaken decision. And he sometimes found that the "mistakes" of leaders have a happy ending.

ROOTS

Every young person at some time in his or her life has an interest in his or her roots. Richards often told about the time his father took him to the old Trinity Methodist church in Denver to hear Bishop Quayle. Quayle described how when he had been a boy he read in a magazine that if he sent in $10 they would check into his family tree and find out if he had descended from royalty.

The lad scrimped and saved, mowed lawns, and did special chores to earn money until he finally had saved up $10. Eagerly he sent it off to the address in the magazine ad.

Every day he checked the mailbox to see if anything had come. At last the time arrived when he found a fat letter in the box.

Opening it up, he discovered that the genealogical people had traced Quayle back until they encountered some lords and ladies, some barons and viscounts and earls, and were just about to get into some real royalty when they ran out of money. Now they suggested that if he would send another $10 they might get him even closer to the throne.

Excited when he read that, he worked hard

17

again, mowed more lawns and did more chores for his parents—any odd job he could find to earn that $10. Finally he sent the letter off and waited eagerly for the response.

Sure enough, when the next letter came, they had traced his ancestry back to marquesses and dukes. It was just a step now from the royal family. But when they encountered a nest of smugglers off the coast of Cornwall, he decided to give up the quest.

Richards always ended his recounting of Quayle's experience by saying, "I may have descended from some men who swung by their necks from telephone poles, but I know I don't have any ancestors who swung by their tails from coconut trees." (He always told the story in his sermon on evolution.)

Richards was interested enough in his family ancestry to search out the family coat of arms. The Richards' family coat of arms consisted of a white dog, brown castle, red and white crest, green emblem with white band, gold sheaves, and the motto *"Veleo et vigeo"* in gold scrollwork with a slate gray overall background.

The name "Richards" was a common one in the Middle Ages, especially in Wales, Cornwall, and Devonshire. It comes from the Old English "ric" for ruler, and "heard" for hard, thus ric-heard, or hard ruler.

Several theories have attempted to explain the popularity of the name "Richard." Some think King Richard the Lion Hearted inspired fathers all over the realm to name their little sons Richard. Others attribute its popularity to Richard, son of Hloohere, king of Kent, in the seventh century who later became a monk at Lucca. When the letter "s" was added to Richard, it signified that its holder was a "son of Richard."

Or perhaps the Richards family descended from Richard, Earl of Cornwall, born January 6, 1209, and died April 2, 1272. He was the second son of King John.

But let's allow H.M.S. Richards to tell us a little about his family tree in his own words:

"My family comes from the west country, Wales and Cornwall. Richards is a

Welsh name. Cornwall used to be called West Wales. The last person that spoke the Cornish language died in 1798. My father's father was born in Redruth, Cornwall, right down in the tin mine country of Cornwall. Cornwall is the extreme western point of southwestern England.

"We are not Anglo-Saxon but Celtic, the ancient Briton stock who were in the British Isles before the Anglo-Saxons came in. It's the same with the Irish and the Scots. After you cross the River Tamar from Devonshire into Cornwall, you go into a different country.

"When the Romans entered England they pushed the Britons back into the western mountains of Wales and Cornwall and the Scots north into Scotland. And they built the great wall across the north to keep the Scots back.

"Then the Anglo-Saxons came in to help Christianize Britain in the raids of A.D. 490—they were savage. [The name Saxon, according to Winston Churchill, derives from the weapon they used, the seax, a short one-handed sword.]

"When I was in England I went down and looked at those old cemeteries and found the name Richards on the headstones again and again. I went to the church in Redruth and found a church book there that dates back to the thirteenth century. There's the name of our family there.

"My father, however, was born in America. His father, William Jenkin Richards, came over here, went to Wisconsin, and sent for his sweetheart, my grandmother. They were married the day she arrived from England.

"My father, Halbert, was born in Mineral Point, Wisconsin, on May 5, 1869. When he was seven years old they took him back to England, but my father always considered America his country."

The Richards first settled in Redruth, Cornwall, their former home, but later moved to Grantham, Lincolnshire, where he went to school in the same room where Isaac Newton had attended.

Because Halbert Richards' health was poor, the family moved to a better climate in the city of Exeter in Devonshire. There his father, William Jenkin Richards, was a lay preacher in the Methodist church. During his growing up years there, even though Halbert was only 15 or 16 years old, his father would send him out to preach in little churches nearby.

H.M.S. remembers hearing his grandfather Richards preach. The man was not an orator nor a great scholar. He didn't have a big library but depended on his Bible as the primary source of his preaching. In his interviews with H.M.S. for his doctoral thesis, Wilbur Alexander records the grandson's evaluation of Grandfather Richards' preaching.

"Every man preaches himself to a great degree. He preaches the Word as reflected through himself. Grandfather's earnestness impressed me because of his total commitment to preaching. I knew that my grandfather could have made a lot of money either as an artist or a jeweler, but he thought the gospel message should go to all the world, and he gave his entire life to preaching in little parishes which other men refused to take. Many times he nearly starved because he refused to hold church socials and suppers to augment his small salary. Instead he worked with his hands to support his family. He was absolutely honest and sincere. I could no more think of my grandfather being dishonest than I could think of the moon falling down to the earth. Each time he entered the pulpit he carried with him the conviction and earnestness he had developed in daily devotion to God."

While living in Exeter, Halbert Marshall Jenkin Richards as a boy witnessed an event that shook not only Exeter, but all of England.

A young man apparently named John Lee was accused and convicted of murder. Though he persistently maintained his innocence, he was sentenced to hang.

The night before his execution, young John Lee had a dream. In the dream he saw himself in the prison on the fateful morning being led out of his cell and down a corridor, then making a turn to the right before reaching to the gallows. In the dream John Lee walked up the 13 steps. A guard blindfolded him and placed the noose around his neck. After Lee received permission to say his last words, the executioner pulled the lever to spring the trap, but nothing happened. Then John Lee woke up.

The day John Lee was to be hanged, young Halbert and his

friends, along with most of the populace of Exeter, circled the prison, watching for the flag to be hoisted from inside to signal that the condemned had met his end. They waited and waited, but the flag never appeared.

Inside the prison that morning John Lee had awakened and everything happened just as he had seen it in his dream. Led from his cell down a long corridor, he made a turn to the right before coming to the place of execution. John Lee walked up the 13 steps, was blindfolded, the noose placed around his neck, and the lever pulled that would send him into eternity. But just as he had seen in the dream the trapdoor refused to open.

After taking John Lee off the scaffold, the guards checked and oiled the machinery. Everything seemed to be in perfect order. They put a sack of sand on the trapdoor and pulled the lever. The sand went hurtling down to the pavement below.

Again they positioned John Lee over the trap, adjusted his blindfold, and slipped the noose over his head. Once more the executioner pulled the lever, but still nothing happened.

A second time the guards led John Lee down the steps while they tested the scaffold, and again they positioned him on the trapdoor. A third time the executioner pulled the lever, but a third time the trapdoor refused to send John Lee to his death.

Visibly shaken, the prison authorities sent a wire to Queen Victoria, asking her what they should do. She responded that since they had tried three times, they should commute his sentence to life imprisonment.

Years later someone else confessed to the crime for which John Lee had been condemned, and the law set him free.

But let's let H.M.S. Richards continue with the story of his father in Exeter.

"My father had tuberculosis as a boy. He was about to die. 'If I can go back to my country,' he thought, 'I think I can be well.'

"Seventh-day Adventist Elders J. H. Durland and Sands H. Lane came to

the city of Exeter in Devonshire just to try out a few meetings in a hall. No one had ever preached the Adventist message in Exeter. [Lane had accepted a call in 1885 to hold meetings in England.] The first subject they advertised was 'Where Are the Dead?' My father was thinking a lot about that. Sixteen years old, he faced death from TB. He saw that sign in the window in Mol's coffee shop on the south side of High Street in Exeter.

"He said to his father, 'Father I want to go and hear that.'

" 'Aren't you afraid to go out at night, son?'

" 'No, I want to hear that.' So they wrapped him up and let him go. He was convinced that what he heard was the truth, including the Sabbath as well as the condition of a person in death. The two American evangelists only stayed there a few nights, but my father, a Salvation Army Captain, and an old woman accepted the message they heard—the three of them.

"His father tried to convince him that Sunday was the true Sabbath. He was a lay preacher in the Methodist church, but when he realized that his son was determined, he said, 'If that's what you believe, I will help you keep it the best I can. I won't stand between you and God.'

"My father was so ill the doctor told his father he couldn't live. But my dear old grandfather, a very godly man, went in alone and prayed for my father, and he seemed to get a little better after that.

"Now father wanted to return to America. He just knew he'd be better if he could go back to his home country. Since he was 17, they let him come alone. He arrived in New York on Sunday, July 4, 1886, and because it was a holiday, they wouldn't let him go through customs. So he had to wait till the next day.

"When he finally was processed through customs, he had only 35 cents in his pocket and a train ticket out to Milwaukee where he had a few relatives.

"My father had learned the jewelry trade in England, and when he reached Wisconsin he started to mend watches. I have one of his original cards he handed out from door to door. He kept the Sabbath faithfully and became the head of a little group of believers there in Wisconsin, but he couldn't secure enough work to really support him.

"Then he went to Atlantic, Iowa, where an uncle had a jewelry shop. When he arrived there, he became the watchman in the shop. One morning—I think it was his very first night in town—he woke up and noticed a big commotion across *the street from the jewelry shop. It was an Adventist tent going up, and Elders Hankins and Willoughby held meetings there. How delighted he was to once again be in the company with fellow believers in his own faith. From the fruits of that tent meeting a little company started, and my father was appointed their leader, even though neither he himself or any of them had been baptized."*

It was early spring and still extremely cold when ministers came to baptize them. Even though he was desperately sick with the flu, young Halbert decided he must be baptized. He still suffered from what they called consumption, now known as tuberculosis. They advised him to wait until later in the spring, warning him that he might die if he was baptized in that cold water, but he would not be dissuaded. They broke the ice in Troublesome Creek near Atlantic, Iowa, and Halbert M. J. Richards was baptized in that icy stream. Ever afterward he testified that when he came up out of the water, he was healed. Perhaps he was.

The young man continued as leader of the little group of 34 believers in Atlantic for a time, then the local conference sent him to Ottumwa, Iowa, to work as a colporteur. He continued his jeweler trade part-time in order to raise enough money to bring his parents back to the United States.

Soon the conference leadership asked Halbert to assist Elder J. S. Washburn in a series of meetings in Davis City, Iowa. Washburn decided to play matchmaker to the watchmaker preacher, and sent his young assistant to check in with the local elder of the Adventist company of believers in Davis City.

When Halbert knocked on the door, he met a young woman who, when he saw her, took his breath away. He testified ever after that it was love from the very first moment.

Berta Captolia Sylvester was the daughter of Jasper Newton Sylvester, town blacksmith. Not only beautiful, but smart and talented, she taught public school in Iowa for seven years and served as the organist in several of the local churches in town.

Perhaps in a conspiracy between J. S. Washburn and Halbert M. J.

Richards, Berta Sylvester was asked to be the pianist and organist for the evangelistic meetings.

One afternoon as they were planning the music for the evening meeting, Halbert persuaded Bertie to come up on the platform, and there he proposed marriage. She didn't play coy and ask for time to think about it, but accepted his proposal on the spot. He was a handsome young man, serious and sensible, and she liked what she saw. Sensing, however, that as the people became aware of the flourishing romance it would disrupt the meetings, she resigned as its organist.

The next spring, May 17, 1893, Bertie and Halbert were married. Their marriage would last 63 years. From it a baby would be born who would some day become a familiar name to the ears of millions of Seventh-day Adventists.

"HIS MASTER'S SERVANT"

Late in the summer of 1894 a perspiring young man, dressed in black, coattails flying, flagged the eastbound freight.

"What do you mean, young man, by stopping this train? We don't take passengers," an irate brakeman growled.

"I know, sir, but I've just received word that my wife has given birth to my firstborn son in Davis City, and I would be most grateful for a ride."

The stern expression melted into an understanding smile. "Hop on board, parson. My guess is you're a preacher, and this time the ride is our treat."

Bertie had gone out with her new husband to hold evangelistic meetings in Iowa right after their wedding, and had been with Halbert until just about the last minute. "I grew up with the smell of canvas in my nostrils," Richards often said. "I came almost being born in a tent. My mother just got home in time."

A few hours after boarding the freight, the anxious young father swung down from the caboose, waved at the sympathetic brakeman and

25

engineer, and headed down the country road toward home.

"He shall be the Lord's baby boy," he said after he had put his hands on the tiny head. The life of Harold Marshall Sylvester Richards was launched.

In his growing up and adult years he must have been often ribbed about those high-sounding initials. "What's that 'H.M.S.' stand for, boy? His majesty's ship? Did your dad hit you over the head with a champaign bottle at the christening?" But as an adult he always preferred to say his initials meant "His Master's Servant."

The words spoken in dedication by his father on first seeing his little son, and the words his mother uttered in an agony of anxiety two years later, had a profound impact on young Harold as he grew up.

At age 2 he crawled out of the house while both mother and grandmother were busy, and busied himself under the apple tree in the backyard. Only a mother knows how far little legs can carry a baby in an incredibly short time. By the time the women finally discovered his hiding place he had consumed a large quantity of green apples.

The doctor didn't think the little boy would live, but mother prayed. "Lord, if you heal my baby, I'll give him to you. He'll be your boy in a very special way."

All during his growing up years his parents reminded him of his father's prayer of dedication and his mother's anguished petition for healing. "The knowledge of that was a great deterrent to me when I was going over 'fool's hill,'" he said. He urged parents to protect their sons and daughters, not only by prayer, but by reminding their children of their prayers.

As an infant Harold went along with his parents to the tent meetings. "From the time I was born until I was ordained, there was never a summer when I didn't smell canvas," Richards said. "I was in a tent as far back as I can remember."

In *Man Alive,* Virginia Richards-Cason's book about her father, she captured the essence of young Harold's life during his first two years.

"In the years following his birth, Dad often accompanied his parents on their many evangelistic crusades. Grandmother told me how she used to lay pillows and blankets in a box, which she put on the saw-dust floor next to the organ. She would put the little fellow to bed in the box, play the hymns for the service, then take the box and slip out of the tent during the sermon. She would go into the family's little living tent, which was pitched beside the big one, and put her baby to bed for the night. All the while she would listen through the canvas as Grandfather preached. When he neared the end of his sermon she would come quietly back into the larger tent to play the closing song.

"When Dad got too big to be cared for so easily, he was left with his grandparents in Davis City. By this time he had a little brother, Kenneth, who was getting used to the same bed-in-a-box upbringing."

Young Harold had a loving mother and father, but was also blessed to be living in the same town as his mother's parents.

In between tent meetings Halbert and Bertie would move in with Bertie's parents in Davis City. It was during one such interim that Grandmother and Grandfather Sylvester acquired the unique handles, "Twopops" and "Twomoms."

A little visiting neighbor girl noticed that Harold and his brother Kenneth had two women and two men who seemed to have equal authority over the boys. In bewilderment she pointed to the two women and said, "You have one mama and two mamas." Then turning to the men, "and one papa and two papas." From that time on, Grandfather and Grandmother Sylvester were "Twopops" and "Twomoms."

When Richards turned 43 years old, "Twomoms" wrote him a letter filled with her memories of that summer day when he was born.

"To the little boy that came to us when they were playing base-ball over in the meadow.

"Twomoms' own precious baby boy. Now Twomoms is looking back. What is it, 43 years, to a lovely comfortable home with big roomy rooms, plenty of them? And a big bay window to the south of the stairs in Twomoms' and Twopops' room. And a lovely young mama (to be) oh, so sick on Twopops' and Twomoms' bed. Of course, whenever she was so very sick she had to be on poppy's and mommy's bed.

"There was a big north window, and a west one, but the big bay window was to the south. All of them were open that hot August day. Aunt Jule, Dr. Stella Norman's mother was there, and Dr. Horner. And some boys were playing baseball right over in the meadow south. Anyone could see them plain. And hear them from our window.

"But Twomoms could not see them, or hear them until there was a little cry, and Dr. Horner said, 'We have a baseball player.' Then Twomoms could hear that and could see through her tears. And the lovely and loved baby's mama lay so still and white.

"But Aunt Jule and Twomoms went downstairs with that little bundle. We had a fire and warm water. Aunt Jule turned back the wrappings and put the little bare body by the stove, Twomoms hovering over it. And Aunt Jule said, 'Ha ha. The water works are all right.'

"It's all as plain to me today as if it was yesterday.

"Twomoms has always said you were born in my bed and in my arms and have never been out of my arms and my heart.

"That was a beautiful home and how joyful Twopops did look when he came to the house and found that little baby boy that filled his heart to overflowing always. And when you cried with the tummy ache, my, how Twopops would scold us. 'Can't you do something for that baby?' Then he would get up any time of the night and walk the floor with you held up close to him, to help your tummy ache feel better. Something he never did with his own babies. And his love never lessened as you grew out of the wee babyhood.

"I will leave you to guess if it has lessened with the years with Twomoms. If you think it has, you are very much mistaken. Granny loves her baby dis the same, only more."

Once Harold went with Twopops to St. Joseph, Missouri. While there young Harold preached his first sermon. Wilbur Alexander tells about it in his doctoral thesis on H.M.S. Richards.

"Richards remembers preaching his first sermon at the age of four. He had been taken to St. Joseph, Missouri, to attend the funeral of his great-grandmother Sylvester. In the living room of the family home he noticed a large bowl of oranges. When he was not invited to help himself, he began to talk most earnestly about the New Jerusalem, how wonderful it was, the great tree there that had all that fruit on it, and how it had 'oringins' and 'oringins' on it all the time. The sermon was highly successful, as measured by results, for the boy preacher was given all the oranges."

During the boy's growing-up-years his grandfather Newton Sylvester probably had more influence on him than even his own father did because Halbert was gone so much of the time.

"Newt" Sylvester was a blacksmith. On his father's side, H.M.S. was English, but his mother's family was 100 percent American. Joseph Sylvester, Newton's own grandfather, had fought under George Washington from the siege of Boston to the surrender of Cornwallis at Yorktown. Harold was the son Newt never had, and he treated the boy as he would have his own son. Twopops was young Harold's hero. Though he cherished his English heritage, Richards' early bonding with Newt Sylvester created in the young boy a fierce patriotism for his own birth country. Years later he would remember and cherish the memories he and Twopops had together.

"My grandfather was in the Pikes Peak gold rush of 1861. He rode in a wagon train across the plains and fought with the Indians. Then he went to the big gold rush in Virginia City, Montana.

"When he returned to Iowa he was about 30 years old. He was a handsome man. His hair turned grey when he was 20. Six foot one inches tall, he was a crack shot with a six-shooter. When grandmother wanted to cook a chicken, Twopops would ask her to choose which chicken in the flock she wanted. Instead of wringing the neck, he would take his revolver and shoot the head off of the chicken she wanted.

"My grandmother was only 17, a little bit of a thing when they first met. He fell for her. Taking her to dances, she'd ride on a horse, and he'd walk alongside and hold her feet to keep them warm. It was 30 degrees below zero.

"All my grandmothers and great-grandmothers could stand under their husbands' arms. My great-grandmother was so fiery she'd slap her husband's face, but she'd have to go get a stool, and he'd wait for her to come so she could slap him.

"When Grandfather Sylvester first went west, he got as far as the Missouri River. It was flooded and he couldn't get across. So he stayed there and set up a blacksmith shop in Davis City, Iowa.

"A Methodist preacher arrived in town and people attended his meetings. Someone came to my grandfather and said, 'Newt Sylvester, don't you know why the young men of this city won't go forward in these meetings?'

" 'Why?'

" ''Cause they worship you. If you'd go forward all the young men in town would follow you. They're watching to see what Newt Sylvester does.'

" 'Well,' he said, 'if I'm responsible for the morals of this town, maybe I ought to go forward.'

"And he did. Sure enough, when Newt Sylvester went up to the front, all the young men came parading behind.

"Later a young Adventist preacher pitched a tent. He was 21 years old. The town had just one church, a union church. My mother played the organ.

"A Mormon challenged the Adventist preacher to a debate. When the debate concluded, the young Adventist said, 'How many of you believe what I've preached is the truth?'

"The whole town stood up—everyone.

" 'Now how many of you are going to obey it?' Only two people responded— my grandfather and grandmother."

After he had been working in the Iowa conference as a lay preacher for several years, the leadership ordained Halbert Richards to the gospel ministry on May 30, 1897. His conference president, Elder Morrison, encouraged him to attend a school of evangelism in Battle Creek, Michigan, where his instructors would be A. T. Jones, E. J. Waggoner, Uriah Smith, W. W. Prescott, and Mrs. Ellen G. White. The Iowa Conference had not paid Richards anything for his work as a lay evangelist helper, but gave him $50 with which to attend the Battle Creek school.

It was there that Halbert Richards learned the great doctrine of the 1888 spiritual awakening, righteousness by faith. He testified later that sometimes a revival would break out during classes at

Battle Creek, and the young men and women would begin a prayer meeting that would last long after the class period was supposed to be over.

Harold Marshall Sylvester Richards was about 4 years old when the family moved to Battle Creek, Michigan. Twomoms had become sick, and the family wanted Dr. John Harvey Kellogg to operate on an abscess on her hip. The only anesthetic Dr. Kellogg used was a few swallows of hard liquor and a turkish towel for Twomoms to chew on during the cutting. She was a tough little Scot-Irish woman. When she recovered, the Battle Creek Sanitarium put her in charge of its sewing room.

While the rest of the family was in Battle Creek, Newt Sylvester found himself caught up in the Klondike and Alaska gold rush fever.

In August of 1896 George Washington Carmack, an American prospector, and two Indian friends had made a rich find of gold on Rabbit Creek in the Yukon. The news didn't reach the outside world until the following July, but when it broke, thousands of men from all over the world raced to the Klondike to get rich.

The people of Davis City got up a grubstake for Newt Sylvester and Lon Bullock, another young man from town. Newt packed up a portable blacksmith forge, and he and Lon headed for Skagway with the other gold seekers, enduring the agony as they packed over the White and Chilkoot passes.

The letters that came from Alaska to Battle Creek, some of them water-stained from falling through the ice in the frozen Yukon River and being fished out, were exciting grist for the minds of two little boys who idolized their Twopops. They would set up chairs in the living room and pretend they were dog sleds. The boys called their game "Twopops out on the trail."

Life was hard in the Klondike. The two men lived in a little tent pitched inside a bigger tent, but things got so tough that Lon Bullock finally couldn't take it anymore and went back home to Davis City. Newt stuck it out, making more money shoeing horses at $10 apiece than he did finding gold. He would hammer horseshoes out of gun barrels the men brought to him. He even made the tools to pull his own teeth.

Newt went on from the Klondike to Alaska when someone discovered gold at Nome, but finally returned to Davis City. For years afterward people would remember the tall blacksmith who would hand out religious tracts up in the Alaska gold-rush country.

In Battle Creek the two boys, Harold and Kenneth, when they tired of playing "Twopops on the trail," would pretend to preach. Harold would always end up the preacher and 2-year-old Kenneth, the audience. Harold's mother remembered one sermon that always seemed to capture their imagination—the story of the raising of Lazarus. Four-year-old Harold would tell how "Jesus came and found Lavruth in a deep hole with a big rock over him, so He shouted with a loud voice, 'Lavruth come forth,' and Lavruth, he comed."

The family thought young Harold was old enough to start kindergarten when he was about 5 years old. His doting Twopops and Twomoms had already taught him to read, but his first terrifying day soured him on kindergarten or school for several years thereafter.

He had been left alone in a big empty room. It may have been only a moment before the teacher arrived, but to the frightened little boy it seemed like an eternity. All around him in that cavernous empty room were imagined dangers—a forbidding stairway in one corner that seemed to lead down into a dark spooky basement. He was sure lions and snakes and other hungry creatures lurked down in that dark hole, just waiting for some little boy to come within striking distance. It may have been that chilling experience, as well as his mother's fear that school would only incite him to read more than he should, that then impelled her to hold him back from school until he was 8 years old.

Because of his persistent trouble with his old respiratory problem, Halbert Richards moved his family to Denver, Colorado, in 1899 when Harold was 5 years old. It was in Colorado that young Harold's real education would begin, and to Richards, Colorado was home the rest of his life.

H.M.S. RICHARDS AND ELLEN G. WHITE

Every time he would drive, fly, or travel by train over or through Colorado, H.M.S. Richards would become nostalgic at the sight of Pike's Peak and Long's Peak and the majestic Rocky Mountain range visible from Denver and cities up and down the range line.

H.M.J. Richards, because he was having recurring respiratory trouble, transferred to Denver, Colorado, when Harold and Kenneth were 5 and 3 years old. Though he was too young to remember it, an event that happened early in his father's Denver ministry shaped his entire life. Let him tell the story as he no doubt heard it recounted dozens of times by his Father, and as I have heard it told by him.

"H.M.J. Richards, my father, was just a young man when he became pastor of the West Denver church. One Sabbath morning, just as he was ready to start to preach, the door opened and in came Ellen White, her son Willie, and Sarah MacInterfer, her companion and nurse. Immediately, father asked Mrs. White up to the platform to preach.

"She said, 'Elder Richards, did you plan to preach today?'

" 'Why, yes.'

" 'Did you pray for God to give you a subject?'

" 'Yes.'

" 'Do you think He answered your prayer?'

" 'Yes.'

" 'Did you study it?'

" 'Oh, yes.'

" 'Why,' she said, 'I wouldn't think of preaching today. If the Lord has given you a sermon, I want to hear it.'

"She sat on the platform and made him preach.

"When he finished she took him aside and told him that she had been blessed by his message. But then she continued and said, 'If you keep talking the way you use your voice, the way you strain your voice, you'll die young.' Then she gave him instruction on how to speak, how to breathe as a public speaker. People nearby wanted to talk to her, but she gave him a 15-minute voice lesson.

"Later he said, 'In those 15 minutes, I learned more about how to speak, how to breathe, than I did in all my courses in preaching in Battle Creek College.'

"She was kind in helping young preachers that way. When he was 87 years old, people still loved to hear him speak. He had such a gentle sweet voice, because he had followed the principles she'd taught him. She told him how to breathe from his abdomen.

"That day while she was there, he asked her, 'Sr. White, how should I use your writings in my preaching?'

" 'When you are preparing a sermon,' she replied, 'pray that the Lord will give you the subject the people need. Then study that subject from the Bible. Read everything the Bible has to say about it. After that,' she continued, 'go to my writings, and find all I have been given on that subject. Then preach it to the people from the Bible.' "

The counsel that Ellen White gave to his father became a way of life for H.M.S. Richards. His long-standing habit of Bible reading gave him a depth of understanding of what the Bible says. He was also an ardent student of the writings of Ellen G. White, but he never preached with a stack of the red books piled high on the pulpit. He presented his message from the Bible.

H.M.S. Richards was deeply committed to the prophetic ministry of Ellen G. White, yet years later, when I received the assignment to help prepare daily broadcast scripts, he advised me, "Never put anything on the air you cannot defend from the Bible." He knew our Adventist temptation sometimes to try to support doctrinal positions by relying on her writings, and he knew if we fell into that trap, we would have a hard time answering letters that challenged our teachings. He was determined that everything we put on the air could be defended from "The Book."

Although the writings and the character of Ellen White powerfully influenced him, he also had common sense enough to know she was a fallible human being, that she made mistakes.

When all the furor over the accusations that she had plagiarized from other authors shook many in the church some years ago, Richards remained unperturbed. "They haven't discovered anything new," he said. "All those charges are old. I heard them all 40 years ago. They were all discussed at the 1919 Bible Conference."

He reminisced about the Bible Conference held July 1–21, 1919, in Takoma Park, Maryland, followed by three weeks of meetings with the Bible and History Teachers Council, in which church leaders discussed the recurring charges of plagiarism.

In addition, they examined Ellen White's statements on history and science, some of which had been shown to be incorrect. They referred to Willie White's statement in which he said, "Regarding Mother's writings and their use as an authority on points of history and chronology Mother has never wished our brethren to treat them as authority regarding details of history or historical dates."

Elder Arthur G. Daniels wanted to bring these things out in the open, but some of the more conservative leaders were afraid it would shake the faith of the people. Against the advice of Daniels, the General Conference president, they elected to keep the whole issue quiet—a decision Richards always thought was wrong. It was his view that the Adventist people have a lot of common sense and can be trusted with the truth. "If they had opened the issue up in

1919, much of the trouble that plagued the church in the 60s would have been avoided," he said.

At the end of the 1919 conference those attending it requested "the General Conference Committee to arrange for another conference of this character in 1920." Their request was never honored, and the minutes of the Bible Conference were lost until December 1974 when Elder Don Yost came across the brown-paper-wrapped package in the General Conference office, containing 2,400 pages of manuscript transcribed from stenographic notes taken at the Conference.

Not long after the 1919 Bible Conference, the next General Conference session voted Elder Daniels out as General Conference president. Many think it was at least partly because of the stand he took at the 1919 Bible Conference.

Richards recognized that Ellen White was a human being, subject to human frailties and mistakes. Even in her writings she sometimes made errors.

He was aware that Ellen White read history and science books widely, and that she sometimes quoted passages that were incorrect. It didn't bother Richards that Ellen White sometimes confused the Herods of New Testament history, attributing things to the wrong Herod. And it didn't shake his faith in her prophetic gift that she didn't understand the underground workings of volcanoes. It never for a minute diminished his faith in her as God's prophet. He felt that it was a positive thing for her to be well-read. She had in her library D'Augibne's *History of the Reformation,* Wylie's *History of Protestantism,* Conybeare and Howson's *Life and Epistles of Paul,* Edersheim's *Life and Times of Jesus,* and hundreds of other wonderful historical and devotional books. Richards would have been disappointed if she had not been eager to read such works. He recognized that she used material from those books in an intelligent way to form a bed on which she presented God's messages to her.

He applauded F. D. Nichol's 1951 book *Ellen G. White and Her Critics,* but felt it was not necessary to try and show that she never erred. She herself accepted the message of Jones and Waggoner in 1888, even though their view of the law in Galatians was contrary to some things she had written earlier. Again and again Ellen White urged that to find doctrinal positions we should go to the Bible, not to her writings.

H.M.S. Richards accepted her for what she was and what she herself claimed to be. It protected him from the disappointments some men and women experienced who held an unreal view of what a prophet and prophecy should be.

He was 15 years old when he remembered seeing and hearing Ellen White for the last time.

"I saw Ellen White at a camp meeting in Boulder, Colorado. The meetings were held in a big octagon building with an iron roof. The last time I saw it, it was still standing on the campus of the University of Colorado in Boulder, right up against the red rocks.

"Ellen White came there on Sabbath with Willie, her son, and Mrs. MacInterfer. She arrived in a tasseled surrey with horses pulling it. The place was packed. Of course, just about all of the Adventists from Colorado were there, but most of the people in the building were not Adventist members. They filled up the building and wanted to see this Adventist prophet, having heard about her.

"When the time came, she stood to preach. She spoke just like a dear old Christian lady talking. I was only about 15 years old, but I counted the texts she used and discovered that she employed more than 100 texts in her sermon. Like a schoolteacher she'd use her finger and turn the pages of the Bible, but she didn't have to read it. Instead, she'd refer to one after another and quote them from her heart.

"In the middle of the sermon it began to rain on that iron roof. There was no public address system, no microphones, but we could hear her voice above the sound of the rain on that iron roof. It was just like a silver bell cutting through all the noise.

"Finally after she had talked about 35 or 40 minutes, her son came up to her and said, 'Mother, you've got long journeys ahead of you. I don't think you ought to wear yourself out any more. You've got a lot of other talks to give, and you're going on to other cities. Maybe you'd better rest now.'

"She said, 'Oh, not yet. I haven't prayed yet. I want to pray before I sit down.'

"So in just a minute or two she finished her talk. Then she kneeled down and started to pray. I can remember those words distinctly. 'O, my Father'—not our

Father—'my Father.' She hadn't prayed for two minutes, before I was afraid to look up. A mighty power came over that audience. There was no excitement. Nobody screaming. But you could hear people begin to sob all over that audience. The power of God came in there. I was afraid to look up for fear I'd see God standing right there talking with her. She forgot all about us as she was in the presence of God talking with Him. My boy's heart melted, I tell you. I was in tears, too.

"God honored her as His special servant before all those people. She had many revivals and it was not excitement that moved the people. It was just by praying, things like that. The power of the Lord would come in there, convert people, and change their lives. Many became preachers and missionaries and workers that took their stand for Jesus in places like that.

"After her prayer, her son came and helped her up, and she was just a dear old Christian woman again.

"I know all the Bible arguments for the Spirit of Prophecy and I believe in them, but I would believe she was gifted as a prophet if there were no such arguments, because I was there and experienced that power in my own heart and saw it happening to other people as well.

"I never did see her again after that, but when we heard she had died, we all felt like orphans. She'd always been such a tower of strength to the Adventist work."

Arthur G. Daniels was president of the General Conference of Seventh-day Adventists during many of the years of Ellen White's strongest ministry to the church. As a result of her messages, he had seen the church spread worldwide. He had witnessed the health and medical programs advance by following her lead, building hospitals and sanitariums on virtually every continent. And he had seen the church become a pacesetter to the world in the field of education. Daniels was not disturbed that Ellen White quoted Conybeare and Howson, or Wiley, or D'Aubigne. He offered his own testimony concerning the evidence that God had called Ellen G. White: "I believe that the strongest proof is found in the fruits of this gift to the church."

Until the day he died H.M.S. Richards said, "Amen and amen!"

LITTLE BOY GROWING UP

When the Richards family moved to Denver, Twopops was still in Alaska. After the gold-rush fever had abated somewhat, he returned to Davis City, Iowa, with the intention of packing up Twomoms and going back to Alaska. He loved it there. It was his kind of frontier.

They started west and got as far as Colorado to say goodbye to the family. But something about the mountains looming up against the sky, the rushing river plunging through Big Thompson Canyon, the wildness of it all, appealed to Twopops. And besides, his favorite little grandson lived nearby. He and Twomoms settled in Loveland a few miles north of Denver in a ranch house on the northwest edge of town, just below the dike that held back Lake Loveland.

Near that house a wild cottonwood tree grew so that the branches shaded the room where Harold and Kenneth slept when they were at their grandparents' place, as they were most of the time.

Later Harold could remember as a little boy looking out that window at the wild turkeys roosting in the branches of that tree, even in the bitter cold winter. They wouldn't stay in the chicken house with the chickens but would sit in a row on one of the branches of that cottonwood, facing into the wind, their heads tucked under their wings.

Often when Father was away preaching, Mother would still be there at Twopops ranch. Richards' poem, "When My Mother Tucks Me In," recalls those childhood days.

> "How the changing years have borne me
>   Far away from days of home!
> Now no Mother bends above me
>   When the time for sleep has come.
> But it gives my poor heart comfort,
>   And it brings me rest within,
> Just to dream that I am little
>   And my Mother tucks me in.
>
> As I kneel there with my brother
>   By the bed above the stairs,
> And I hear my gentle Mother
>   Whisper, 'Boys, remember prayers!'
> Then she comes and prays beside us,
>   'Father, keep them from all sin.'
> Oh! her kiss is tender, loving,
>   When my Mother tucks me in.
>
> When at last the evening finds me
>   And life's busy day is done,
> All the bands of earth that bind me
>   Shall be broken one by one.
> Then, O Lord, be Thou my comfort,
>   Calm my soul Thy peace to win;
> Let me fall asleep as gently
>   As when Mother tucked me in."

As the boys grew, their mother planted in their hearts a love for poetry. She would read or repeat to them Eugene Field's "Divine Lullaby," or "Armenian Lullaby." Sixty or more years later the lilting lines of "Armenian Lullaby" would come bubbling out of his mind's treasure house almost letter perfect.

"If thou wilt shut thy drowsy eyes,
My mulberry one, my golden son!
The rose shall sing thee lullabies,
My pretty cosset lambkin!
And thou shalt swing in an almond tree,
With a flood of moonbeams rocking thee—
A silver boat in a golden sea,
My velvet love, my nestling dove,
My own pomegranate blossom!"

He learned to love the melodic swing of those words.

"The stork shall guard thee passing well
All night, my sweet! my dimple-feet,
And bring thee myrrh and asphodel,
My gentle rain of springtime!
And for thy slumberous play shall twine
The diamond stars with an emerald vine
To trail in the waves of ruby wine
My myrtle bloom, my heart's perfume,
My little chirping sparrow!"

"Think of those words in there," Richards would say. "How many adults know what they mean? Or do they mean anything? They're just beautiful."

"And when the morn wakes up to see
My apple bright, my soul's delight!

The partridge shall come calling thee,
My jar of milk-and-honey!
Yes, thou shalt know what mystery lies
In the amethyst deep of the curtained skies,
If thou wilt fold thy onyx eyes,
You wakeful one, you naughty son,
You cooing little turtle."

That was one of the poems mother sang to her two little boys. They knew it was something nice, something she loved, and so they loved it in turn. A loving mother or father can make a good imprint on growing minds, an imprint that will shape their lives for as long as they live.

Richards remembered that out the back door of that ranch house, about 50 or 60 feet from the house, was a half-buried brick root cellar. It was cool in summer and warm in winter, and, in those days before refrigerators, Twomoms kept her milk there. Five little toads lived down there and kept the fly population down.

Twomoms fiercely protected those little toads. One day she entered the root cellar just in time to see a snake slithering away with five bumps along its carcass. It had swallowed all five of those toads. Twomoms' anger at the snake overcame her fear of it. Racing over to it she put her foot on its head before it could escape through a hole, and the snake started to wind itself up her ankle. She began to shout for great-grandfather.

"I'm a-comin'," he said as he hobbled out toward the root cellar, "I'm a-comin'."

He cut off the head of that snake with his pocket knife, then slit it open and let the toads out. Four of them survived, but one was too far gone.

Another time Twomoms rescued her chickens. Out back near the lake was an icehouse. In winter they would cut ice from the lake and cover it with sawdust. The ice would stay frozen all summer.

Later they turned the icehouse into a chicken house. One night

42

the family heard a tremendous racket out back. Fearless little Twomoms got a lantern, and away she went. She opened the door of the chicken house to find feathers flying everywhere. In the light of the lantern she saw two big, luminous eyes glaring at her. At first she thought it was a mountain lion and began to scream. The same old great-grandfather came to her rescue. He was about 85 then, and carrying a good-sized cane. He swung at the "mountain lion," and it turned out to be nothing but a big owl.

Twopops took care of the farm, enlisting his grandsons to help. He never liked farming—preferred trapping and hunting. Money was hard to get in those days, and he sometimes would take little Harold with him when he visited his trap line up in the mountains.

Richards remembered one time when he and Twopops were on just such a trek.

"I was just a little fellow, and when I would get so tired I couldn't walk any farther, he would pick me up and carry me on his shoulders.

"One time we had been visiting the traps, walking all day long. Night fell but he still had a few places to go further up a canyon in the mountains. 'I'm going up there,' he told me, 'but it won't take very long. It's too dark for me to carry you. I don't want to risk it. You're too sleepy.'

"Twopops knew about a big rock that had a split in it about 4 and a half feet above the ground. Just about my size.

"'I'm going to put you on this shelf and you can go to sleep,' he said. 'Nothing's going to get you here. Don't worry about the coyotes. They just make a lot of noise. I'll come back and get you.'

"I trusted him implicitly. He'd never deceived me. Never told me anything that wasn't true. I had not the least doubt when he told me everything would be all right. So he put me up in that cleft of the rock. The last thing I remembered was the coyotes howling, the wind sobbing all around me. A lonely place if there ever was one.

"Next thing I knew he was back, waking me up. He put me on his shoulders and carried me 10 miles back to the farm. Hiding in that cleft of the rock was an experience that I remembered when I began to teach about Jesus hiding us in the cleft of the Rock."

Twopops had two daughters, but no sons. Harold became the son he never had. And it filled a vacancy in the boy's life, for he never had his own father around much to bond with.

But he would always remember the times his father came home from preaching and walked along the shore of Lake Loveland to where the son was fishing. For a few hours father and son sat together, fishing and talking.

"I never will forget what it meant to me, that he would come out just to see me and fish with me and be one with me." It was a rare time—a time Richards cherished in his hall of memories.

But his growing up days were emotionally bonded with Twopops. In her book *Man Alive* Virginia tells of an experience Harold and Twopops had at Dunravin Glade. Twopops and Twomoms had taken up a homestead about 30 miles west of Loveland in the foothills of the Rockies and built a rough little cabin, while still keeping the ranch at Loveland.

Harold and his grandfather had gone hunting for game in the mountains above the cabin. The powdery snow was knee deep, and they stopped to rest a few minutes under a tremendous old dead pine tree. The wind was picking up, and they could hear it moaning in the trees. As they rested, they looked up through the branches of that monstrous old pine above them. Lightning had struck it, and its naked arms clawed at the snowy whiteness.

After they moved on, they heard a tremendous "crack" and a thunderous roar as the old pine came crashing down. When the dusting snow settled, they saw that the tree had fallen where they had been standing only seconds before. Both Harold and Twopops sensed that the protecting hand of God had been over them that day.

"I became a son to Twopops. He treated me like a son all through my life. He died in 1913 right in my arms.

"The night before he died, he got up out of bed. I was alone with him. He was a very strong man, too strong for me even though I was 18 years old. I couldn't stop him. He went to the sideboard, got his Bible, and came back and sat down.

" 'Now, you're going to be a minister of God,' he said, holding his Bible. 'I don't know how this thing is going to turn out. I may not be here for long.' He opened his Bible to First Corinthians. 'If you're going to be a preacher, you've got to be a spiritual man. "Spiritual things are spiritually discerned," it says here. For a man of the world they're only foolishness unto him. You can't understand the Scriptures, no matter how learned you are, unless you're spiritual.' "

"His last words to me were Romans 11: 'O the depth of the riches both of the wisdom and knowledge of God.' Twopops died on January 3, 1913. I had those words put on his tombstone."

Once when the Richards boys were 8 and 10 years old, they and Floyd Wright, a neighbor boy, were mud-crawling in an old irrigation ditch that ran through Twopops farm. Father was off preaching, as he often was. The boys found an old muzzle loader musket in the mud at the bottom of that ditch. The wooden stock had long since rotted away, but the rest of the gun was intact, though covered with rust. That ranch had been there since buffalo days, and the gun no doubt was a relic from that time.

Boys that age have a love affair with guns. They hauled it out of the mud and cleaned it up, scraping rust from its barrel. But what good is a gun unless you can shoot it?

Along the ridge of the barn a lot of pigeons paced back and forth. The boys decided they'd prop that old gun against a log, aim it at the ridge of the barn, fasten it with bailing wire, and shoot those pigeons.

Floyd remembered that his dad had some blasting powder in his barn that he'd been using to blow up stumps. They filled a tin can with black powder, big grains like small peas.

Not knowing how much to put in the gun, they pounded the pellets into powder with a rock and poured six or eight inches into the barrel of that gun, probably enough powder to blow up a stump. Then they put in shingle nails and rocks for bullets until they could see the load almost reaching the end of the barrel.

They knew that an old-fashioned gun like that had to have some wadding to hold the charge in, so they stuffed some old rags into the end of the barrel. Next they mashed up a few grains of powder for the flash pan near the touchhole. They planned to string a fuse, light it, and run away.

Just then Harold saw his father walking up the road, coming home from a six-week or more trip. The boy knew if he waited to string the fuse they'd never get to shoot off their gun, so he quickly struck a match and held it up to the powder in the touchhole. That was just about the last thing he knew for a while.

The Lord's blessing and the good workmanship of the men who made that gun held it together. It's a wonder it didn't blow up into little fragments of shrapnel. The burning powder came back out of the touchhole with just about as much force as from the muzzle of the gun, spraying burning powder right into Harold's eyes. Here's how Richards later remembered it.

"My father saw the explosion and heard me yell. He dropped his satchels and came on the run up the road to a welcome home.

"Although my father was very strict he was also very kind. He said not one word of condemnation to me about the incident. I had to be a Christian with such parents as I had—and such grandparents. I could just see light a little bit in one eye. Running in circles, I cried, 'I can see light! I can see light! I can see light!'

"Our little town only had one doctor. He was very good if you could catch him when he wasn't drunk. Father took me to town in the old buggy since nobody had autos in those days.

"The doctor laid me on the table and with a pair of tweezers started picking those little pieces of burned powder out of my eyes for what seemed like an everlasting age. I paid for my fun, I'll tell you.

"'If you'd been a few inches nearer,' he told me, 'you'd never have been able to see again.' That powder was just like little bullets. Always after that my eyes weren't very good. Years later I had a detached retina in my left eye. I know that childhood prank was responsible."

That bit of boyish foolishness could have cost Harold his life, and did destroy the sight of one eye, leaving him blind in the left eye with about half vision in the right for the rest of his life. In spite of that, he did more with that half an eye than most of us do with two good ones.

He regularly read his Bible through twice a year—once in January, then as he put it, once leisurely during the rest of the year. In addition to that, he read *Time, Newsweek,* the Los Angeles *Times,* the *Review and Herald,* plus dozens of books and magazines every year.

And Richards always felt that a minister ought to be acquainted with the classical literature of his own language. For him that included Shakespeare, Milton, and all the great English and American poets. "A minister is really a poet," Richards would say. "Ought to be. That's why half of the Bible is written in poetry. Poetry reaches the deepest part of the human heart. It also gives a minister tremendous command of the more delicate shades of the English language."

As a growing youngster, like most siblings, Harold loved to tease his brother, Kenneth. He remembers that it became such a bad habit that it began to affect his brother's nerves. All he had to do was point his finger and his brother would yell, "Quit!"

Again and again his mother would reprove, rebuke, and exhort him to stop, and he sincerely tried, but then the old habit would creep up on him and his mother would hear Kenneth screaming.

Finally she became desperate. "Harold, you've got to stop teasing your brother. I've asked you to stop, I've begged you to stop, I've commanded you to stop, but you go right back at it again. I've spanked you, but you're getting too big to spank now, so I've got to do something else to make you remember.

"It must be that I've failed as a mother for you to keep doing this all the time. The next time I hear you teasing your brother, you're going to have to punish me."

Young Richards loved his mother and couldn't bear the idea of striking her. He vowed in his heart never to do that again. But one day the inevitable happened. Once more he began teasing Kenneth who started screaming for him to stop.

When Harold heard his mother's voice, he couldn't believe it had happened again. It was like a nightmare.

"Harold, I warned you. Now we've got to go through with the punishment."

Young Richards knew from experience that when his mother or father made a promise, either a good one or a bad one, they always followed through. Now the thought of whipping his mother sent chills through him. But she insisted he go down to the creek and cut a switch.

"Oh, I went down there," he said, "but I stayed a long time. I just couldn't find a switch that I could imagine hitting mother with. Finally, I came back, but she said, 'Oh, that'll never do. That's too small. That wouldn't even hurt,' so she made me get another. I must have gone down three or four times.

"When she was satisfied with the switch I brought, she pulled back the collar of her dress and commanded me to whip her across the back, but I just couldn't do it. She commanded, and I raised my hand, but I couldn't bring it down. While I was used to obeying, my love for my mother and my duty to obey were in such conflict I was in hysterics. I was about to have a breakdown.

"Mother finally saw that I couldn't do it. She sat down with me and told me the story of Jesus, how He suffered with the guilty, by the guilty, and for the guilty. I learned the gospel from my mother that day. It was a lesson I never forgot. And to my knowledge, I never again disobeyed mother about teasing my brother."

As the boys grew older, their father couldn't bear to see them attending public school. His worry and consternation opened a new chapter in the life of young Harold Richards.

"WE NEED AN ACADEMY"

"Elder Watson, we need an academy for our young people here in the Colorado Conference, and I propose that we put it in Loveland."

It was 1906 and H.M.J. Richards was for a time vice president of the Colorado conference, which included the territory of New Mexico. The vice president traveled all over the conference as a kind of troubleshooter for the president. (H.M.S. Richards, with a chuckle, described his father's position as vice president in the conference. "That was in the days before conference presidents became afraid that a vice president might want to take their jobs from them.")

The elder Richards had been urging a school for Colorado so often and so persistently at every conference committee meeting, that finally conference president Watson got tired of it.

"Richards, if you're so concerned and so determined over this thing of an academy, why don't you go out and raise some money for it?"

"Is that a committee action, Elder Watson? Make it a committee action, and I will." They did, and he did.

The leadership never thought he'd do it, but

he raised what in those days was a tremendous sum: $8,000. Then old W. A. "Daddy" Hankins gave 13 acres of land three and a half miles south of Loveland. It was the beginning of East Colorado Academy, later Campion.

That meant the boys had to walk from Twopops' farm to school each day. The best and closest route was by the railroad track.

One day, walking home from school along the railroad track, his books carried with a strap across his back, Harold was deep in thought. From the school to Loveland, going into town, it was down grade, and the trains would coast along almost silently. All at once the boy felt the ground shake and leaped to the side just in time to see the train rush by.

In the summer of 1907 Harold's father, with Elder L. A. Spring, began tent meetings on the outskirts of Loveland. Since attendance wasn't good, their father expected Harold and Kenneth to attend every evening to help swell the crowd. When the series of meetings was half over, his father developed a skin infection and Spring had to continue alone.

One Sabbath afternoon the two boys were there. Richards remembered that "Brother Spring was no great orator. He was a quiet man and spoke diffidently. But the power of the Lord came into that little meeting. He appealed to us to take our stand for the Lord and His work, and to give our hearts to Christ."

At the close of the meeting the group sang a song from the *Christ in Song* hymnbook.

> *"There is a gate that stands ajar,*
> *And thro' its portals gleaming,*
> *A radiance from the cross afar,*
> *The Saviour's love revealing.*

> *"O depth of mercy! Can it be*
> *That gate was left ajar for me?*
> *For me, for me?*
> *Was left ajar for me?"*

The boy knew that song carried a message just for him, and when Spring made a call for all to come forward who wanted to give their lives to the Lord, Harold stood and walked to the front.

In her book *Man Alive,* Richards' daughter Virginia described what happened afterward. "When he got home, he told his mother what he had done. Without a word, she led him into his father's room where he lay ill. There followed a touching scene as Grandfather learned what had happened at the meeting, and with soft weeping and praise to the Lord he prayed with his young son."

Sometime after the boy's birthday that summer Harold's father led him down into the water of Lake Loveland. The surface of the lake that day was glassy and perfectly reflected the majestic Rocky Mountains to the west. There with the boy's beloved Long's Peak looking down on him, H.M.J. Richards lowered his son into the water in baptism.

Soon after the family had moved from Denver to Loveland, a small school building had been moved onto a vacant lot about two miles from Twopops' farm. At first just the Richards and Sylvester families and one elderly woman attended the little church. Later converts began to swell the congregation. As he was growing up, Harold was Sabbath school secretary, Sabbath school superintendent, deacon, and elder.

The little group had no regular pastor. An old layman and local elder, George Ragan, conducted the meetings most of the time. But not from the pulpit—that was too holy a place for him. He stood down off the platform on the floor with the congregation.

The young boys loved him. Although an uneducated man, he was sincere and loved the boys back. Once on a Sabbath school picnic on a mountain near the head of Big Thompson canyon, he stopped, tears filling his eyes.

"Boys, do you see that big pine tree up there. I did a terrible thing there once." Of course, that had their attention. "I killed an Indian right at the foot of that tree." Harold and Kenneth were wide-eyed. "The Indian had his gun pointed right at me. I had to shoot him first, or he would have shot me. I shot him, and he fell off his horse right there."

Ragan paused, unable to continue for a moment. "I left as soon as the Indian hit the ground because I knew there would be others around, but I came back a few days later. The Indian was gone and so was his horse. But I found his bridle with silver mountings on it. I've asked the good Lord many times over to forgive me, and I know that He has."

Another experience helped young Richards sense the protecting power of God. A group of boys were out hiking in the mountains and came across an old mine shaft. They entered, and as their eyes became accustomed to darkness, saw what they thought was the form of some animal. Boylike they began to throw rocks at the dark silhouette. It made no movement. Creeping a little closer, they finally discovered it was a big pile of old dynamite sticks—200 or 300 of them. Old dynamite can be very unstable, and if a rock had struck in just the right way, every one of those boys would have been blasted out of that cave like a shot from a cannon.

In 1908 Richards heard William Jennings Bryan speak in Loveland about the Sherman Antitrust Act and the efforts on the part of the courts to interpret the Act "reasonably." Bryan attacked the Republican position of softness on the trusts and monopolies—that anti-trust cases should be decided "reasonably." He asked his audience what would have happened if God had said, "Thou shalt not steal, unreasonably. Thou shalt not kill, unreasonably. Thou shalt not commit adultery, unreasonably." Young 14-year-old Richards thought it was a good argument.

In those early days of the twentieth century Richards sometimes heard the family talk about the mortgage on the farm, and the threat to their personal welfare brought about by big business and the great "trusts." Twopops was a Populist, and often spoke heatedly against big business. The boy, though not fully aware of all the political ramifications of what was going on in government, was captivated by Teddy Roosevelt, whose motto was "Speak softly and carry a big stick." That was the kind of action politics that appealed to a boy.

It was a high point in young Richards' life when he saw Teddy Roosevelt come out of the Brown Palace Hotel in Denver one day and climb into a carriage. "When I finally got to see Roosevelt himself and heard him speak, I was thoroughly captivated by him," Richards said. "And I do think that he influenced me as a speaker a great deal. I wanted to be like him; I wanted that vitality, that vigor, that directness. And the way he'd double up that fist of his—I'll tell you, he was a ball of fire. I often thought about him as a public speaker."

When William Howard Taft was elected president November 3, 1908, it was a sad day for the boy. He was disappointed that his hero Roosevelt hadn't run again, and that Taft was president. At this time he read Roosevelt's six-volume history, *The Winning of the West.*

Early in his young life he even contemplated becoming a lawyer and entering politics. His grandfather's cousin, John Forrest Curry, was secretary of state in California from 1899 to 1911, but the boy also felt a pull to be a minister.

His grandfather, William Jenkin Richards, had been converted by Salvation Army General William Booth, and had become a lay preacher. In later years H.M.S. Richards would often say that "my father was a preacher, and his father, and his father, and his father, right back to Mr. Richards who traveled with John Wesley."

Richards loved stories about Wesley. "Wesley is my favorite character outside the Bible," he often said. "Wesley saved England from the terrible materialism that gripped it in the eighteenth century."

The boy read Wesley's journals, many of the pages of which had been written on horseback as Wesley traveled from one small Christian group to another. In his sermons Richards often told stories from Wesley's life and experiences.

"My great-great-grandfather was one of the young preachers who traveled with John Wesley. He heard him preach to 10,000 men in the mine pits around London. Wesley saved England from a revolution similar to the French Revolution.

"Wesley always fell in love with his nurse when he was sick. Unfortunately, he

married the last one instead of the first. All his life she was a trial and a torment to him, yet never a word of criticism or complaint about her appeared in his private diary.

"His diary was not written for publication. He and his brother worked out a special private shorthand that only they could read. All during his married life not one word of complaint appeared about his wife, even though she made life a terror for him.

"One day one of his young ministers happened to come to the house and found her dragging John Wesley around the house by his long hair. The young man later told his friends, 'I never came closer to murder than I did that day.'

"Another time Wesley was preaching about the Ten Commandments. He said, 'Brothers and sisters, I've been accused of breaking every one of the commandments except stealing.'

"Just at that moment his wife jumped up in the audience and said, 'John Wesley, you know you stole sixpence out of my purse just last week.'

" 'Well, ladies and gentlemen, that completes the list.' On the day she died, he simply entered the words in his diary, 'My wife died today.'

"If you want to know the eighteenth century, read Wesley. Wesley had a cool head and a warm heart. The last sermon he ever preached, when he rose to speak it was the only time he ever broke down. His brother, Charles, had written more than 8,000 hymns. As Wesley announced one of Charles' hymns for the congregation to sing, his loneliness suddenly came over him. As he began to read that hymn he suddenly broke down and burst into tears. Charles had gone. All his old companions had already died. He sobbed for a few moments, then preached his last sermon.

"Just before he died, he spoke to all of his young preachers gathered round him. His last words were, 'And the best of all is, God is with us.' "

In September of 1910 Harold Richards entered the academy as a freshman. It was a happy time for the boy. Later he loved to tell about what happened one Halloween.

"The school had a bell tower over the main entrance of the main building. During chapel period that day Principal Farnsworth closed the announcements by saying, 'Now, I hope no one tries to ring that bell tonight. It's been done other times, but it's not going to be done this time. Remember that.'

"Of course that was just a challenge. I recruited some of my friends and we determined to ring the bell that night and not get caught.

"First we went to Loveland and bought two balls of binder's twine. When we returned to the school, we established ourselves in an apple orchard across the railroad tracks from the school.

"It had a perfect, but secure, view of the bell tower. We tied a rock to the twine and tossed it over the power lines. Then after dark one of the other boys and I sneaked onto campus. We managed to get up in the bell tower without anyone seeing us, then tied another piece of string to the clapper of the bell. After threading it through the lattice work around the tower, we then dropped it down the wall of the building to the ground below.

"That done, we casually walked across campus, innocently greeting everyone we met. When we reached the twine that we had thrown over the power lines, we tied the two pieces together, then gave the twine a little tug so that our co-conspirators in the apple tree could pull the twine tight high over the campus where no one could notice it.

"Once we had all that done we rejoined our friends in the apple tree and gave the twine two or three good pulls—bong, bong, bong. Just as we expected, Elder Farnsworth with his troops came swarming out of the building and over to the classroom building to catch whoever was in the bell tower. Of course, by this time we had given the twine a yank, breaking it so we couldn't be traced to our hiding place in the apple tree.

"Twice more that night we rang the bell. The last time the string we had threaded through the lattice broke, ending our fun for that night.

"Next morning in chapel the principal said nothing about the bell-ringing incident until just before the closing bell rang.

" 'Oh, by the way, if I'd been the one ringing the bell last night, I'd have strung some wire through the lattice in front of the bell so the line wouldn't have broken. You're dismissed.' "

Those boys loved E. E. Farnsworth, and he loved them. One time on Farnsworth's birthday seven of the boys decided to give him a birthday spanking. Virginia Richards-Cason tells about it in *Man Alive*.

"It was during summer vacation, so the group was primarily the boys who lived off the campus, including Dad, and two or three boys from the dormitory who stayed through the summer. A big alfalfa field separated the academy buildings from Farnsworth's home. A path between his house and the school was worn smooth through the alfalfa and here the boys crouched, waiting in ambush while one of their friends called Farnsworth on an old crank phone.

" 'You're wanted right away at school, sir.' It was about six o'-clock on that summer evening. The boys waited and waited, but Farnsworth did not appear on the path. Then, suddenly, they heard him shouting at them from the other side of the field. Evidently he had somehow seen them hide and now he was taunting them to come and catch him.

"With one motion the seven boys straightened and began to run. Leaping over the alfalfa, tearing through it, the seven boys charged toward their principal. Once they caught up with him, he quickly used his 250 pounds to send them sprawling one after the other. He was like a bear attacked by a pack of wolves. The boys somehow managed six good spanks on him before he grabbed one youngster around the neck with one arm and latched onto another with the other arm, pulling both of them to the ground. The other boys kept trying to roll him over, but in their efforts a couple more of them were caught by Farnsworth's legs and they were pinned in a wrestling hold they could not break. In this position—two boys held by his arms, two others pinned between his legs, and the rest too tired to do anything—the principal began to tell them stories of adventure, of faith, and of daring action. Every once in awhile the struggle would resume, but always ended with Farnsworth in control."

The bond between boys and principal never unraveled. Years later, when Richards accepted a call from Canada to California, E. E. Farnsworth, then retired in Fresno but still the beloved principal of his boy, warmly welcomed H.M.S. into his home.

During most of his Campion school days, both in grade school and academy, Harold considered Twopops' ranch as home, but in 1910 H.M.J. Richards and sons built their own home in Loveland, halfway between Twopops' ranch and Loveland. But they only stayed there six months, for his father had heard that they could obtain land on the Ute Indian Reservation west of the Rockies. He moved the family to Palisades on a homestead.

It was while the family was at Palisades, Colorado, that young Richards first met the old Adventist pioneer, J. N. Loughborough. Let's let him tell about it in his own words:

"I remember hearing him at the General Conference in 1913 in Takoma Park. Only weighing 120 pounds, he was a little short fellow. They had to put him up on a table so they could see and hear him at the session.

"But I had heard him even before that. He had promised to stop over and speak at Father's tent meeting in Palisades on his way east from California. It was right on his way—right on the Denver and Rio Grande Railway between Salt Lake and Denver. He was going to Washington for some reason, but he couldn't come at the time planned because of some big washouts and floods between California and Colorado. It delayed him two or three weeks.

"When he did arrive I remember Father took me with him down to the railway station to meet him. Just as he got off the train, father said to him, 'Well, I suppose you're quite surprised that you didn't get here when you planned to.'

" 'No, I wasn't surprised,' he said. It seemed to me like a strange thing to say. Father waited until we were sitting at the dinner table, and he asked him, 'What did you mean when you said you weren't surprised that you didn't get here when you planned to?'

" 'Well, Brother Richards,' he replied, 'I don't talk about this because it's just for me and nobody else. You see, I'm an old man. I have no wife, no family, and live all alone in a room at St. Helena. When I go on these journeys, I don't know what's going to happen to me. Things might disturb me or worry me. Just for me and nobody else, before I start on a journey like this, I always have a dream, and I see all the main things that are going to take place during that journey. I saw the whole thing in a dream. I knew it was all right. Everything was going to come out all right.'

"That was the testimony he gave. The Lord gave him those dreams to provide him peace of mind while he was traveling for the Lord."

In the middle of Harold's years at Campion Academy, the Pennsylvania Conference invited his father to lead there. Since the two boys were in school and Twopops wasn't well, Harold's mother and the boys stayed in Loveland for a while. After Twopops died in January 1913, his mother rejoined her husband in Pennsylvania, leaving Kenneth and Harold with Twomoms at Campion until summer.

Immediately after school ended, the two boys took the train from Colorado to Washington, D.C., to join their parents at the 1913 General Conference in Takoma Park just outside of Washington, D.C. At that General Conference Richards saw some of the pioneers of the Seventh-day Adventist movement, as well as men he would work with in future years. That was when he saw old Elder J. N. Loughborough again—the man who had visited their home in Palisades. One day the rain came down so fiercely on the tent roof that nobody could hear the preacher. It was in the days before public address systems. During the downpour the audience began to chant—"Prescott! Prescott!" They knew that W. W. Prescott with his big booming voice could be heard above the most violent thunderstorm. Before many years H.M.S. would find himself in a head-to-head confrontation with W. W. Prescott.

After the General Conference session concluded, the family went back home to 4910 Arch Street in Philadelphia, but Harold took the train back to Colorado that summer to finish his final year at Campion.

Harold loved his classes at Campion, though, strange as it might seem, he received his lowest grades in English and public speaking and his highest grades in agriculture.

Campion days were full of more than just schoolwork. Though he never did settle seriously on one girl, several caught his eye. And there were the GGORs—"Giggling Girls on the Roof," who would sit on the roof and giggle every time the boys went by.

Though he didn't get his best grades in public speaking, Harold did sharpen his speaking skills through the Saturday night debating teams. His first debating partner was Victor Price, but Harold and Victor became so skilled and so consistently won their debates, that the school finally put them on opposite teams.

Harold loved music, singing bass in a male quartet at Campion. They called themselves "The Scrapiron Four." But one of the big musical events of Harold Richards' academy years was the performance of the cantata "Queen Esther." Teresa Reed-Gosmer, the music teacher at the academy, directed it. Harold received the lead role of King Ahasuerus, and was listed in the printed program as H. Sylvester Richards. Twomoms made the costumes for King Ahasuerus and his bride, Queen Esther. The student actors and chorus gave a triumphant performance at the Majestic Theater in Loveland, as well as in other locations in the area. It was such a success that people asked the school to repeat it again in the community the next year.

Richards later loved to list all the offices he held in the senior class. He was the president, the vice-president, the secretary-treasurer, the valedictorian, and the class. His was a class of one, and he was it. The junior class treated him like a king as they shepherded him through the commencement ceremonies. Professor W. A. Gosmer gave the commencement address on the subject of Christian education. As Richards sat there listening to the sermon, he couldn't dodge any of the arrows shot out by the preacher. He couldn't assume they were aimed at the other members of his class. They were all for him.

The sermon so impressed Richards that he determined that he would write a commencement sermon and give it sometime if the opportunity ever presented itself. He received his chance sooner than he expected. The next year the junior class that had treated him so royally in his senior year asked him to return and be their commencement speaker. Twenty-four years later a woman who had attended the graduation exercises that year sent Richards a clipping of the Loveland newspaper that had reported on the event. The graduating class of Campion Academy in 1915 consisted of four students: Reathel Colleen Jenkins, Alice Adelle Crooks, Llewellyn E. Aufderhar, and Howard K. Halladay.

The title of Richards' sermon to the class was "The Worth of a Man." Here's how he began:

"Two sailors stood on the deck of a ship and looked at a sail on the sea. They were both looking at the same sail. One said, 'It looks small and far away.' The other said, 'It looks large and near at hand.' They were both looking at the same sail. They were both right, for one was looking through the big end of the telescope, and the other through the little end.

"Two philosophers stood on the mount of vision and looked at a human being. One said, 'He looks as insignificant as an atom.' The other said, 'He looks as big as the universe.' They were both looking at the same man, and they were both right. One was looking at his reputation and the other at his character."

The Loveland newspaper article that reported the graduation exercises also carried the full text of a poem Richards wrote especially for the occasion. It was entitled "The Measure of Humanity."

> *"Adam saith to Seth his son*
> *When Adam's life was nearly done,*
> *'I'm the first man that e'er was made,*
> *And yet a failure, I'm afraid,*
> *But you are young and life is thine.*
> *You have a chance that ne'er was mine,*
> *When at last I give up the fight,*
> *Go in and make the old thing right!'*

> *"And after years had passed away*
> *When Seth was old and bent and grey,*
> *He called for Enos, gay and young,*
> *For Enos was his only son,*
> *And showed him how he'd failed to do*
> *The job that Adam told him to.*
> *Then muttered low with failing might,*
> *'Go in and make the old thing right.'*

> *"But Enos failed to do the work*

For like his pa he'd rather shirk;
And pass it on from son to son,
Abhorred by all and loved by none,
Until in some far distant day
When there was just no other way
And men were driven on by fright,
They'd all rush in and make it right.

"And thus it went, as ages fled.
The daddies told their sons, 'tis said
The reason they'd not done the stunt
Was because their tools were old and blunt.
But boys are mighty like their pas,
So they put it off with 'Hees' and 'Haws'
Until in this, our generation
We demand of the next, the reformation.

"And so it goes—we sit and talk,
But when it comes to work, we balk,
And always hope that those who follow
Will take the nasty dose and swallow;
And so this class, the Mighty Four,
Will do what we have not before.
Their loyalty has scaled the height,
And when they go, they'll make it right."

At Campion Academy the boys who were planning to become ministers formed "The Little Leaven League." They took the name of their club from Jesus' parable recorded in Matthew and Luke: "Whereunto shall I liken the kingdom of God? It is like leaven, which a woman took and hid in three measures of meal, till the whole was leavened" (Luke 13:20, 21).

But that opens the door to another chapter in the life of the young, sprouting preacher.

SPROUTING PREACHER

During the summer between school terms at Campion Academy young Richards would go out with his father to help with tent meetings. During the summer of 1912 they held evangelistic meetings in Ft. Lupton, Colorado, north of Denver. It was at this series that young Richards preached his first real sermon. His father knew he would feel less self-conscious if he and Harold's mother weren't around for their son's first sermon attempt, so he arranged to be absent that day.

"Harold, I must be away this Sabbath. I'd like for you to take the sermon at the tent while I'm away."

"What shall I preach about, Father?"

"Why don't you preach about angels?"

"Is there enough in the Bible about angels to make a sermon?"

"You look in your Bible and see what you can find on that subject."

When Harold began to search through his Bible, he was surprised at how much he found about angels. He couldn't begin to use it all. So that Sabbath afternoon he spoke on angels.

Afterward he felt that he had failed miserably and decided he would give up preaching. It gnawed at him for several days. A few days later an elderly woman approached him.

"Young man, I just want to tell you how much your sermon about angels did for me. I live alone away over on the other side of the tracks and often get frightened that someone will hurt me or steal my chickens, but after you talked about angels, it comforted me. I know now that angels watch over me, and I'm not afraid anymore."

"Oh, how much that did for me," Richards later said. "Sometimes people think if they compliment a young man for his sermons he'll get bigheaded. A young man needs encouragement sometimes. Oh, I don't mean to flatter him, but just tell him his sermon was a blessing to you if it was."

More than 60 years later H.M.S. attended a Campion Academy Homecoming. An elderly woman 93 years old came up to him and told him she was there in Ft. Lupton when he preached that first sermon. "She got so excited," Richards said, "that the dear little thing just grabbed me and kissed me and wept like a baby." She would have been 31 years old at the time.

That same summer at Ft. Lupton the evangelistic team had a strange experience the night Harold's father preached on "The Great Red Dragon" of Revelation 12. Here's how Richards remembered it.

"My father held a tent meeting and I was his tentmaster that summer, my first time on the conference payroll. It was my responsibility to look after the tents. I lived in a small tent in back of the large tent. Almost impenetrable brush and weeds covered the lot behind my tent.

"Father's tent was pitched on a corner lot. On two sides stood large trees spaced quite closely together. On one side up near the tent was a little shoe mending shop.

"On this particular night Father was preaching on 'The Great Red Dragon.' He always warned the people, 'I never preach on "The Great Red Dragon" without something happening. Something exciting takes place.' Of course, that helped to bring a bigger crowd.

"It was a hot August night. Father had asked me to put all the sides of the

tent up so the air could come through. People were sitting on their front porches in the houses around. It was a sleepy night.

"Of course, nobody had automobiles in those days. Only horse-drawn vehicles. Wagons, buggies, horses with saddles on them, all were tied up around the tent. I'd patrol around every little while to see that everything was all right while Father preached.

"He had almost come to the close of the sermon, and nothing unusual had occurred. I was outside checking things out. All the horses were standing around with their heads down. One big white horse, tied to a tree, was sound asleep.

"Suddenly, just as though someone had stuck a sword into him, that horse gave a snort and leaped right up in the air. He broke the rope that had fastened him to the tree, and started to plunge right toward the entryway of the tent. One more leap would have taken him right into the congregation.

"Father heard and saw this commotion and said, 'You're dismissed!' He did it so people could run out, but it happened so fast no one had time to move from their chairs.

"Just as the horse reached the entryway to the tent, he reared back and turned almost as though he were on a swivel, just as though some unseen guard were there. He ran off and got all tangled up in the brush behind the big tent and couldn't free himself.

"While this was happening, two horses on the other side of the tent broke loose and darted toward the entryway, trying to gallop into the tent with their buggy behind them. The thing happened so fast. Just as they got there they reared up and turned away. Kicking the buggy to pieces, they ran off into the brush and became tangled up.

"While this was going on another horse broke loose up the street, taking two or three boards off the side of the shoe shop with the wheel of its wagon. He tried to get into the tent that same place, but turned away just as the others had been, also ending up in the brush. Everything happened so fast the people were still sitting there in the tent. They had no time to move.

"The farmers had to come the next day and haul away the pieces of broken buggies and wagons. It was a very strange experience—something I'll never forget. I was supposed to be keeping order, but I couldn't do a thing. I'm convinced that only the angels guarding the tent saved the people from a serious accident."

One of Richards' closest boyhood friends in school was Kenneth Gant. Both members of "The Little Leaven Club" at Campion, they looked forward to becoming ministers. They began holding Bible studies in the little schoolhouses around Loveland. The boys were unsure of themselves, so one of them would speak for a while until he ran out of steam, then the other would pick up the reins and go until he was out of ammunition.

They had their first taste of the joys of evangelism when one woman in Loveland responded to their Bible studies. Every night before they went into her house, they'd stop by a mailbox and have prayer together. Richards often said, "We didn't know what we were doing. If she'd ask us a question and we didn't know the answer, we'd tell her we'd look it up and bring the answer next time. In spite of all our fumbling, she accepted the Lord. She just walked right over us into the church."

One summer between academy school terms Richards and Kenneth Gant inveigled the conference into letting them try their wings at holding evangelistic meetings. The conference sent them to the northeast corner of the state. That was where the "shaggy dog" story happened.

"I don't think any of the committee had ever been up to Holyoke, Colorado. They just put their finger on the map and said, 'Send them out there.'

"It was my first experience in which it was my tent and my responsibility. We soon discovered we had a little round 30-foot tent full of holes. We had to borrow seats from the courthouse. The first night 19 people attended—one girl and 18 men, and they all sat on the back row. My grandmother—she was a widow by this time—rented a room in a house nearby and would cook for us. I owe a tremendous lot to my grandmother, Twomoms. She kind of took care of me till I married.

"A Methodist preacher's place backed up against our lot, and he had seven cats—an old mother cat and her six kittens. Every night just as we'd get started preaching, those cats would walk down the aisle and right up on the platform and rub around our legs. Finally we solved the problem by putting the cats in a big food box we had in our little tent behind the main one. Then after the meeting we'd let them out and they'd go home.

"It was summer time, and almost every evening away up there on the plains, rolling thunder would come up, and sheet lightning would begin to flash. About 7:00 or 7:30 a few drops of rain would begin to fall just when people were beginning to arrive. They'd get scared and wouldn't come, or if they did show up, they'd then leave, because they knew the tent would leak.

"Unable to keep a crowd, we were having a terrible time. It got so bad that I finally said, 'I'll go to the conference office in Denver and bring back another tent top. They say they've got a good one there. I'll bring it on my ticket as baggage.'

"A camp meeting was in session at Boulder at the time, and there was a girl up there I wanted to see. Her name was Huldah Schultz. I thought I could visit with her briefly, then bring down the tent top. I accomplished this, but found in the process she was already engaged to another fellow.

"Obtaining the tent, I arrived back to Holyoke just about sunrise Sunday morning. Kenneth and I took the leaky tent down, and put the other tent top up. A tremendous job, it took us all day long. We were as tired as we could be by meeting time that night.

"But we had a big crowd. I'd told the people I was going to speak on the subject of 'The Great Red Dragon,' and that whenever my father or I preached on that subject something strange always happened. They came out to see if it would.

"It was lovely weather, but sure enough, just as soon as I got to preaching that old thunder began to roll again over the prairie. People looked around nervous-like, but I said, 'Don't worry. We're told this tent top is perfect, and there's no danger. If you're here, let it rain.'

"I started preaching again—it's terribly hard to resume preaching when someone interrupts—but I finally got going again.

"Sure enough, the rain came roaring down. You couldn't hear a thing. I had to stop.

"But you know, that tent wasn't like a sieve at all—it was like a colander, worse even than the other one. The rain came straight through. People had to get up on the chairs. The water ran in streams on the floor it was such a downpour. There were just a few spots where the people could get out of the rain.

"Finally, not more than five minutes later the rain stopped, and I had tried to get started again. 'Now, there's no use to go home,' I said. 'Some of you are wet anyway. It's a warm night, and it won't hurt you.' Well, they took it gracefully, and most of them decided to stay. I struggled to find the thread of my thought.

"During this terrible gully washer a big shaggy black dog—and I mean big and shaggy—wandered in the front door of the tent to get away from the rain and lay down just inside the canvas wall of the tent.

"Just about the time I got started again the third time—managed to get the attention of the people and back onto the subject of 'The Great Red Dragon,' the dog stood up in the back of the tent and for a moment looked right at me. Then he started stiff-legged down the aisle toward me—gazing right at me. The closer he came the more nervous I felt. Of course, most of the people didn't see him until he passed where they sat. By the time he reached the front everybody was watching him—and I was looking at him and still trying to talk. With something like that getting nearer and nearer, you naturally find it hard to keep on your subject and hold the people's interest—that's a pretty hard job to do.

"Well, the dog stood right in front of me. I was on a little platform only about a foot high with nothing between me and him except a row of posts with a flat board nailed to the top. There he waited just gazing at me.

"I was about to stop when he seemed to be satisfied, and flopped down against the front of the platform right there at my feet.

"Getting up steam again, I started to regain control of the audience again. Suddenly the dog jumped up, whirled around, and looked at me just as if he was going to leap right onto me. I just couldn't continue. As I paused, he began to shiver and shake until he just flopped down there in the sawdust with one great convulsive shake. He was dead.

"When he hit the ground a woman on the front row screamed. 'I told you something was going to happen here tonight,' I told the audience. 'This is the third interruption.'

"That broke the tension. Then a little bald-headed man—I can see him now, but I've never learned his name—came creeping up, afraid that dog might be still alive. Reaching out, he took the animal by the tail and dragged it backward underneath the wall of the tent, then dropped the wall back down again. Now I had to finish the talk.

"That's one example of what happened to me when I spoke on the subject of 'The Great Red Dragon,' but it's not the only one by any means.

"Kenneth Gant and I finished those meetings in Holyoke, but they were a *complete failure. Every night we'd go out on the prairie and pray that God would deliver us from that discouraging place. We got one convert, and she wasn't very bright. When we returned to school that fall we didn't feel like big preachers. Instead, we crawled in the back door. It was probably the best thing that could have happened to us. If we'd been successful, it might have ruined us.*

"The next summer the conference didn't know if they wanted us or not. No doubt they thought those two fellows don't amount to much, but they said, 'Send Richards up with John Turner in the east part of the state, and send Gant down to'—I think it was Elder Farnsworth. 'If he doesn't need him, let him go canvassing.'

"Gant and I were such bosom friends that we met in the conference office in Denver. We went down in the basement and had prayer together, shook hands, and had our pictures taken together. Then we said goodbye, thinking we'd maybe never see each other again.

"Going upstairs to get my satchel, I had my hand on the doorknob, starting out, when the telephone rang in the conference office. Ralph Emery, the conference treasurer, answered it.

" 'Wait a minute, Harold! Wait a minute!'

"The telephone message was from Elder Altman, father of Roger Altman, later an officer in the General Conference. He was calling from Colorado Springs, and the conference wanted someone to hold meetings at Woodland Park near Pike's Peak.

" 'Say, you fellows want to be together. Why don't you hold a meeting there.'

"Just that quick we were a team again. The conference told us about an old dance pavilion up there on a lake. We found an old tent wall we could put around the outside of the dance pavilion for some privacy as we preached. We got that rolled up, had our tickets changed, and were actually on the train for Woodland Park within 40 minutes.

"That little town had only 100 people, but we got 14 of them for the Lord— 14 percent of the population. We had a wonderful experience there. I could almost write a book on it.

"There in Woodland Park an old man with a long white beard sat in the front row, and just the moment I'd start preaching he'd go off into a tremendous wood-sawing, snoring slumber. He was a nice old man, but people would begin giggling.

"One night I cured him. As I walked back and forth on the platform, first to one side then the other, I worked my way over until I was right in front of

him. *Leaning over almost in his face, I said, 'Ladies and gentlemen, the church is asleep today. It's time for it to WAKE UP!' He never knew what hit him, because I was away over on the other side of the platform by the time he snapped awake.*

"Then I felt ashamed of myself. The next day he brought me eggs and milk and things. I guess someone must have told him what happened.

"It was in Woodland park that I had my first funeral. The Lord taught Kenneth Gant and me a great lesson.

"One night Kenneth awakened me early in the morning. 'Harold, wake up!' he said. 'Wake up! Something terrible's happened! Mrs._____'—and he told me her name—'Mrs. _____ committed suicide.' They'd fished her body out of the lake and put her right there on my platform—a woman who'd been sitting in front of me every night.

"We'd gone down the previous Sunday to her house to see her. She had a lovely home, a husband, and children. But a stranger was visiting with them that day. 'Well, there's company,' Kenneth and I told each other, 'so we won't talk about God. We won't pray. We'll go on and come back again another time.'

"The Bible says, 'Preach the Word; be instant in season, out of season.' There on the desk of the dance pavilion where we held our meetings was a note from her that I was to preach her funeral sermon.

"That visitor we'd seen was an old sweetheart. When she saw him, she just lost control of herself, left her husband, her children, everything, and came up to our meeting place. I could see where she'd tried to wade into the lake, but lost her nerve. Then she jumped from the pavilion into the deep part of the lake.

"We hadn't talked to her about God. Imagine how Gant and I felt that morning. A woman that we should have talked to and prayed with—and didn't. A couple of young preachers did a lot of heart searching, I'll tell you. We did a lot of weeping before the Lord.

"Her mother arrived to have the funeral and brought a Methodist preacher with her. She said she didn't want an old so-and-so Adventist preacher doing her daughter's funeral. My, I was glad of it.

"I'll never forget his text: 'There shall be no more sea.' When the funeral ended he came right to me and said, 'Richards, I know you Adventists forgot more about the book of Revelation than I know. I don't suppose that was the real mean-

70

ing of that text.' He'd taken the sea to mean a symbol of separation. 'Come on out and help me at the grave.'

" 'No,' I said, 'you're doing just fine.' "

Those meetings in Holyoke and Woodland Park, before he'd even been to college, got H.M.S. Richards' feet wet in public evangelism. It set the tone for the rest of his life. To the end of his days the smell of wood shavings or canvas were like the scent of smoke to a fire horse. He'd be raring to get to preaching again.

After the successful meeting at Woodland Park, Kenneth had to return to Campion to finish his senior year, and Harold joined up with John Turner, the man he had been scheduled to join before Kenneth and he went to Woodland Park.

John was holding meetings in a little schoolhouse in Ford, not much more than a crossroads in the northeast corner of Colorado and just a few miles from the Nebraska line. I remember visiting Ford some years later while traveling with the Voice of Prophecy group and listening to "the Chief" tell us stories of what went on that winter on the bleak plains.

One man who came to the meetings made an especially negative impression on John and Harold. His wife had pressured him into coming. The fellow was a nasty looking specimen who chewed tobacco. The tobacco juice flowed in an ugly brown river down the sides of his mouth onto his vest.

Every evening during meeting he would sit in the very front desk of the little schoolroom, radiating antagonism. John and Harold would speak on alternate nights, but this fellow was impartially and equally rude to both of them. After almost every point made in the sermon, he would shake his head violently. From time to time he would conspicuously haul out a big watch during the sermon and sometimes even shake it to determine if it was still running.

During the schoolhouse meetings Harold received word that Twomoms was ill with pneumonia. She was still living in Holyoke a few miles away, where she had come to help take care of him and

Kenneth Gant when they conducted their ill-fated meetings there. When he reached Holyoke, he saw at once that it would be necessary for her to get to a hospital as soon as possible. Harold really feared for her life.

He took her on the train from Holyoke to Denver in a driving snowstorm, then on to the Boulder Sanitarium where he left her in the capable care of Dr. Green and his staff.

When Richards arrived back at Ford, Colorado, two weeks later, a fine-looking man met him at the railroad station. His face was vaguely familiar, but Harold just couldn't seem to place him. As he stepped off the train the man called him by name.

"Have we met, sir? I'm afraid I can't recall your name or who you are."

"Oh, yes, we've met."

"Help me. I can't remember."

"Oh, yes, we've met many times at the schoolhouse at Ford. I'm the man with the watch."

I'm sure he couldn't have missed the look of absolute astonishment on Harold's face as he tried to pull it all together. That man had accepted Jesus while Richards was gone those two weeks to Boulder with Twomoms, and the transformation, both physical and spiritual, was nothing short of a miracle. It was a lesson of encouragement to both Harold and John to see what unbelievable things God's power can do in a human life.

More than 60 years later H.M.S. met a man in Paradise, California, named Johnson who had attended the schoolhouse meetings in those sand hills near Holyoke, Colorado. He reminded Richards of the time when Harold and young schoolmate Aufderhar rode out to the schoolhouse on a motorcycle to preach and were dumped roughly when they hit a stretch of deep sand right in front of all the people waiting for them outside the door. He said Richards and John Turner had planted the seed in his heart in those meetings that finally brought forth fruit many years later. When Richards saw him in Paradise, he had become a believer. "We thank the Lord,"

H.M.S. wrote in his diary of this seed that waited 60 years to sprout and grow.

Before the meetings in Ford ended, the East Pennsylvania Conference invited Harold to come back to work there. His father had become president a couple years before, and there were great opportunities for evangelism.

One of his first assignments in the spring of 1915 was in the little village of Millerton in Tioga county just a mile or two from the New York state line. Harold had literally to fight for a place to hold his meetings there. Here's how I heard him tell it.

"I was sent to a little town in Pennsylvania to hold meetings. The only members were a few women who met in the Odd Fellows Hall above a drugstore. The chief mogul in town was Mr. Miller, the county undertaker. His wife was an Adventist. Miller hated all preachers—Adventist ones in particular.

"The only suitable place to hold the meetings was that Odd Fellows Hall, and in order to get it, I had to see Mr. Miller. I decided the only way was to beard the old lion in his den.

"When I knocked on the door, Mrs. Miller met me. She was terrified, but ushered me into the living room in which her husband was reading the evening paper. When she introduced us, he only looked up, grunted, and kept on reading.

"As I sat there trying to figure out what to do next, I noticed he had the sports section open. It was the spring of 1915 and the papers were full of the upcoming fight between Jack Johnson, the Black heavyweight champion, and Jess Willard, the challenger. Johnson had won the championship on Christmas day, 1908, in Sydney, Australia, and his victory led to a public clamor for what the boxing world called a 'White hope' to dethrone the Black champion.

"To try and get some conversation going, I said, 'Who do you think is going to win between Jack Johnson and Jess Willard?'

"Miller quickly put down the paper. 'You interested in boxing?'

"'Oh, not particularly. I just spar around a little,' I answered.

"'Would you like to go a few rounds with me?' he asked.

"I could see he wanted to whip the Adventist preacher and crow about it to all his friends around the county. In those days he was in fine shape—weighed about

73

200 lbs. I weighed about 160, but was light on my feet. Although I didn't really want to fight him, I didn't have much choice.

" 'All right, I wouldn't mind, but don't hit me too hard.'

"He agreed.

"By this time I could see Mrs. Miller was pale as a ghost. She just knew her husband was going to kill me.

"Miller sent his wife to get a neighbor woman to act as our seconds in the fight. We pushed back the coffins in the big mortuary display room to form a regulation ring. The women tied on our gloves and kept time. We had regulation three-minute rounds, with a one-minute rest between.

"Fortunately during my last year at Campion I had been friends with a boy who had done quite a bit of boxing. I tutored Victor Price in some of his classes and in return he gave me boxing lessons. He had taught me to dance around and wear out my opponent. By the end of the school year, Victor gave me a pair of boxing gloves and I knew how to defend myself.

"During the first few rounds I pretended I was left-handed, led with my right, and kept the left back by my chin, cocked and ready for a big punch.

"Right from the start he showed that he was going in for the kill. But as we sparred around for the first round or two, I could see that he was beginning to get a little winded, so I just kept away from him, dancing, feinting, boxing, backpedaling. When he went back to his corner at the end of the fifth round he was puffing.

"Just before the beginning of the sixth round, I offered up a little silent prayer. 'Lord,' I said, 'this fellow needs a licking. He needs one if ever anyone did in this world. For his wife's sake, for the truth's sake, and for the fact that I need a place to hold my meetings, help me to teach him a lesson.'

"As I came out to meet him in center ring, I switched to my natural right-handed stance, and I went right after him. Before he'd been chasing me, but now I went after him and it seemed to confuse him for a moment. His face was red and he was puffing harder. A minute into the round I saw an opening and caught him with a lucky punch. He went down.

"When Miller climbed to his feet he was fighting mad and forgot all about the science of boxing. He came up flailing, trying to kill me. That played right into my hands. A few seconds later he hit the floor again. Again he staggered up red-faced and swinging like a wild bull. The third time he went down and stayed down.

"A minute or two later he raised up on one elbow and shook his head to clear the cobwebs. 'It's them blankety-blank cigarettes," were his first words as he slowly stood to his feet.

"After the women had untied our gloves, he stuck his hand out to me. 'Preacher,' he said, 'if you ever come to this town and don't stay at my house, there's going to be trouble.'

"I got my meeting hall, rent free. We had 26 baptisms out of that meeting and started a fine church.

"More than 30 years later the quartet and I were traveling in Pennsylvania. 'I want to go through Millerton on the way home and see if old Mr. Miller is still alive,' I said.

"It was about 8:00 at night when we reached the town. Everything was different, but I went into a store and asked if Mr. Miller was still alive.

" 'Yes, he's still alive and lives just down the road.'

"I went and sure enough there was the old house. After I knocked on the door a humped-over old man opened it and looked at me.

" 'You don't know me,' I began.

" 'Yes, I do. You're that preacher that knocked me down. Come in here.'

"I had a wonderful time with him. We spent about an hour together and I had prayer with him before we left. He was my dear friend until the day he died."

Harold held some evangelistic meetings with Howard Detwiler in Blossburg, Pennsylvania, and in Tioga County in the coal mining country. The two of them started a church there. Later Harold teamed up with Harry and Anna Rahn, a Pennsylvania Dutch couple. Harry would lead the music and Anna would cook for the two of them and visit interested people and give Bible studies. They held some tent meetings in Mansfield. Later Richards loved to tell about how they slept in a haunted house there.

"We had just come into town and had already pitched our tent, but were trying to find a place to live. Harry and I were at the tent when Anna returned all flushed with excitement.

" 'Harry, Harold. Good news, I've found a house. It's a beautiful house and

it's only $5 a month.'

"The big house stood majestically in a little grove at the end of a tree-canopied lane. To Harry and Anna Rahn and to me it looked like a full-grown fairy castle. We had been camping—the three of us—in a single room in town while hunting for more comfortable and spacious quarters. Naturally we had rushed out to see the mansion Anna had discovered. Now we stood at the entrance to the lane and surveyed it.

" 'You know, I can't figure it out,' Anna said, breaking our reverie. 'Why did they let us have it so cheap? After all—$5 a month . . .' She threw up her hands in bewilderment.

"We decided to close the deal quickly, before the owner changed his mind. It didn't take long to move our 'furniture' into the house. Our entire homemaking equipment consisted of three single cots, some folding chairs, our trunks, and a rickety table.

"It was glorious! The house was one of those sprawling old-fashioned mansions, with a full basement, 18 rooms on two floors, and a huge attic. I set up my cot in one of the immense parlors while Harry and Anna settled in a big room opening off the kitchen.

"We all went to meeting early that night. I was to preach on the subject of 'spiritism,' my old 'great red dragon' sermon, and I wanted to make a few last-minute arrangements for the program. Anna liked to visit with the people as they came in.

"Just before I went forward to preach, I saw her coming up the aisle, her face ashen.

" 'Oh, Harold,' she whispered hoarsely. 'I just found out something terrible. That house we moved into today—it's haunted! That's why we got it so cheap.'

"Imagine how I felt. There I was, ready to preach on 'spiritism' only to learn that the house where we were to sleep that night was haunted! As I walked to the pulpit and turned to face the audience, there sitting on the front row was the only spiritist medium in the county, mumbling to herself as she rocked back and forth with her eyes closed.

" 'Lord,' I whispered a prayer, 'give me the victory over this thing. Help me, Lord.'

"The Lord came through as always. I preached with great freedom. And all during the sermon the spiritist medium sat on the front row in a trance, 'peeping and muttering.'

"The moment I finished, she jumped up, put her hand to her head, and shouted so that the whole audience could hear: 'Don't I know this is the truth! Don't I know this is the truth!' Then she ran out as if the devil were after her. I thought about Jesus and the man with the unclean spirit who said, 'Art thou come to destroy us? I know thee who thou art, the Holy One of God' (Mark 1:24).

"After the crowd had gone, the Rahns and I slowly—very slowly—made our way back to our new home. As we walked up the lane in the darkness, the house looked much different than it had in the morning. Now it loomed black and ominous against the night sky.

"The front door creaked frighteningly, and our footsteps made hollow echoes as we walked through the empty rooms. None of us said much.

"Harry and Anna went to their room at the back of the house, and I to my parlor 'bedroom,' where I soon huddled under the covers, listening to every creak and groan of the old house.

As I lay there a long time, listening and staring wide-eyed into the darkness, all at once I began to think how I could scare Anna. As I became engrossed in my mischievous plans, I lost all my own fear.

"Creeping out of bed, carrying my shoes, I made my way as silently as I could up the creaky stairs, all the way to the attic. When I reached the top, I put on my shoes and started down the stairs—clunk, several seconds pause, clunk, pause, clunk, pause, clunk—clunk—clunk.

"Downstairs, Anna was petrified with fear. Harry got up quickly and ran to my parlor army cot. When he saw that I was gone, he guessed instantly what was going on, but went along with the joke and kept quiet. All the while those heavy footsteps crept closer, closer, closer—clunk, clunk, clunk! Anna was practically in hysterics. When she finally saw who and what the ghost was, she was too relieved to be angry.

"Right there, in the middle of the night, she cooked us a big dinner—scrambled eggs, fried potatoes and gravy—the works! When we had finished eating, we all felt more cheerful and went to bed, sleeping peacefully the rest of the night.

"That wasn't the last of the troubles with the haunted house. Sometimes the wind would whistle through the trees outside, and the whole house would moan as if it were some giant animal in pain. Anna was ready to move out, $5 or no $5 a month.

"Then we discovered the secret of the ghostly groans. Hanging over the roof of the house was the limb of a tremendous elm tree. When the wind was just right, *the limb would rest on the ridge of the roof and saw back and forth like the bow to the strings of a giant violin. It had frightened away all previous tenants. With the enigma solved, the Rahns and I could listen—and laugh."*

As Harold continued to work in Pennsylvania, he held meetings in Philadelphia and other Pennsylvania towns with young J. S. Washburn and Elder R. A. Harter.

One night during the Harter meetings a big rainstorm threatened to blow the tent down. Harold and the other men ran from one tent stake and rope to another, trying to loosen the ropes to keep them from pulling the tent stakes out of the soggy ground. Every time the lightning would flash, blue streaks would run down the ropes, giving the poor man wrestling with them an ugly jolt. It was only by the mercy of God that one of them wasn't killed.

By 1916 two years had gone by since Harold had graduated from academy. Twomoms was putting the pressure on him to go to college. His father joined in the urging. But Harold didn't want to go. He loved the excitement of preaching. But that's another chapter.

BACK TO SCHOOL AGAIN

"College! Why should I go to college?" Harold protested. "I'm already doing the Lord's work, holding meetings and raising up churches. College would be just a waste of time. Four years out of my life. You never went to college, and you're a conference president," Harold shot back in answer to his father's urging. The young man intended it to be the coup de grace, the final sword thrust to end the argument. But his father had an appropriate answer.

"That's true, I never went to college, but I never lived and worked as a young man in the twentieth century, either."

Harold decided to attend, but didn't think he'd be staying very long. As a result he chose first to take the courses he needed most, so that he could leave quickly and get back to work.

The war was raging in Europe in the fall of 1916 when 22-year-old H.M.S. Richards arrived at Washington Missionary College not far from the nation's capital. He reached Washington, D.C., in time to see Woodrow Wilson, the president of the country, during the final days of his campaign for reelection.

Leading a parade down the District of Columbia's streets, the president was dressed in a blue coat, white trousers, and a straw hat. His campaign slogan was "He Kept Us Out of War!"

Four years before, while Richards was still a teenager and a junior in Campion Academy, Woodrow Wilson had won the Democratic nomination for president of the United States after a long and bitter battle with James Beauchamp "Champ" Clark of Missouri. When Wilson had been nominated at the Democratic convention in the Baltimore, Maryland, armory, his supporters released baskets of white doves. They proceeded to flutter up into the rafters of the building, generously bestowing their droppings on the heads of the delegates. Clark held his lead in the voting 440 to 324 over Wilson for the first 10 ballots, but as day after weary day passed, Wilson began to nibble away at Clark's lead until he finally captured the nomination on the forty-sixth ballot. William Allen White, a political reporter at the Baltimore Convention, confessed that it was the longest convention he had ever observed during his career.

In the 1912 election that followed Wilson won over President Taft and Teddy Roosevelt, primarily because Roosevelt had split with Taft and the Republican party by running in his own newly-formed Bull Moose party.

Then on June 28, 1914, just days after Richards' graduation from academy, the assassination of crown prince Franz Ferdinand of Austria in Sarajevo, Bosnia, kindled the first flames of World War I. On August 4, England declared war on Germany and the Central Powers. Wilson was able to keep America out of the fight for a time, but when the German submarine U-20 sank the passenger liner *Lusitania* in May of 1915 with a loss of 139 American lives, former President Teddy Roosevelt echoed the sentiment of many Americans that we should jump into the war and teach the Kaiser some manners.

The United States reelected Wilson in November 1916, and he continued to resist entry into the European war, but the inconceivable blundering of the German war machine by attacking United

States shipping and attempting to incite Mexico against the United States little by little raised American anger until on April 2, 1917, Wilson made his war speech to congress and it voted to declare war.

This made young Richards eligible for the draft. It began to dawn on him that he might have his college life and future ministry cut short or at least postponed by the army. Though he had to sign up, for some reason he was never called even though two of his college classmates were drafted. Had he actually been called up, though, it is doubtful that he would have had to serve because of his blind left eye and limited vision in the right.

That September of 1916 Harold Richards enrolled in Washington Missionary College, signing up for classes in European history, Greek I, philosophy, advanced Bible doctrines, and advanced college rhetoric. His grandmother "Twomoms" Sylvester sold the little homestead cabin in Dunravin Glade, Colorado, for $500 to help pay his college expenses and volunteered to come keep house for him.

They lived in a little third-floor apartment, and in order to pay the rent Richards got up at 4:00 winter mornings to fire the furnaces for six apartment houses.

Though young Richards already held ministerial credentials issued by the East Pennsylvania Conference, and he was still a student in Washington Missionary College, the District of Columbia Conference Executive Committee voted him a ministerial license in the fall of 1917 and added him to its roster of permanent conference employees.

A few weeks later the committee offered the following assignment to the young ministerial student: "VOTED that we ask Brother Harold Richards to undertake supervision of the work at Arlington and Ballston for the present, devoting Sabbaths and Sundays and such other time as he finds possible in connection with his school work, to the work there; and that we allow him for such services a salary of $5.00 a week." The following month the conference asked him to conduct the annual week of prayer for the Kilmarnock church.

He and D. A. Rees, another young minister, held evangelistic meetings in Laurel, Maryland, during his summer vacation in 1917. Rees later received another assignment, leaving Richards to continue the meetings with no one to help him but a young lad who took care of the tent. He did the preaching, praying, led the singing, and took up the offering all by himself. In addition to conducting tent meetings, Richards took classes by correspondence during the summers of 1917 and 1918 so that he could complete all his college requirements in three years.

In September 1917 he signed up for courses in advanced English literature, the Epistles, European government, history of antiquity, introduction to philosophy, major and minor prophets, economics, Greek II, the history of Greece, and ethics.

During February 1918 the conference committee voted further that "in view of the fact that Brother Harold Richards has undertaken the duties of Elder of the Capitol Hill Church, taking full charge of the regular services and Sunday night meetings at that place, it was VOTED that the salary of Brother Harold Richards be increased to $10.00 per week plus the usual 20 percent bonus."

For the duration of his college life Richards continued to be the pastor of the Capitol Hill Seventh-day Adventist Church in downtown Washington, just under the eaves of the nation's capitol. He had to ride the streetcar twice a week from Takoma Park to get to his church, involving an hour and a half journey with two transfers. Never one to waste a minute, he studied Greek and other difficult subjects while traveling to and from his church.

One day while Richards was on his way to church something happened that stuck in his memory for the rest of his life. A distinguished-looking couple was about to board the streetcar at one of his stops. Thinking a little Black boy behind them had brushed against his wife, the man became enraged. Knowing her husband's fierce temper, his wife hustled him aboard the streetcar to avoid an embarrassing scene. As the red-faced husband slid into his seat by the window, the little boy still stood outside the streetcar. Before his wife could stop him, the man jabbed his umbrella out the window of the streetcar right into the child's eye.

As the screaming boy fell to the ground, the motorman locked the breaks of the streetcar and jumped out to help. A crowd quickly gathered, and a police officer arrested the man.

The court subpoenaed Richards as a witness at the trial. When the lawyer called him to describe what he had seen, Richards told the court what he thought of a man who would do such a cruel thing.

"Objection, your honor. Please instruct the witness that we aren't interested in what he thinks, only what he saw."

One of the other witnesses was a school teacher. When the attorney for the little boy asked her to tell what she had seen, she testified that "when this man leaned out the window of the streetcar, his face looked just like a demon!" The lawyer for the defendant immediately jumped to his feet. "Objection, your honor. This witness has no idea what a demon looks like."

For years after that, Richards would use the incident to explain that we as Christians are witnesses. We are not called to share with the world our fine-spun theories, but what Jesus has done for us. He would emphasize that Jesus had said, "Ye are my witnesses," not "Ye are my lawyers!"

Richards and some of his student minister friends would often go into downtown Washington to hear well-known preachers. One was G. A. Gordon, pastor of the Washington Congregational Church. They saw that Gordon used notes, but could never catch him turning a page. One night they came with binoculars and sat in the gallery. Sure enough, they noticed him cleverly sweeping a page over as he was making gestures to emphasize a point. With the binoculars they could see that his notes were written in large letters, but on closer examination recognized that they were in Hebrew.

On December 18, 1917, the night the United States Congress passed the Prohibition Amendment to the constitution and sent it on for ratification by the states, Richards and some friends went down into Washington to hear Billy Sunday, the well-known American evangelist.

Born in Ames, Iowa, Sunday had been a professional baseball player, but after his conversion left baseball and took to preaching. With songleader Homer Rodeheaver, he held 300 great revivals across the United States, and is estimated to have spoken to 100 million people, bringing many of them to Christ.

Though some considered him crude and vulgar, he was an energetic and enthusiastic champion of prohibition, and no doubt had a great influence in the passing of the Eighteenth Amendment. "I hope the time will come," he would shout, "when America is so dry you'll have to prime a man before he can spit."

In the summer of 1918 Richards was again in a tent, but this time had young D. A. Rees as a coworker. They held tent meetings in Arlington, Virginia, and from a tent campaign in Laurel, Maryland, established a church.

One day while they visited with interested people from their meetings, a storm came up. Rees and Richards hurried back to the tent to try to save it, but were too late. They found it in shreds. That night Richards preached under the stars on the topic "The Battle of Armageddon."

On one of the nights in the Laurel campaign, Richards and Rees had lined up a special attraction. A missionary from India would show slides. The tent was packed, but the guest never showed. Richards had to stir up a sermon on the spur of the moment.

They rescheduled their India guest for a later night, but by 8:15 p.m. he had still not appeared. Just as they were about ready to give up hope, an automobile chugged up to the tent in a cloud of dust. Their guest got out and in a flurry of activity began to set up his projector. When it was ready, he turned to Richards and Rees with an embarrassed confession.

"Men," he said, "I forgot to bring my screen. Do you have something here we can use?" All the young evangelists could come up with was a sheet that had to be stripped from the bed of bachelor Richards. With great chagrin he pinned up the wrinkled linen that had been on his army cot for several days. All this preparation consumed half an hour. By 8:45 the guest was ready to go—they thought—until he turned and confessed to the audience that he had forgotten his slides.

The summer of 1918 was a time of great emotional and spiritual turmoil for Richards. It was the occasion we mentioned earlier of his anger and resentment against the president of the Columbia Union Conference. Whenever I heard him tell the story, he would preface his remarks with "I won't go into the rightness or wrongness of what happened, but . . . " His father never spoke of it to either of his sons, but young Richards was perceptive. He could sense that something had brought sorrow and anguish to the mother and father he loved. When they would visit him at college that summer, he would often see that his mother had been crying, and he would hear whispers from others about what had taken place.

At this date it's impossible to know with certainty what the problem was, but his father was not reelected as president of the East Pennsylvania Conference that year. It is altogether possible and even likely that the young man felt that the Columbia Union Conference president had not supported his conference president with enough vigor, or more likely had been a part of the movement to have him dropped from his office.

The succeeding year H.M.J. Richards served as president of the Ontario Conference, then after one year moved on, accepting a position as president of the Texico Conference with headquarters in Clovis, New Mexico, in 1919. He only held the position for three years and was not reelected. Then he remained in limbo for a year before becoming president of the Arkansas Conference.

After little more than three years in Arkansas, the elder Richards was once again not reelected as a conference president. In his diary for May 3 of that year, Harold Richards wrote: "Granny writes about a man that wrote a harsh letter to Father. Criticism. Somebody else wants the job maybe. It's the only scar in this work—the enemy of leadership."

In another entry for the next day, May 4, 1926, Richards comments, "No word from Father yet. I fear he is depressed over the attitude of his union president. Why does a successful work have to be hindered that way? May the Lord interfere and deliver from all evil."

H.M.S. Richards was a devoted son, and through the eyes of love may have failed to recognize that his father had difficulty in his personal relations with fellow church employees.

H.M.J. Richards continued to bounce from place to place in succeeding years—chaplain at St. Helena Sanitarium in California; pastor of the Mountain View Seventh-day Adventist Church; pastor briefly in Long Beach, California; chaplain at the Glendale Sanitarium, and finally as an assistant to his son in the Voice of Prophecy ministry. By then he was in his late seventies.

It was a well-known fact that none of the women in the office wanted to be the secretary of the older Richards. Del Delker (popular contralto soloist on the *Voice of Prophecy* broadcast for years) finally received that unpleasant assignment. She recalls how one day he rebuked her for changing and editing one of his letters.

"Elder Richards," she replied, "a good secretary tries to make her boss look good. You had a lot of repetition in your letter, and I took it out. If you want the one who gets your letter to think you're a doddery old man always repeating yourself, I'll be happy to type your letters exactly as you dictate them."

He never troubled her again about what she did to his letters, and they became fast friends. Those of us who knew him, admired him and loved him, but recognized that he was often abrasive and curt with associates. He criticized Voice of Prophecy employee social events, considering them frivolous. Sometimes he would attend them, no doubt because Bertie, his wife, insisted, but likely as not would dourly show his disapproval by his body language.

On one occasion, Jerry Dill, bass in the quartet, took a photo of him at one such social event and later as a gesture of friendship presented it to him. He took it, looked at it for a moment, then without thanking Jerry, tore it in two.

Was he a bad person? Not at all. He was a rigid old Englishman when I first knew him, somewhat lacking in a sense of humor, very conservative, yet in many ways was totally without guile. I remember one time we members of the quartet were complaining to him about something we thought needed to be changed in connection with our music department. After listening patiently, he offered a bit of sage advice. "Boys, be patient," he said, then quoted the wisdom of von Logau. "Though the mills of God grind slowly, yet they grind exceeding small." It takes all kinds to make a world.

Young Harold Richards was ordained to the ministry on September 21, 1918. Though it is unusual for a young man to receive ordination before he even finishes his seminary training, in Richards' case it was totally appropriate. He had already been actively preaching for more than five years, and had demonstrated unusual ability and dedication. Richards took 1 Corinthians 2:1, 2 as the guiding text for his own ministry. "And I, brethren, when I came to you, came not with excellency of speech or of wisdom, declaring unto you the testimony of God. For I determined not to know anything among you, save Jesus Christ, and Him crucified."

During that final year at Washington Missionary College he took classwork in Greek III, sociology, pastoral training, Rome and the Middle Ages, American history, and international law.

Richards was attending classes one day when church bells began ringing and the factory whistles blew. It was the eleventh hour of the eleventh day of the eleventh month, 1918. World War I was over! The Armistice had been signed. No more worry that the draft would interrupt his school work. Peace had come at last. Richards with his classmates joined in the celebration in downtown Washington, D.C.

But on January 9, 1919, Richards received a blow that was to him almost as painful as if a member of the family had died. Theodore Roosevelt, his boyhood hero, suddenly and without warning, died in his sleep. Many of Roosevelt's friends including young Richards, and no doubt Roosevelt himself, had wistfully hoped that he would be nominated for the presidency once again in 1920, but it was not to be. The old warrior was dead.

Richards was active in extra-curricular activities, even though he had worked his way through school, earning most of his expenses. He was president of the Quadrangle Club, leader of the Ministerial Band, and assistant editor of the school paper, *The Sligonian*. His fellow students elected him president of his class in both his junior and senior years.

The college annual for 1919 had a page dedicated to Harold Marshall Sylvester Richards, senior class president. Beneath his picture were these words:

> *"The general voice*
> *Sounds him for courtesy, behavior, language,*
> *And every fair demeanor, an example;*
> *Titles of honor add not to his worth,*
> *Who is himself an honor to his title."*

The school paper quoted part of his president's address to his senior class:

"These are days big with promise and freighted with destiny. The gates of service are wide open, and the call is loud. War is over just now, and men prophesy times of peace. As the Four Winds clear away the smoke of world conflict, the Seven Seas make wide a pathway to the ends of all the earth.

"We do not mistake the meaning of this hour. We understand to a degree its serious import and its unexampled opportunity. And we accept the challenge. We cannot do otherwise than be true to our Alma Mater for she is the Gateway, not to careers, but to service. The '19 legion has its orders, and they are simple—Forward March!

> *"From here and there and everywhere,*
> *To northern woods and southern seas,*
> *From old Arcturus to the Pleiades*
> *The way leads still; from dark to dawn;*
> *On, Class of '19, Onward! On!"*

Elder Arthur G. Daniels, president of the General Conference of Seventh-day Adventists, preached the baccalaureate sermon for Richards' graduation. After the service, Richards asked him, "Elder Daniels, where shall I go to work?"

"Well," Daniels said, "two big fields are opening up—Canada and the Deep South."

"If I were your son, where would you recommend that I go?" Richards continued.

"Canada," was Daniels' immediate answer. The next week Richards wrote a letter to the Ontario Conference of Seventh-day Adventists, and their reply set in motion a chain of events that would change the course of Richards' life, not only for the next seven years, but permanently.

He had been too busy to think much about marriage during college days. Some girls had tried to attract his attention—girls whose company he sometimes enjoyed on social occasions—Loretta Taylor, Elmira Lothrop, Frankie Bliss. With Frankie he even entertained thoughts of marriage, but something kept their relationship from progressing beyond being just good friends. Had he only been able to look into the future, he would have seen that God had a special girl waiting—a girl he would meet in a foreign land, a girl who would change his life in a wonderful way forever.

HARMONY CORNERS

Ottawa was a great disappointment. The Ontario Conference had led Richards to believe that his first assignment would be in a new church in the capital city of the great northern neighbor of his home country. What met his sight when he arrived was a little tarpaper church with 20 members and a discouraged pastor, Elder W. J. Hurdon, the man with whom he was to work.

When he and Elder Hurdon began to search for a lot on which to pitch a tent for their meetings, they ran into further disheartening news. The only available lot was on a corner about a half mile from the center of town, with huge billboards obscuring the site where they would put the tent. He made the best of a bad situation by advertising their location as "Behind the Billboards," and suspending a large banner between the two tent poles that were barely visible above the billboards.

When the meetings began, Richards hired a young fellow to lead the music and take care of the tent. Wilfred Belleau confessed to Richards that he wanted to become a preacher, but didn't know what to do to improve his speaking ability.

91

"Look, Wilfred, in the morning after your work is done, put the tent walls down, and preach to an empty tent. Pretend it's full of people."

One day Richards noticed the tent walls down, and heard someone talking inside. He suspected it was Wilfred practicing, so he quietly slipped in and sat down on the platform behind him. After a bit, when Wilfred said something that stirred his heart, Richards boomed out a loud "Amen!" Startled, the young man almost leaped off the platform.

In her book about her father, Virginia Richards-Cason tells about one family that accepted the Lord from those 1919 Ottawa meetings. Mabel MacDougal, a young government employee who had been attending, had decided to be baptized, but she had a great burden for her Scottish mother and her 10 brothers and sisters. Mabel persuaded Richards to go with her by train up-country to the MacDougal farm to visit the family.

"John runs the family, along with Mother," she told him on the train, "but it is really Edna who is the key to this group. If you can persuade Edna to listen, you'll get the rest of the family."

When they started the Bible studies in the big family kitchen, Mabel arranged her family around the table with Edna sitting directly across from Richards. Edna, from the start, manifested a deep interest, and responded positively each time Richards and her sister Mabel returned to the farm for a Bible study. Surprisingly, only the mother held back. She wasn't convinced of the necessity of baptism by immersion. Richards didn't push her.

When the day came for two of the girls to be baptized, they were all ready to leave for the service when they noticed that their mother was dressed up as though she too were going somewhere.

"Mother, where are you going?" they asked.

"Why to be baptized, of course," the woman answered.

In time the entire family of 12 MacDougals joined the Seventh-day Adventist church.

The Ottawa church operated a small church school on the premises, but late summer of 1919 they received word that the teacher scheduled to teach that fall had become ill and wouldn't be able to come. The conference quickly scouted around for a substitute teacher and found a girl who had been selling religious books down in the Niagara peninsula, but would be willing to take the position at least for a year.

When young Pastor Richards, along with one of the deaconesses in the church, met the train, he saw a stunning young woman alight from the coach. Mabel Annabel Eastman captured Richards' heart from the very first sight he had of her. She was wearing a dark blue suit, with a black velvet hat. Unable to take his eyes off of her, he thought she had the pinkest cheeks he had ever seen.

From that day on, the little church school with its nine students and pretty teacher had the most attention it had ever received from a pastor. He visited the school just about every day to make sure everything was progressing in a satisfactory way for those nine children.

Twomoms, who had come to Ottawa to keep house for her favorite grandson, also noticed with approval, and from time to time invited the school teacher to meals at their little home.

The members of the church began to be aware of the pastor's unusual interest in the church school as well, and even the students watched with wide eyes and knowing glances. They even cooperated by studying quietly alone for an hour or two from time to time when the pastor took their teacher to a concert at the nearby Musicians Guild Hall during school hours.

As the year progressed, Richards began to hear rumors that Mabel's father, the treasurer of the Canadian Union Conference of Seventh-day Adventists, was planning to accept an invitation to transfer to Boulder, Colorado, and young Richards feared that he would take Mabel back to the States where some young buck south of the border would snap her up.

Thus it happened that on Tuesday evening, March 23, 1920, Mabel and Harold were returning from one of their visits to her parents' home in Oshawa near Toronto. As the Canadian National train clickity-clacked toward Ottawa that evening, Harold led Mabel back to the parlor car at the end of the train. There he moved two of the big chairs close together, and they talked of what she might be doing the next year after school concluded.

Then he invited her out onto the observation deck to watch the sunset. In the rosy glow of the setting sun, Harold Richards took Mabel's hands in his.

"Mabel, I love you," he said. "Do you think you could be my wife. I haven't riches or lands to offer you; only the love of a struggling preacher. Can it be enough for you?"

When she began to cry, Harold knew her answer was yes even before she spoke the words.

Three weeks later, on Wednesday, April 14, Harold and Mabel were back in Oshawa, Ontario. There in a quiet private ceremony in a tiny suburb of town felicitously named Harmony Corners, Mabel and Harold promised they would love each other forever. Elder A. V. Olson, president of the Eastern Canadian Union Conference of Seventh-day Adventists, performed the ceremony. Twomoms was there, along with Mabel's mother, father, and sister, but Father and Mother Richards were in faraway Clovis, New Mexico, and not able to attend.

Harold Marshall Sylvester Richards forever after that declared that a loving heavenly Father had been guiding his life, saving Mabel for him. "She had a rose in her hand when we were married," he said. "She was the sweetest thing I have ever seen."

Their honeymoon was the train ride back from Oshawa to Ottawa. Some of the church members might have guessed that something special had happened back in Harmony Corners, but young Pastor Richards didn't announce their marriage and introduce his bride until the end of the school year a few weeks later. One of Mabel's little students burst out, "Oh, goody," and danced around, clapping her hands.

Twomoms didn't stay long after the wedding. She was sad to leave her beloved grandson, and he urged her to stay, but she wisely responded, "In the early years of marriage, every young couple needs some time to be alone."

Harold Richards kept busy during his years in Canada. After the

94

tent meetings in Ottawa in the summer of 1919, he held evangelistic meetings in the church during the winter.

In the summer of 1920 he and Mabel went down to Kingston where he conducted a series in a tent with his friend, George Belleau. Wilfred, George's brother, was the young man who had helped Richards the summer before in Ottawa. George and Harold began to notice things being pilfered from their tent. They decided to string up a long heavy wire from one end of the tent to the other, then fasten George's ugly and fierce-looking bulldog to a chain on the wire so he could roam the tent and frighten away any prospective thieves. It was a great idea and worked fine until one day someone stole the bulldog. Belleau finally got his dog back from a local judge to whom the thief had sold him.

That winter Richards returned to Ottawa where he and F. W. Stray, the Eastern Canadian Union Conference president, held meetings in the Regent Theatre. The next summer found Richards and Stray together again in a tent in Ottawa, and the winter of 1921 in the Orange Hall. The Orangemen were an Irish Protestant organization active in Canada. Though Richards was still pastor in Ottawa, the city had been transferred out of the Ontario Conference and now belonged to the Quebec Conference with Elder D.J.C. Barrett as conference president.

The summer of 1922 Harold Richards and Mabel, along with Harold's mother and father, boarded a train out to the General Conference of Seventh-day Adventists session in San Francisco. It was the first time for either Harold or Mabel to visit the Far West. Neither of them knew that in just four short years they would be making their home in California, and it would be there that Richards would launch his broadcasting career.

After returning from the General Conference, Richards held a tent evangelistic campaign with his friend E. D. Lamont. It was the first of several meetings they would conduct together in Canada. Richards and Lamont opened up the first of their meetings in the Star Theatre in Carleton Place that winter, about 30 miles southwest of Ottawa. In

March they concluded their last meeting in the Star Theatre and moved to Chosen Friends Hall, a second floor room above some stores.

In those days Richards often had to deal with ministers of other denominations who would attack Seventh-day Adventists as soon as he pitched his tent and released his advertising. After one such attack by a Reverend Phillips, Richards answered him on the front page of the local newspaper, *The Sentinel*. Another time in Carleton Place, the Reverend Bonsworth of St. Matthews Church warned his congregation about Richards. The opposition only served to excite interest. When Richards would advertise that he would answer the criticism, he would invariably get a full house in his tent or meeting hall.

On May 1, 1923, Mabel received a telegram that her mother was seriously ill. Richards borrowed $150 from a church member and put his wife on the Canadian National train. She would transfer in Chicago to a Boulder, Colorado, train. The next 12 weeks were lonely ones for the young evangelist. He no longer had Twomoms to take care of him, and now his wife was gone. May 2, the day after Mabel left, he wrote in his diary: "Most lonesome day I've ever spent." May 3: "No word from Mabel." Friday, May 4: "My, how I had to work trying to press trousers and get ready for Sabbath. Truly a woman has the hardest end of all things—a dull round of monotony."

While Mabel was away, Harold performed his first wedding service for a young preacher friend, Albert Millner, and his bride Rita May Wells. The bride was so nervous that Richards had to calm her down, and in the process soothed his own jumpiness.

He remembered a few years before, when he and another young minister crony, Howard Detwiler, had conducted evangelistic meetings in Blossburg, Pennsylvania. Neither of them were ordained ministers at that time. "Harold, do you think we have the authority to marry people?" Detwiler asked. "A young couple has asked me to marry them, but I don't know if I can."

Harold urged his friend to perform the wedding. "I read in a Pennsylvania law book the other day that any minister can perform a marriage ceremony. It didn't say he had to be ordained. You're a minister. You have a ministerial license. Go ahead."

"You do it, Harold. Your dad is president of the conference."

"Oh, no. My dad would be tougher on me than he would on you. You do it."

It was getting late when they finally decided it was all right to officiate. Howard reluctantly did the ceremony and Harold served as one of the witnesses.

A few months later the two young ministers were walking by the young couple's home. "Harold, do you think they're really married?"

"Well, Howard, I certainly hope so."

Whether that young couple was legally married no one ever knew or confessed, but the knot for Albert and Rita Millner stayed tied for a good long time, and the Millners were not only his lifelong friends, but would become close coworkers just a few months later in the town of Renfrew, Ontario, about 60 miles up the Ottawa River.

Finally, on July 24, Harold received a telegram from his wife that she would be on the 7:15 p.m. train. "Got house cleaned as well as a man can," he wrote in his diary for that day, and he had a vase full of sweetpeas on the table to greet her when she came in the door. "What a joy after separation since May 1," he confessed to his diary.

On August 3 that summer he was shocked when he learned of the death of President Warren G. Harding. He had met Harding as a Senator in 1918. The next day (Sabbath) after Harding's death, Richards preached a sermon on Micah 6:8, Harding's presidential oath of office text. "He hath shewed thee, O man, what is good; and what doth the Lord require of thee, but to do justly, and to love mercy, and to walk humbly with thy God."

A couple weeks later a diary entry on Mabel's birthday expressed his frustration at not being able to treat her in what he felt was the manner she deserved. "Mabel's birthday, and I penniless. Well, she knows I love her more than ever, and I know she loves me increasingly and that's enough for any mortal."

Word was getting around about the young preacher in Ottawa, Canada. In November 1923 Richards received a telegram from

Frederick Griggs, president of Emmanuel Missionary College in Michigan, requesting him to come to the college immediately and preach twice a day for a week for the school's Week of Prayer. Harold arrived by train and for the next week spoke morning and evening to the students in their chapel. At the end of the week he wrote in his diary: "Good revival and souls saved, I believe."

Invitations began to come asking him to be pastor and evangelist in Chicago, Kansas City, New York, and other places, but Harold and Mabel felt it was important to stay in Canada, at least for the present.

In January 1924, Richards, in the dead of winter, with Albert and Rita Millner and Elder Joyce, another young preacher, began an evangelistic series in Renfrew in the O'Brien Theatre. They continued until summer, when they pitched a tent in the same town. By this time W. A. Lindsay, who would become a lifelong friend and associate, had joined him.

During February 1924 Mabel and Harold traveled to Kingston to attend an Eastern Canadian Union Conference session. Elder William A. Spicer, president of the General Conference, had come to the meetings, and the leadership assigned Richards to write up his morning devotional talks for the Canadian Union church paper. After the meetings, Spicer went through Ottawa on his way west. Richards' entry in his diary for February 24 reported that "Spicer came to visit on way through to Oshawa. Elder Spicer seemed to appreciate my books more than anybody I ever had here. He is so kind in home to us—a good man and full of the Holy Ghost."

The next January, Richards, Lindsay, and Millner would open a series of evangelistic meetings in the Majestic Theatre in Pembroke, another little town 100 miles up river from Ottawa. Opening night the temperature dropped to 20 degrees below zero.

On April 9 of that spring Richards wrote his diary entry in red ink. Why? Because it was what he called "a red-letter day in his life." At 4:00 a.m. Mabel awakened Harold with the news she was feeling her first labor pains. Since they didn't own an automobile, he called a taxi and at 4:30 a.m. got her to the hospital. The doctors and nurses all assured the young couple that the baby wouldn't arrive for 12 to 24 hours. Virginia Dale Elizabeth Richards surprised them all by making her appearance much earlier. Richards' diary entry for that day reported that "the finest baby in forty counties came to town at 7:10 a.m., Dr. J. Fenton Argue presiding. We are happy and thank God for the light labour and healthy child. May we ever be led of His Spirit to guide her feet aright and be true parents."

The child was the joy of his life. Three given names had become a tradition in the Richards family. Dale and Elizabeth honored members of the family—Dale from an aunt and Elizabeth from his beloved Twomoms. Virginia was the name of the wife of a favorite poet, Edgar Allan Poe. For a while the proud father made an effort to call her Dale, but the name didn't stick. She finally ended up responding to GeGe.

Five days after Virginia's birth Harold and Mabel celebrated their fifth wedding anniversary. The diary entry for that day was jubilant. "Five years of married life end today! Best years I ever lived!"

The new dad bought a baby carriage at a second-hand store for $10 and painted it with Japanese lacquer. "As good as a new one for twice the price" he noted in his diary for April 22.

But as much as he would have loved to stay at home and spoil his new little daughter, the life of a pastor and evangelist had to go on. Richards commuted by train from Ottawa to Pembroke all spring to continue the meetings in the Majestic Theatre.

In May he had to leave the preaching to Millner and Lindsay while he responded to invitations to preach baccalaureate sermons in Mount Vernon, Ohio, and Oshawa, Ontario. Even though it meant long hours on the train and lost sleep, Richards couldn't say no to Kenneth Gant, his old Campion crony who requested that he come to Ohio. He arrived Friday afternoon, but discovered when he checked his luggage that he had left all his sermon notes at home. "Had to stay up till 1 a.m. last night—Lord helped me—had pretty good freedom at 11 a.m." Although he arrived home by train the following Tuesday, he had to leave again on Friday to preach the baccalaureate at Oshawa on Sabbath, then return to Pembroke and his meetings on Sunday. It was only a drive of 107 miles, but in a friend's Model T Ford it took them five hours.

Later that same week, Lindsay, Millner, and Richards pitched a tent in Pembroke and started their meetings. Virginia Cason described some trouble they had at the Pembroke tent meetings.

"One night someone poured sand into the oil line of Lindsay's car. When it was started, the sand was pumped through with the oil and ruined the engine. Lindsay offered a $500 reward for information regarding the 'prank,' but no one came forward. After some tent ropes were cut and various other incidents of harassment occurred, the two preachers decided to post a guard outside the tent while the meetings were in progress. Dad and Lindsay took turns preaching and guarding.

"One Sunday afternoon a mob of twenty to thirty young fellows approached the tent during the service. Since it was Dad's turn in the pulpit, Lindsay was standing guard outside. With him was the husband of a lady who had already been converted. The man was a big, muscular fellow, and he and Lindsay were prepared for trouble. They had parked Lindsay's new car close to the tent, pointed toward the street. The gang advanced toward them, cutting tent ropes as they came and shouting threats. The two guards noticed that the leader seemed to be a man about thirty years of age. As the mob came still closer, they began throwing rocks. The defensive strategy had been planned to the last detail. Suddenly, Lindsay signaled his helper and yelled, 'Get him!' With one motion the big man grabbed the leader and forced him into the waiting car. Lindsay jumped behind the steering wheel, revved the big engine, and the car began to move. The rest of the gang quickly surrounded the car and tried to keep it from moving, but the powerful engine was too much for them. The car picked up speed, bouncing across the bumpy lot to the street.

"'Aw, come on,' the gang leader pleaded with the two men in the car. 'We didn't mean no harm.'

"Lindsay's answer was to apply more pressure on the accelerator. 'Tell it to the judge,' he said."

Since it was a weekend, they had a hard time locating a local magistrate, but when they finally found him, he wasn't too pleased at being disturbed.

"I've already got you on two or three counts, fellow," he told the man. "The only place for you is Kingston." The Canadian federal penitentiary was at Kingston. By this time the judge had the man really scared and begging for his life.

Finally, the judge relented, putting the man on probation. "I'm not forgiving you," he said. "If anyone—and I mean anyone—throws another stone at that tent, or cuts one more rope, or makes a disturbance of any kind around there, I'll hold you personally responsible. You'll find yourself in Kingston before the week's over."

Needless to say, no more trouble occurred at the Pembroke tent meetings. At its conclusion the evangelistic team baptized 13 people in the nearby Indian River.

That September the conference asked Richards and his little family to go to Montreal. It was hard to leave all the friends they had made in the six years they had been in Ottawa. The little Ottawa church held many memories for both Harold and Mabel.

But before moving to their new place of labor, the little family took a leave of absence from Canada for several months, lasting from September to the following January. Richards' father had invited him to hold a series of meetings in Little Rock, Arkansas, but the family decided that on the way to Arkansas they'd take a side trip to Colorado where Mabel's father and mother now lived.

When they crossed the border from Canada into the United States, Mabel's father met them with his brand new Studebaker coach at the old Eastman family homestead in Charlotte, Michigan. On Monday, September 14, 1925, Mr. and Mrs. Eastman, with Harold, Mabel, and baby Virginia, piled into the new Studebaker and headed toward Colorado.

Driving across country in the fall of 1925 was nothing like now. Going through Nebraska they encountered heat and rough dirt roads. Richards' diary for September 19 remarks over the marvelous change in the roads after crossing the Colorado line. "What a difference!" he says. "Fine smooth gravel roads!"

The nostalgia began to sweep over him later that day as he saw the first dim outline of Long's Peak, Pike's Peak, then the whole outline of the Rocky Mountain range. "What memories! The sweet aroma of sagebrush! The wonderful sunset curtain across the West—this was dear old Colorado again!"

Out in Colorado, away from his home conference, a telegram reached Richards asking if he'd be available to come to Ohio as a pastor and evangelist. The answer was no, not yet anyway.

While in Loveland he persuaded his father-in-law, Fred Eastman, to drive him up to the old cabin at Dunravin glade. "Cabin still standing," he wrote. "I could have stayed there for days. It was more like old times than anyplace we've visited."

During his stay he saw many old Campion friends and visited Twopops grave. On Sabbath the Boulder Seventh-day Adventist Church invited him to preach. He entitled his sermon "Who Broke the Sacred Heart of Christ?"

Before he and his family left Colorado on the Rock Island Railroad for Kansas City, the president of the Colorado Conference invited him to pastor at Pueblo, and his old friend John Turner urged him to join the Intermountain Conference on the western slope of the Rockies. Word was getting around that H.M.S. Richards would be a marvelous asset to any conference. Again he had to say no to both invitations.

When the family arrived by train at Gentry, Arkansas, his mother and father waited for them at the station. "Mother met us and forgot all else when she saw the baby," he told his diary on October 5, 1925.

On Sunday night, November 8, they opened their meetings at the KKK tabernacle in Little Rock. The crowd was so large that Richards had to give his opening sermon on evolution twice. Attending the meeting that night was a Mr. Titus, the oldest living telegraph operator. Ninety-three years of age, he had been with Samuel Morse when he sent the first message by telegraph, "What hath God wrought?" in 1844.

The diary entry for December 13 of the series: "Spoke on 666. Got $6.66 in the offering." During the Little Rock meetings Richards suffered from migraine headaches. The December 6 entry in his diary said: "Afternoon—fine crowd on 'Seven Seals' and in evening, headache and freedom on 'Sabbath' to biggest crowd so far. Never had audience listen to that topic so earnestly and respond so fully—too sick to answer all questions."

He was able to have his old friend and music leader, Henry de Fluiter, with him for the Little Rock meetings, though before the meetings finished, de Fluiter had to rush back to Colorado to be with his daughter whose child was dying.

As the close of 1925 approached, telegrams and letters flew to Canada and back again. Elder C. F. McVagh, president of the Eastern Canadian Union Conference, urged H.M.S. Richards to return quickly to his work there to finalize plans for a big evangelistic thrust, while the Little Rock people wired McVagh to allow Richards to stay longer and finish what had been started there.

The pressure from Canada became so insistent that Richards had to leave earlier than he had planned. An ultimatum from McVagh stated that he could stay in Little Rock six more weeks if he would commit to remain in Canada at least another year. That was a promise Richards did not feel at liberty to make. The Little Rock meetings had some baptisms, but not as good as he had hoped.

On New Year's Day, 1926, Richards wrote an entry in his diary that sounded an almost eerily prophetic note. "In the name of the Lord, Amen! This year's life I dedicate to God and His cause on earth! . . . I hope the year will mark the greatest advance step in the work ever known and a new emphasis on real preaching of the Word."

Neither Richards nor any other human knew of events that would begin that year that would profoundly influence not only the life of H.M.S. Richards, but of the entire Seventh-day Adventist Church organization.

CHANGE IS IN THE AIR

Eleven days into the new year found the Richards family on the Rock Island Railroad heading back to Canada. After a brief visit with his brother, Kenneth, in Washington, D.C., Harold and his family arrived in Montreal at their new place of work. Their lodgings were in the second floor of the church building, and consisted of a kitchen and one other big room divided by a half-partition. The bedroom-living room shared a wall with the church pipe organ, and the organ blower motor sat in the bedroom where little Virginia would have to sleep. A church caretaker lived in a room off the balcony of the church and shared the kitchen with them.

Richards had high hopes for a vigorous series of meetings in that great French-Canadian center. He and Lamont found they could rent the big His Majesty's Theatre in downtown Montreal, but McVagh, the union president, opposed it and urged that they hold their meetings in the church. In his diary Richards described McVagh as "a good and spiritual man—but seems to put a damper on my spirits. We have no promise of permanent help—I feel it's the wrong way to stir Montreal."

Before beginning meetings in the church, Lamont and Richards paid a contractor $100 to clean and decorate it, also against the advice of McVagh. He wanted them to wait until after the meetings, but Richards was appalled at the condition of the church "which was very dirty indeed."

The church meetings opened on Sunday evening, January 31, 1926. "There were 65 present," his diary reads. "That is about 35 besides our folks." His subject was evolution.

It wasn't going to be easy living in the same room with a pipe organ. Sometimes the church organist would practice until 10:00 or 11:00 at night. This didn't fit into little 10-month-old Virginia's sleep schedule, especially during the days and weeks when she was running a 102-degree temperature and cutting two front teeth.

Little by little the crowds at the church began to grow, and to build up interest in the area, Richards and Lamont began holding meetings also in Pt. St. Charles and Verdun, suburbs of Montreal.

On April 9, 1926, Virginia celebrated her first birthday. "God has given us a precious treasure," Richards confided in his diary, "and she has been so well, and our hearts cannot praise Him enough."

A few days later, on April 17, a wire came from W. W. Prescott at Washington, D.C., that threw Richards into a mental and emotional turmoil. The General Conference had approved a request for Richards to teach evangelism at Union College in Lincoln, Nebraska. Elder McVagh, the Eastern Canadian Union Conference president, gave his consent.

Two days later Elder Prescott arrived by train to put pressure on Richards to accept the invitation to Nebraska. Prescott had been interim president at Union College the previous year, and was at that time head of the Bible department. He spent the whole day with Harold and Mabel, leaving only after they had given a tentative consent.

But all was not well. In his diary Richards confided: "I fear that kind of work. Don't think would be as free as evangelistic. Am writing to Father. How glad I am I have him to go to."

For the next few weeks Richards wrestled over the decision. "Have felt disquieted since yesterday," he wrote on April 20, "but am seeking light from the True Source." His friend and coworker, E. D. Lamont, did not want him to go. While all the preaching and pastoral work had to continue, a deep undercurrent of unrest surged through Richards' heart.

May 2: "I pray many times a day for divine leading and am looking for it," he wrote.

May 3: "No word from Father yet."

May 4: "No word from Father yet."

May 8: "Neither McVagh or Wilson will advise me to go or stay."

When his father finally did respond, it was only to tell his son that it was a decision that he would have to make with the Lord's help.

Complicating his decision, Richards now realized that the East Canadian Union was not going to be able to fulfill their promise to him to finance large scale evangelism. Finances were too short. Richards knew they would now have to leave Canada and find another place of labor, even though their seven years in that delightful country had resulted in wonderful experiences and had earned them many friends.

Richards turned to Mabel, his faithful companion, but she couldn't and wouldn't tell him what to do. Finally the pressure became so intense that Richards secluded himself in the attic of the old church. There he spent several days wrestling with the Lord, praying for some kind of divine sign, but as is sometimes the case in our lives, no direct message from heaven came.

At last, in desperation, he made his decision, and on May 10 wrote to Elder C. K. Myers of the General Conference and to W. W. Prescott at Union, declining the invitation from the college. Once he had made the decision and mailed the letters, Richards felt an immense burden roll off of his heart. He knew then he had made the right choice, but he still didn't have a place to land, and he knew he would be leaving Canada. Although he was in limbo, he was in the Lord's hands and that was a place he always felt comfortable.

But it still didn't stop the pressure that continued from both Washington, D.C., and Lincoln, Nebraska. Myers wrote from Washington that the General Conference still wanted him to go, and Elder W. A. Spicer, General Conference president, supported it, too. But once he had made the decision, Richards never flinched again.

But the Lord didn't leave him hanging long. When a phone call came from Elder E. L. Neff, president of the Central California Conference, inviting him to come as an evangelist, Richards' inner voice said, *"This is it! Take it!"*

Six weeks after he had first begun to wrestle with the call to Union College, Mabel, Virginia, and Harold boarded the train from Montreal to attend the General Conference session in Milwaukee, Wisconsin. There he saw Prescott and reaffirmed his decision not to go to Union College. "He said very little," Richards told his diary in an entry for June 1. "I felt I had disappointed him."

Years later, looking back on this trying time, Richards could see God at work. One of the men with whom he would have closely labored with, P. L. Thompson, president of Union College from 1928 to 1931, resigned and accepted a position as president at Shurtleff College, a Baptist institution. Thompson's abandonment of the Adventist faith had an extremely unsettling effect on many of the teachers at Union. Richards, knowing his own penchant for loyalty to his coworkers, had a deep inner feeling that it would have been shattering to him as well.

During that General Conference session Richards confirmed with Elder E. L. Neff that he would join his Central California Conference in the fall.

June 12 was the last day of the session at Milwaukee. Elder Carlyle B. Haynes sang "What Never Part Again" to close the meetings, as he would sing for many General Conference sessions in years to come. It was hard for Richards to say goodbye to his father and mother, and it was hard for them to bid farewell to their first little granddaughter.

Upon returning to Canada, Richards began planning for a tent evangelistic campaign in Verdun, a suburb of Montreal. The East

Canada Union approved a good team at Verdun—Richards, Lamont, Henry de Fluiter to lead the music, a woman named Crate as Bible instructor, and one named Patch as health lecturer.

The meetings began on August 1 in a 40-foot by 60-foot tent. They had good-sized audiences from the start, but downpours drenched everything on the second Sunday. The dikes they had put around the tent were not high enough, and after the rain six inches of water covered the lower end of the tent floor, but it didn't stop the crowds from coming.

The next day they spent the whole time digging trenches to divert the water from the tent, and brought in two big wagon loads of straw to cover the floor.

All during August the crowds continued to fill the tent, even though on August 30 the wind nearly tore it down. After spending the next day repairing it, they raised it again just in time for the meeting on Tuesday night. Throughout September the crowds continued.

On September 26 people packed the tent again, and Richards was scheduled to speak but had one of his nauseating migraine headaches and had to go home, leaving the preaching to Lamont.

By the end of September the weather was beginning to feel like winter in Canada, and the team switched from the tent to a hall. On September 30 Richards worked all day getting the new hall ready for the meeting, ran home, ate supper, then rushed back to preach the first meeting in the new hall—and his last sermon in Canada. He had planned on staying until the end of the campaign, but McVagh, the union president, said the funds were low and they could not continue his salary that long. In the last entry in his diary in Canada, Richards wrote, "I must not think of being away from Canada. I love this land and people!"

The diary contained blank pages from October 1 until Sabbath October 16, 1926, when he wrote from the train, "Awoke this Sabbath just before coming into Kansas City."

The California chapter was about to begin.

CALIFORNIA, A NEW START

Excitement filled H.M.S. Richards' thoughts as the family rolled westward on the train—and apprehension as well. What would life be like in California? Would he be accepted? What would it be like to hold evangelistic meetings there? Would the people respond more readily than the people in the East?

But for the moment the new sights and sounds of the West filled them all with wonder. As they stood on the south rim of the Grand Canyon, Mabel, and even 18-month-old Virginia, seemed to respond to the grandeur. "No words can depict the majesty and awfulness of eternity that overwhelmed me when I looked out over that vast signature of God ground a mile deep in solid stone," he wrote in his diary that day. ". . . We had to leave after only 20 minutes, as we had no money to stay. I surely hope to see this and absorb some of it again." Little did he know then that in a few years he would be racing back and forth across the country hundreds of times in a Voice of Prophecy limousine on old Route 66, thus able to visit and "absorb" both the South and North Rims of the Grand Canyon to his heart's content.

The next morning, at 8:30 a.m., they arrived in Los Angeles. Richards phoned Mabel's father and told him friends were at the station passing through and would like to see him between trains. It was a surprise when Grandpa Eastman saw his daughter, son-in-law, and granddaughter.

Because of Richards' naturally curious nature he was eager almost immediately to begin soaking up all the sights southern California had to show him. On the way to Loma Linda they drove through miles of what was reputed to be the largest grape vineyard in the world. On Sabbath afternoon friends gave them a ride down the coast from Santa Monica through Manhattan Beach, and no visit to Los Angeles would be complete in those days without a stop at Aimee Semple McPherson's Angelus Temple. "I think she is a talented, forceful, magnetic, proud, determined, and passionate woman," Richards wrote of the fiery founder of the Foursquare Gospel Church. "Her trial is a typical latter day phenomenon. All in the Temple pleased the eye—perfect organization—one-and-a-half hours preparation for sermon—two spotlights on HER."

Richards' allusion to her "trial" referred to certain sensational charges made against her, resulting in a court trial, in which she stood accused of immoral charges, including running off to a motel in northern California with an associate. None of the charges were proved, and her followers remained loyal.

His first Friday night in southern California the pastor of the Glendale Hospital church, his old Campion public-speaking professor, William G. Wirth, asked him to give a talk. His subject, "The God of the Valleys as Well as the Hills," reflected his preoccupation with the magnificent scenery that now surrounded him in California.

But sightseeing quickly had to come to an end. It would be years before the Richards' family would own an automobile. They had to do all travel by public transportation or in someone else's car. A week after arriving in Los Angeles, Richards left his wife and daughter with her parents and boarded the train for Fresno, headquarters of the Central California Conference of Seventh-day Adventists, his new employer. He arrived in Fresno tired and sick after an all-day ride on the train that had to labor up and over the Sierra Madre Mountains through Tehachapi Pass into the Sierra Nevada mountain range, then make a swift descent into Bakersfield with brakes smoking.

The next day he took a streetcar, and walked them out to the home of his old Campion principal, E. E. Farnsworth. "They treated me like a son!" he told his diary.

That evening he took a bus south to Visalia, where he would soon be holding evangelistic meetings, and for the next week scoured the town for a suitable house or apartment into which he could move his little family. "Most no good and others too high," he recorded.

Finally, after Mabel and Virginia had come up from Los Angeles by train, they together settled on a furnished apartment at 627 E. Mineral King. It was on the road east of town used by the forty-niners to reach their mining digs in the Sierras. The apartment had two palm trees in the front yard, an item significant enough to record in his diary entry for November 2, 1926, and the apartment would cost them $30 a month.

On his first Sabbath in Visalia he preached at the church about three miles out of town in the vineyards on the subject "The Book of Life." Mr. and Mrs. Bev McCulloch invited him to dinner. Bev would turn out to be a lifelong friend and confidant. "He has 2,300 hens," he wrote of that day, "so we had plenty of eggs. Gave us grapes, prunes, dried peaches, corn—most of people agricultural here. Find a friendliness that is lacking in the East."

A few days later, after the Wednesday evening prayer meeting at the Visalia church, he noted in his diary entry for November 10 that "Brother McCulloch invited us to go to Big Trees—start 6:30 a.m. tomorrow."

The next morning's entry reported: "Red letter day! Brother and Sister McCulloch took Mabel, Virginia, de Fluiter, and me up to Sequoia giant forest. Two hours after leaving oranges, pomegranates, and roses, we were viewing the oldest living thing, 'The General

Sherman' tree through a snowstorm! I had to remove my hat before its majesty. A life that has been pulsating for possibly 3,000 years. Almost a symbol of eternity. I received one tiny cone dropped from that giant tree. Its seeds are as small as wheat grains, but flat and frail."

They soon located a lot at the edge of town on which to build their evangelistic tabernacle. "People here have cars and will come," he wrote. Then he betrayed a flair for the dramatic that would bring him sometimes grief, sometimes success in his evangelism. "Wish I could get a balloon to send up with a light, or send rockets up every night."

By November 15 they had their permit to build the tabernacle on the corner of Oak and North Jacob. Elder G. A. Grauer, a German man, accepted the responsibility of constructing the tabernacle, and had men on the grounds by 7:30 a.m. ready and eager to work, some of them driving 80 miles to help. During the next few years Elder Grauer would erect or remodel nine tabernacles for Richards' evangelistic campaigns in California. Even Elder Neff, the conference president, was on hand in work clothes and with a hammer. Two days later, on November 17, Richards reported to his diary: "Tabernacle about done! Wonderful spirit among men. A real Bethel." On Sabbath, November 27, less than two weeks after they had received their permit, they dedicated the structure in preparation for the grand opening.

Sunday evening Richards wrote enthusiastically in his diary: "First night came at last! The Lord was good. Six hundred plus present—Elders Neff and Fulton also [Fulton was Pacific Union Conference president]—latter made wonderful prayer—said he enjoyed my sermon and was glad I was speaking on Daniel 2 to start. He is a real Christian—all young preachers have confidence in him.

"Brother de Fluiter's music leading was superb—nearly half of Shafter church here. My great longing is for God's leading—my life wholly His!" Everything about evangelism in the Far West was an exciting change from his disappointing recent experiences in Montreal.

About two weeks later C. C. Ellis and his wife Marie joined Richards. Ellis would organize the visiting program, and also would help out during the song service with his trumpet or French horn. From time to time he would fill in for Richards as speaker for the meetings. It would be an association that would continue for five years until Ellis and family left as missionaries to Costa Rica in August of 1930.

For the next 12 weeks Richards spoke six nights a week, giving himself, his team, and his audience a rest only on Monday evenings. On Friday night, New Year's Eve, he held a service until midnight, greeting the new year in perfect Richards' fashion—preaching!

Richards later liked to tell a comic story about what happened one night during the Visalia meetings. He was preaching about how Jeremiah illustrated the point of one of his prophecies by smashing a clay pot on the ground in the Valley of Beth Hinnom south of Jerusalem. Richards had bought a clay flower pot at a nursery and planned to smash it down on the platform to demonstrate how Jeremiah did it, but when it hit the stage it just landed with a dull thud and bounced around. "The choir kept straight faces with great effort, and C. C. Ellis almost died of a coughing fit," Richards remembered chuckling.

A list of his topics during the 1926 Visalia campaign gives us a clue to his style of evangelism in those early years:

November 28, Sunday: "Crash of Nations—Will Mussolini Succeed Where Others Failed?"
November 30, Tuesday: "Satan—Why Does God Allow Him to Exist?"
December 1, Wednesday: "Second Coming of Jesus."
December 2, Thursday: "Signs of the Times."
December 3, Friday: "Crime Wave a Sign."
December 4, Saturday: "Increase of Knowledge."
December 5, Sunday. "Turkey and Russia."
December 7, Tuesday: "Evolution."
December 8, Wednesday: "Peter, the Rock."
December 9, Thursday: "Heaven."

December 10, Friday: "Angels."

December 11, Saturday: "Protestant Purgatory."

December 12, Sunday: "Spiritism."

December 14, Tuesday: "Seventy Weeks."

December 15, Wednesday: "The Sanctuary."

December 16, Thursday: "Cleansing the Sanctuary."

December 17, Friday: "The Judgment."

December 18, Saturday: "The Scapegoat."

December 19, Sunday: "The Millennium."

December 21, Tuesday: Guest speaker—Elder Blunden.

December 22, Wednesday: "The Sabbath."

December 23, Thursday: "First Day Texts."

December 24, Friday: "Peace on Earth."

December 25, Sabbath afternoon: "Star of Bethlehem," and "Question Box."

December 26, Sunday: "Daniel 7."

December 28, Tuesday: "The Surest Sign of All."

December 29, Wednesday: "The Seven Seals."

December 30, Thursday: "The Great Red Dragon."

December 31, Friday: "Eleventh Hour Conversions." Service till midnight.

January 1, 1927, Saturday: "The Next World War."

January 2, Sunday: "Change of the Sabbath."

January 4, Tuesday: "Why So Many Denominations?"

January 5, Wednesday: "The Return of Jesus."

January 6, Thursday: "The Prophet Elijah."

January 7, Friday: "The 144,000."

January 8, Saturday: "Three Woe Trumpets."

January 9, Sunday: "The Mark of the Beast."

January 11, Tuesday: "The Seven Last Plagues."

January 12, Wednesday: "The Two Covenants."

January 13, Thursday: "666."

January 14, Friday: "The Thief on the Cross."

January 15, Saturday: Guest speaker, F. D. Nichol, "Evolution."

January 16, Sunday: "The Unpardonable Sin."

January 18, Tuesday: "What and Where Is Hell?"

January 19, Wednesday: "The Weight of a Soul."

January 20, Thursday: "Did Christ Descend Into Hell and Preach?"

January 21, Friday: "The Rich Man and Lazarus."

January 22, Saturday: "Is Anybody in Heaven Now?"

January 23, Sunday: "United States and Japan."

January 25, Tuesday: "Tithing."

January 26, Wednesday: "Millions of Heathen."

January 27, Thursday: "The Round World and Sunday."

January 28, Friday: "Message of the Pillar of Salt."

January 29, Saturday: "Baptism."

January 30, Sunday: "Blue Laws."

February 1, Tuesday: "Questions."

February 2, Wednesday: "God's Three Memorials."

February 3, Thursday: "Protestant Confessional."

February 4, Friday: "Sabbath Reform."

February 5, Saturday: "The Promises of God."

February 6, Sunday: "Why I Am a Seventh-day Adventist."

February 8, Tuesday: "What Is Jesus Doing Now?"

February 9, Wednesday: "The Two Laws."

February 10, Thursday: Baptismal class.

February 11, Friday: "The Spirit of Prophecy."

February 12, Saturday: Guest speaker.

February 13, Sunday: "Seven Words That Smashed the League of Nations."

February 15, Tuesday: "Peter's Religion."

February 16, Wednesday: "Man With 1,000 Wives."

February 17, Thursday: "God or Gorilla."

February 18, Friday: "Spirit Radio Signals."

February 19, Saturday: "Heaven's Standard of Rest."

February 20, Sunday: "Heaven's Last Call."

Richards illustrated the sermons by 4-inch x 4-inch glass slides that he projected on a large screen back of the pulpit. When he preached on controversial subjects, Richards would bring a stack of books written in opposition to the subject he was presenting that evening. He would read from the books to give the other viewpoint, then read from the Bible, and one by one would toss the secular books to the floor and hold up the Bible to graphically demonstrate that "God's Word is above the word of man."

The last night meeting at Visalia—Sunday night, February 20, 1927—Richards preached on "Heaven's Last Call." At the baptism of 59 people in a pool at Mooney's Grove, Richards stood in the cold water that winter day for more than an hour. Bev McCulloch and another big man had to almost drag him out of the water afterward. At the entrance to Mooney's Grove is the famous statue of the Indian sitting on his horse, the heads of both man and horse hanging in weariness, entitled "The End of the Trail." Richards thought to himself, *I think I know how that old Indian felt, but I'm not at the end of the trail, yet. This isn't the end of the trail. It's just the beginning, and I'm glad.*

Two weeks later, on March 6, Richards opened another series of meetings in Bakersfield, and continued for 100 nights straight, again giving the crowds a rest only on Monday nights, as he had done in Visalia. Their meeting hall was in a large rough wooden tabernacle built by the famous woman evangelist, Aimee Semple McPherson. The owner allowed them to use it for nothing if they consented to make certain improvements. The improvements included a baptistry 10-feet square.

Virginia Richards-Cason tells that during this series the amazed ranchers watched Richards, Ellis, and de Fluiter driving madly all over Kern County in Ellis' little convertible as they visited interested people. They would start early in the morning, drive 50 miles out in the country, then work their way back into Bakersfield, stopping along the way at various ranches. At times they would arrive late, hot and dusty, and without supper, just in time to walk up on the platform. Other times when they would get in a little early they would go to the tabernacle, lock all the doors, and take a quick dip in the baptistry.

In Bakersfield Richards first experimented with radio, using it to advertise his meetings. Midway through the campaign, he invited J. W. McComas, a fiery evangelist from southern California, as guest speaker. Of course, he filled the papers and even radio full of announcements of the coming spectacular. The day McComas and his choir arrived, Richards met them with a police escort at the foot of the Grapevine, 26 miles south of Bakersfield. "The Grapevine" is the name of the final steep mountain descent from the Sierra Madre Mountains into the San Joaquin Valley. The entire cavalcade sped back into Bakersfield with sirens wailing. Was it any wonder that people packed the hall that night? Henry de Fluiter had his choir in the seats on the floor in front of the platform, and McComas had his choir behind the speaker. Even though Richards had already baptized 144 people, McComas made an appeal at the end of the sermon for listeners to give their hearts to the Lord, and 25 more responded.

About a week later, Richards and his team traveled south to Los Angeles to participate in McComas's evangelistic series. They went in 25 cars and were met at the southern terminus of the pass with the same fanfare Richards had given the McComas team the previous week. In the evening at the close of the meeting, Richards made a call for decisions for Christ and 17 came forward. He said afterward, "I think it's a good thing for different men to preach for one another that way. The Holy Spirit uses different men in different ways to appeal to different people."

While the Bakersfield evangelistic campaign wound down, Richards was already making plans for meetings in Fresno. The team had conducted its baptisms in the pond in Mooney's Grove in Visalia, and in the 10-foot square baptistry in the Bakersfield Tabernacle, but for the Fresno meetings Richards would need another big baptistry. Richards, Ellis, and de Fluiter decided to set aside the pennies from the Bakersfield meeting offerings to build up a special fund to pay for fabricating a new baptistry for the Fresno Tabernacle.

By the time they had finished the Bakersfield meetings, Elder Grauer had finished building the thousand-seat Fresno Tabernacle, and they had their new baptistry built and paid for. It was 10 feet long, four feet wide, and four feet deep.

During the Fresno meetings Richards preached every night of the week for nine months straight, with the exception of two nights when he invited Elder Philip Knox of southern California to speak on astronomy and the Bible.

Early in those meetings, a layman named Ackley, custodian of the Fresno Tabernacle, noticed someone putting up some chairs in a little storefront meeting hall down the street and across from the Richards tabernacle. When he asked them what they were planning, they said, "Oh, we're going to be ready when Richards closes his meetings and pick up some of the audience."

"Oh, Richards will be going with these meetings for at least six months, maybe a year," Ackley replied.

"A year! How will he have enough subjects to last that long?"

"Oh, that's not Brother Richards' problem. His problem is that he doesn't have enough nights to preach all the sermons he wants to."

The little group held meetings in their storefront hall for a few nights, then quietly disappeared.

At the close of the marathon Fresno meetings, Richards baptized 120, then packed his evangelistic equipment in a moving van and transferred his team to Merced, where they held their meetings in a large tent. The family lived in a little apartment in back of the Merced church. By the close of the meetings 60 new people had accepted Jesus and joined the little Merced church family.

The fall of 1928 Richards' team returned to Fresno for another series that started on October 14 and continued for about three months. This time "Uncle Henry" de Fluiter painted a tremendous sign across the entire front of Grauer's tabernacle announcing it as the "Seventh-day Adventist Tabernacle." Across the entire length of the building another great sign declared in bold block letters, "Signs of the Times Bible Lectures." By the end of the second Fresno series in early 1929 more than 60 new members had joined the church.

During the Bakersfield, Fresno, and Merced meetings Richards began to have serious problems with the eye injured in his boyhood gun accident. Bright lights would seem to flash whether he had his eyes open or closed. Finally a doctor suggested it might result from a bad tooth, but after the tooth was pulled, the problem persisted.

Finally another doctor prescribed a powerful medicine, thinking a blood clot on the brain might be causing it, but after taking that medicine a short time, Richards knew something wasn't right. When he consulted a third medical specialist, the horrified doctor ordered him to stop the powerful poison at once. "Don't take another drop, Brother Richards. You've been taking enough to kill a strong man!"

Finally, Richards consulted the respected Green Brothers ophthalmologists of San Francisco. The news was disappointing. They told him he had a detached retina, and that if he had come to them sooner, they might have been able to help him recover sight in that eye. Now it was too late. The optic nerve had deteriorated until sight could no longer be restored. "Goodbye and God bless you" were their final not-so-comforting words.

By the time the second Fresno meetings concluded, Elder Grauer had finished another big tabernacle in Hanford, 35 miles south of Fresno. The Richards evangelistic team barely had time to say "Amen, Goodbye" and take a breath before starting again in Hanford. At this time the team acquired a new member, Leta Butcher, as Bible instructor.

Early during the Hanford meetings Mabel Richards received disturbing word that her mother was seriously ill and would require surgery. It was not a surprise. She had never really been well since her lengthy illness years before. Mabel packed a few things and hurried to her mother's side, just as she had six years earlier when she and Harold were working in Ottawa, Canada. Richards and Henry de Fluiter fended for themselves while she and baby Virginia were away. For the next few weeks the men lived on crackers and milk, plus some wonderful pies and cakes provided by some of the sympathetic women in the Hanford church who felt sorry for them.

Mabel's mother didn't survive long after her surgery, and some friends from the Hanford Seventh-day Adventist Church drove Harold Richards to Los Angeles for the funeral.

Soon after the close of the Hanford meetings, Richards had an invitation to the Southern California Conference of Seventh-day Adventists in Los Angeles. He didn't yet know it, but in Los Angeles the career of H.M.S. Richards would take a turn that would make his name known and beloved by millions of friends around the world.

SOUTHERN CALIFORNIA EVANGELISM

"We have an electric refrigerator in our home here at 144 N. Marengo Avenue in Alhambra. First time ever," said Richards' diary for July 1, 1929.

Elder P. E. Broderson, president of the Southern California Conference, had invited Richards to come as a full-time evangelist in the big thriving Los Angeles area. The first meeting they were to hold would be in Alhambra. Richards, as usual, came to town with all wheels spinning.

Two weeks after arriving, Richards and President Broderson spent two hours together. "He is a prince!" enthused Richards. "Backs us up in every way." As time would tell, he wouldn't always have such enthusiastic support from conference administrators. During all the time they worked together, Richards and Broderson enjoyed a marvelous relationship. It would be interrupted by the tragic death of Broderson a few years later, a blow that devastated Richards.

The site for the tabernacle was on the corner of Bushnell and Main in Alhambra. At the permit

123

hearings some of the neighbors vowed to seek an injunction to stop the work, but on July 16, 1929, the evangelistic company obtained their permit, and within 20 days construction started on the building.

On August 18, just 33 days after they had received their building permit, the meetings opened with a tabernacle full of people. "The crowd of 1,100 surprised me," Richards confessed to his diary. His subject for opening night was heaven.

The meetings in the Alhambra Tabernacle continued six nights a week with such great success that it began to stir up opposition. Reverend Foy Wallace of the First Christian Church of Alhambra began putting out handbills all over town, even on the windshields of the cars parked at the Tabernacle, advertising that he was going to reply to "this one-sided debate" of Richards on Monday night, November 18, at the Alhambra High School Auditorium. Word came to them at prayer meeting that the school board had rejected Wallace's attempt to rent the school auditorium. "Surely prayer was answered," Richards wrote in his diary for November 17, but on the next night he attended Wallace's meeting in his First Christian Church.

Wallace tried his best to get Richards to debate with him about the Sabbath, but Richards never felt that debates accomplished much good. It seemed to him that they generated more heat than light. His daughter, Virginia, described what happened the night he attended Wallace's meeting.

"He wanted to hear what the man was really saying about him. He found a place at the back of the church among a group of standing on-lookers. Within a few moments after Dad's arrival, the minister started a string of accusations. He had one of Dad's printed sermons about Paul's meeting at Troas, which said that many people make a mistake about the day this meeting took place. The minister held the printed sermon high as he charged, 'Richards says that text was a mistake.'

"That was not true. This man was saying that Dad had said God made a mistake in His word, the Bible! That could not go unchallenged. In a clear, strong voice that could be heard throughout the room, Dad said, 'That's a lie!'

"The speaker nearly fell off the platform. He had no idea that Dad was there, and since Dad was lost in the group at the back of the church, the minister could not spot him.

"A woman standing near Father turned to him and asked, 'Are you Mr. Richards?'

"'Yes,' he whispered, 'I am.'

"'Oh, good, I want to know more about this Sabbath business. I need to know all about it.' So they moved out onto the steps of the church and Dad gave her a Bible study about the Sabbath right there in front of the place where the minister was preaching against him."

"He is a good speaker," Richards wrote in his diary about Wallace, "and made out a convincing case for those desiring to reject the Sabbath." But then he added, "Since the attack of Wallace a new interest in the truth is evident." Richards was rediscovering what he had noticed in his little meetings in Canada. When someone attacked him, it provided helpful advertising and momentum for his own crowds.

Despite his heavy preaching schedule, he never lost his interest and curiosity about things happening in the world around him. On August 1 he noted that the Graf Zeppelin had begun its round-the-world voyage from Lake Constance in Europe to the United States, and on August 26 he stayed up until 1:30 a.m. listening on the radio for the landing at Mimes Field in Santa Monica. At 9:00 a.m. the next morning Mabel's father took them out to see it before it proceeded on the next leg of the journey in which Captain Hugo Eckener would pilot the huge craft around the world in 20 days, 4 hours, and 14 minutes.

On September 20 he had his old friend J. W. McComas on the platform. In the intervening two years McComas had fallen afoul of church administration for some reason, and Richards, typically championing the underdog, tried to encourage McComas by inviting him to participate in his own meetings. "McComas says he loves the truth, but feels he has been grossly mistreated. Maybe he has—it's altogether possible today," Richards commented to his diary. A few years later the church reinstated McComas, and the man resumed an active pastoral and evangelistic service, thanks no doubt in part to Richards' encouragement, compassion, and understanding.

Monday night each week was their only night off, and the Richards' family and evangelistic team spent every Monday possible at the beach. On August 19 he and his helpers went to Long Beach, but got lost coming home and were late. "Mabel never scolds," he confided to his diary. "Just as sweet as if I had been gone only an hour when I am late." And on September 16: "Water very cold and surf high and fine." It was the kind of exercise and emotional release he needed from his six-nights-a-week grind in the tabernacle.

October 10, for the first time ever, Richards used motion pictures in his meetings, projecting a film made by the Ford Motor Company. He also tried using slides for the song service. "People sing better from the screen than from a few books every night," he said. He was always on the alert to use tools that made the meetings better.

On October 19, 1929, Richards for the first time began a 15-minute broadcast on radio station KNX that he would air several times a week. The Los Angeles *Express* provided the radio time free as a perk for the advertising Richards placed with them every week.

Friday, October 25, was a second Red Letter Day for Richards. As he walked off the platform after his sermon in the tabernacle that evening, Fred Eastman, his father-in-law, greeted him.

"How's Mabel?" Richards nervously asked the older man.

"All right, and you have a little son down in the hospital."

"What a surprise!" Richards wrote in his diary. "Our prayers were answered and all is well. It is my prayer now that the Lord lead us in our duty to this dear little one. If the Lord tarries, may he help finish the Lord's work. As far as I can, I give him to the Lord for that work! God bless him! He was born about 9 o'clock, so on the holy Sabbath day." The child received the name Harold Marshall Sylvester Richards, Jr.

In November Broderson notified Richards that a request had come to the conference for him to go to Hawaii, but Richards turned it down. Things were just getting started in Los Angeles, and he didn't feel it was time to move again so soon.

Sunday evening, December 15, the Alhambra evangelistic campaign closed with 63 baptized and more to come. Helping H.M.S. Richards in the Alhambra campaign and in many following evangelistic efforts in southern California was Bible instructor Lona Brosi. "She deserves credit for every soul we baptized there in Alhambra," Richards said of her. "If you could get a crowd coming to your tabernacle, Lona would assure you of a baptism. She had a study class every night before the meeting began. She'd fill in the cracks and give explanations we didn't have time to give in the general meeting."

At the conclusion of the Alhambra meetings, Richards had the tabernacle moved to the corner of Western and Main in Los Angeles.

Between campaigns Richards and family took a few days vacation in a little cabin back of Mount Baldy. He went fishing just as he had done in Canada between meetings. It was a wonderful way for him to relax and unwind.

The next series of meetings opened January 5, 1930, just three weeks after the close of the Alhambra meetings. Since they still had no car, the family moved again in order to be closer to their tabernacle. Their new address, 3240 E. 27th Street, was just six blocks from the tabernacle on Western and Main.

In this series Richards invited his friend, the noted lecturer Dr. Alonzo Baker, to speak several times. Dr. Baker, world traveler and authority on international affairs, had been a lecturer at the University of Southern California, a teacher of international relations and political science at the University of the Pacific for 15 years, and drew standing room only crowds whenever he spoke at Richards' meetings.

On April 19 Richards had a baptism of 22. "The water was so hot I nearly fainted," he said. These meetings continued until May 11, when he preached on "God's Last Message to the World." They baptized 91 from the series.

Before the next campaign in Santa Barbara, Richards and family attended the General Conference session in San Francisco, meeting many old friends. There he met Elder B. G. Wilkinson who sold him a copy of his latest book, *Our Authorized Bible Vindicated*. "I have always been in favor of the King James Version for the pulpit and this seems to confirm my position. Anyway, it will start a conflict among us as Seventh-day Adventists," Richards said.

Vast crowds attended the session, and the public address system was not very good. The hall was packed, and the people outside couldn't hear well. "The ministers seem to have little if anything to do with the conference," Richards wrote in his diary. His old friend, Arthur G. Daniels, commented wryly to him that "they seem to be wandering around like pelicans in the wilderness."

In preparation for the Santa Barbara meetings, Richards picked out a temporary home for his wife and two children at 225 W. Victoria Street, Santa Barbara. They arrived on the train two days later. The first night the whole house began to shudder and shake. They thought it was an earthquake, but it turned out that it was only night target practice by the big battleships in the straits between Santa Barbara and the channel islands.

On July 25, Richards and Elder E. Toral Seat, a young California evangelist, started meetings in a tent in Santa Barbara. They decided that they would alternate nights preaching, drawing straws to see who went first. Elder Seat preached the first night about the God of creation. Seat mounted his big telescope outside the tent as a drawing card to help bring in the crowds.

The Tuesday after they pitched their tent a strong Santa Ana wind nearly blew the tent down. It scared away most of the crowd, but Richards gave a Bible study "to the brave ones who came inside the jumping, snapping tent."

During the Santa Barbara meetings Richards first began to dream about making a visit to the Holy Land. One woman even offered him a small donation toward such a project. It would be many years before he would be able to fulfill that dream.

One night in Santa Barbara, just as the meeting started, a young man, cigarette dangling from his mouth, slouched into the tent with his hat on. When one of the ushers asked him to remove his hat and put out his cigarette, the fellow was ready to fight, but at last submitted when the usher pointed out to him that his cigarette might set the sawdust floor on fire and burn down the tent. He sullenly took a seat, and in spite of that inauspicious beginning, continued to attend. Before the meetings were over he had accepted Jesus. Later he became a successful radio evangelist, starting his own radio program called *Builders of Faith*. Richards had the pleasure of marrying him to a wonderful Christian girl. Robert Thomas became a lifelong friend of H.M.S. Richards.

One day during the Santa Barbara meetings, Clyde and Marie Ellis drove through town on their way to mission service in Costa Rica. They had been close friends and coworkers since the first California evangelistic days in Visalia and Bakersfield. Richards' daughter and the Ellis girls had grown up together. During the next few hours they spent time remembering the good times they had enjoyed in the past—the time Richards tried to break a pot on the platform in Visalia, the little red convertible they used while visiting interested people in Bakersfield, the swims in the baptistry on hot days, even the time Ellis fell asleep on the platform while Richards was preaching one night. In the middle of the sermon, Richards began to cough and an usher came rushing up to bring him a glass of water. When he tapped Ellis on the shoulder and handed him the glass, Ellis woke up, thanked the usher, and drank the water. The audience watching the little pantomime came unglued.

Mabel, Marie, and all three little girls cried together as they took a few snapshots and waved goodbye. Richards said he would have felt better if he could have cried too.

Young Ray Broderson, son of the conference president, was the tent helper in the Santa Barbara meetings. "Lately I have learned to think a great deal of Ray Broderson," Richards wrote in his diary Sabbath, September 6, 1930. "He is the best custodian we have ever had in any of our tents or tabernacles. I believe he will make a good medical man."

A couple of days later Richards began feeling discouraged. "Some way, I feel so futile—accomplish so little," he wrote. "My eye prevents intense or even regular study or writing. I am in the middle of life [36 years old], and have accomplished nothing. My wages are as big as they ever will be in our denominational work most likely—$5.28 per day—and am I doing anything for humanity, my family, or myself?" His feeling of self-pity may have had its trigger in a statement that day from his friend, President Broderson, who commented critically about the small gift the woman in the Central California Conference had given toward his Palestine trip. Someone had told the Central California Conference president about it, and the individual had written to Broderson complaining. "He spoke about the gift as if it were a source of irritation to the president of the Central Conference—as though they felt they should have it for missions!"

During this time when Richards was closing his meetings in Santa Barbara and planning meetings in Hollywood, his wife was trying to hold the family together. They still had no car, and wherever they went they had to go by bus, train, or other people's vehicles. Just then they had to find another place to rent close to the tabernacle in Hollywood. They had been more or less camping in Santa Barbara, and with house hunting and taking care of the two children, Mabel was running out of emotional energy. Seven months pregnant, she felt exhausted. "Mabel broke down and cried several times," Richards wrote in his diary for September 18. "Not like her usual composure."

The Richards family finally found a place at 4524 Franklin Avenue, Hollywood. Their rent was $65 a month, pretty steep for someone earning less than $30 a week, but it was just a few blocks from their tabernacle on Hillhurst.

In the midst of all this frenzy of activity Mabel went to the White Memorial Hospital. On November 18, 1930, Kenneth Eastman Halbert Richards entered the world. "He doesn't look like Virginia or Harold, Jr., at his age. He is a little towhead. His head is very round for a Richards. Eyes deep blue," was a father's assessment of the new arrival.

A few days later Richards opened his evangelistic campaign in the heart of Hollywood on North Hillhurst, not far from the present site of the ABC TV Center. His subject was the "Coming World War." Mabel arrived home from the hospital with baby Kenneth the day the meetings opened. Some had to stand in the crowded tabernacle. As the meetings began, Richards' voice was just about gone. He had a severe case of laryngitis—he could hardly make a sound, and there would be meetings every night for the next month (only Christmas Eve excluded), with a radio broadcast on KNX three days a week. Fortunately, none of his vocal ailments ever lasted very long.

On Wednesday night, December 31, 1930, New Year's Eve, Richards had what he often called his "Watch Night Service," continuing right on through until midnight and the greeting of the New Year. "More people stayed through till 12:00 than I expected," he wrote in his diary for New Year's Eve.

It was during the meetings in Hollywood that Richards first invited Manuel Mancuso to play a special role in them. He worked in the Hollywood movie studios as an "ape man." When Richards preached on evolution, Manny would don his special ape suit and a uniformed guard would lead him in chains from the back of the hall. As he walked up the aisle toward the platform, the "ape" would at times lunge at a fearful woman sitting nearby. She would scream on cue, and on at least one occasion a woman fainted as Mancuso's "guard" gave a jerk on the chain and led him on up to the front.

Once Mancuso got on stage, Richards would introduce him as "the only ape man in existence." Richards would then remove the ape head and demonstrate that there was no missing link after all. Manny became a regular feature of Richards lectures for many years.

Meanwhile the mail began to come in from the people listening to his radio broadcast. Everyone of his team was excited when they received a letter from far off Idaho where Thelma Merriman Brown had heard the Los Angeles broadcast.

As the letters began to flow in from listeners, Richards found himself swamped trying to answer them all. By mid January he was so desperate that Elder Broderson offered him the use of a secretary in the conference office to answer mail. He dictated answers for nearly an hour. "It was my first experience with a stenographer," he said.

Richards' earnestness and compassionate demeanor disarmed all who came in contact with him. Miss Cook, the woman in charge of the Los Angeles *Express* advertising and assignment of radio time, asked if Elder Richards would pray for her father who was extremely ill. After the meeting that night, he, with Uncle Henry, called on her.

When Richards had an off night from one of his own meetings, he would often go to hear another preacher. On March 12, 1931, he took Mabel with him down to hear John Ford, his brother evangelist, preach in his big tabernacle in Anaheim. "He is a good preacher," Richards reported. "Has a big crowd. Simple style—evangelical. Big neon sign—FORD BIBLE LECTURES."

As the Hollywood meetings progressed, he began to have regular baptisms. February 14: 13 baptisms; March 14: 15 baptisms; March 24: 5 more. By April 5, the last meeting of the first Hollywood series, he recorded in his diary that they had baptized 64.

At the conclusion of the Hollywood meetings, two of his converts approached him. "You've got to hold more meetings here in Hollywood," they insisted. "Hollywood people are slower to make decisions. You mustn't leave. You must stay."

"But there's no more money for another meeting," he replied.

With that Mrs. Angelique Graves and Miss Margaret Ratzer opened their checkbook and gave Richards $1,000 as seed money for a second series.

Three days after closing his Hollywood meeting, he was in Oakland listening to noted evangelist Charles T. Everson preach.

On April 19, just two weeks after ending his first series of meetings in Hollywood on Hillhurst Avenue and operating on the faith of his two benefactors, Richards inaugurated a new set in the same spot with the subject, "Will the World Be Red or White." The

Tabernacle was packed. Only preaching six nights a week in this second series of Hollywood meetings, he took a vacation every Monday.

On April 12, 1931, he began to broadcast on KMPC in addition to his regular KNX programs. He had been on the radio a year and a half now, and the radio programs were growing and absorbing more and more of his time and energy.

It was in the second series of meetings that his fatherly heart was warmed when little 6-year-old Virginia came forward on an altar call. After the meeting she whispered to him, "Daddy, I took my stand tonight." "It made me feel good—the dear little soul," he confided that night in his diary. "Daddy's true sweetheart."

At the close of his second series in Hollywood during the first week of June 1931, and immediately after a 10-day camp meeting at the Los Angeles County Fairgrounds in Pomona, the Richards family took a much needed vacation with friends Charles LaFrance and family. Sleeping in the car and on the roof of the car, the two families had a wonderful time visiting Carlsbad Caverns; Santa Fe, New Mexico; the Grand Canyon; Zion National Park; and Las Vegas— about 2,000 miles in 13 days.

On August 16, 1931, Richards started a third series of meetings in the Hollywood Tabernacle. They used no newspaper ads, but put out 8,000 handbills and opened to a full house. The meetings continued six nights a week until the middle of December, with a brief break in November.

One afternoon as he was studying backstage at the tabernacle, two women who had been critical of church leaders asked for his endorsement of a book one of them had written. "My sister, you have claimed to have the gift of prophecy, but you have given me no evidence that God has given you the gift of prophecy," he told one of them. "Do you know what you're doing, sister? You're doing the work of the devil."

"Why, whatever do you mean?"

"My Bible says the devil is the accuser of the brethren, and you're making his work a lot easier for him. He doesn't have to work nearly as hard because you're doing his work."

The two women backed away sputtering, ostentatiously wiping the dust from their shoes.

After the meeting of October 9 he walked off the platform sick with a fever of 105 degrees, and for the next week other men had to substitute for him, but he was back again at almost full strength on October 18.

When Richards preached his farewell sermon at the Hollywood Tabernacle on Sunday evening, December 13, 1931, he could say, "We have baptized about 170 persons at the Tabernacle here, Brother Ben Allen has sold $3,500.00 worth of books, and Uncle Henry has several hundred dollars in the bank from offerings, above and beyond expenses."

As the year drew to a close on New Year's Eve, H.M.S. Richards and his evangelistic helpers met for an evening of fun and games at the home of Lona Brosi, his Bible instructor. As the clock struck 12:00 midnight, they didn't sing "Auld Lang Syne." Instead, they joined their voices in "Blest Be the Tie That Binds."

As he rode home alone on the streetcar those early morning moments of the New Year, he could reflect on a year of wonderful memories—hundreds of people baptized, a wife and growing family he loved and who loved him. But it was a blessing that he could not see the sorrow and problems that would come to the nation, to Los Angeles, and to him personally in the following months. Suicide and slander, bank failures and national economic depression, a jolting and terrifying earthquake. But neither could he see that God was moving events in His own perfect and inexorable way that would open for Richards a new door of opportunity for his ministry.

RADIO

"Dark day! Dark day! At a social church gathering at home of Dr. Smith of Burbank, word came of the death of my *beloved friend,* Elder P. E. Broderson, a few hours before in the Roselyn Hotel, Los Angeles, by his own hand," Richards wrote in his diary May 9, 1932. "Now I see the end of that awful physical and mental strain of the last two years—and no doubt of his boys' troubles, too. He must have been unbalanced. Never has a death so unnerved me. How the enemies of the cause will triumph! Why! O, why! And to think of him alone in that room, and all of his friends, we who loved him dearly, unconscious of his great need! What a mockery life can be!"

Elder Broderson had recently been elected president of the North Pacific Union Conference of Seventh-day Adventists. The very fact that his close friend and loyal supporter was moving away had caused Richards great uneasiness. He had reveled in the wholehearted enthusiasm Broderson had displayed in their relationship together. The thoughts of wrestling with a new administrator made him apprehensive. Now his friend was gone!

A suicide always gets the rumor mills grinding. Whispers circulated of an affair on a cross-country train a few days before Broderson's suicide, but Richards always believed in his innocence. Months later a brother of the woman who was supposed to have been involved showed Richards a letter he had received from his sister. Her letter confirmed Richards' views. "He was and is innocent," Richards wrote in his diary. "He was a victim of physical and mental breakdown and strain. A year ago he had an operation on his back. At that time they warned him never to be alone in times of depression!" Then he added concerning gossips who are always unwilling to give up on a juicy story, "but what does cruel 'Mrs. Grundy' care for facts!"

The tragedy threw the whole conference into turmoil. G. A. Roberts, the conference president, called Richards and asked him what he thought they ought to do about the funeral. "Don't try for a big funeral," Richards advised, "or a small private one. Just have it." Unfortunately, the conference employees remained in the dark about things.

Richards met the train that came in from Seattle with the family. Broderson's sons had elected not to tell their mother the nature of his death. They felt she would not be able to handle it.

The funeral took place at the Brown Brothers Funeral Chapel in Los Angeles on May 14. The conference president read the scripture, Richards offered the prayer, and Elder J. E. Fulton, the Pacific Union Conference president, preached the funeral sermon. At the grave a quartet sang and Elder A. G. Daniels read Psalm 142.

Mrs. Broderson was unable to get out of the car at the grave site. "On the way back from the cemetery two tires went flat on the funeral limousine in which Sister Broderson was riding," Richards recorded in his diary. "It caused a long wait and was hard on her. What a terrible day! And he might just as well have been alive. All kinds of rumors afloat, but I know that God knows all. My heart is too full to talk or write. Words seem flat and insipid. It is the greatest shock, I think, of my life, because I have always loved him."

Earlier that year Richards had opened with some big meetings in a new tabernacle on the corner of 48th and Hoover in Los Angeles. The first night, January 24, 1932, 1,780 people were present. "Biggest opening ever for me," he wrote.

The family had moved to an old remodeled house on 942 W. 50th street, just a few blocks from the tabernacle. It was within walking distance, since the Richards family still did not own a car.

The business of trying to get everywhere by public transportation had its down side. On February 9, he recorded, "Missed my KNX broadcast. First time in three years. All cars failed me. Took bus and street cars from 50th street to Hollywood. Got there 15 minutes late."

During this series of meetings Richards tried something new. He began a Sunday school class in the tabernacle with Mabel's help, and a Sunday afternoon sermon which he assigned to his young evangelist helper, Reuben Nightingale. "He spoke at 3:30," Richards wrote. "In spite of the rain, he had a good crowd and did well. He'll make a good preacher I believe."

Richards was right. Reuben Nightingale became a successful evangelist, a conference president, and before he died, the president of the Mid-America Union Conference of Seventh-day Adventists.

On some occasions Richards would invite guest speakers to keep his crowd coming. F. C. Gilbert, noted Jewish convert spoke in February, Earle Albert Rowell presented the dangers of narcotics in March, and one night Richards was surprised to see his old friend, Evangelist O. O. Bernstein from Illinois sitting in the audience.

Bernstein was not afraid to try different things to hold his audience. Once while he was preaching on what happens to people when they die, Bernstein arranged to borrow a casket from a funeral parlor and use it as a prop on the stage of his tabernacle. That proved to be a little much for some of the conservative members of his congregation. Bernstein also had a model of the Israelite wilderness tabernacle. He used it when preaching on the sacrificial system and dramatically explained how it pointed forward to the coming of Jesus.

When he read that Dr. Herbert Booth Smith of the Immanuel Presbyterian Church on Wilshire in Hollywood had invited Sabbath-keepers to hear him speak on the change of the Sabbath, Richards was there in person. In his presentation Booth mentioned Richards' name and pointed him out in the audience, demonstrating that the preaching of the young evangelist was having an impact on the whole metropolitan area of Los Angeles. A few days later, when Richards advertised that he would make a two-hour reply to Booth Smith's sermon, he had an overflow crowd in his tabernacle.

One week later Richards spoke in his tabernacle on H. L. Mencken's recent editorial in the *Mercury* that "If the Bible is true, Seventh-day Adventists are right."

In May 1932 Richards presented what he called his "Three Hour Sermon on the Sabbath." The tabernacle was full and he held his crowd the full three hours.

After five months of meetings, six nights a week, Richards preached his closing sermon of the campaign in the Los Angeles Tabernacle on June 19. Dozens had been baptized.

To unwind emotionally and physically, Richards spent a week in a cabin in the mountains with four young friends. "Never shaved the whole time," he wrote.

In 1932 the summer Olympic Games came to Los Angeles. Richards rechristened his tabernacle at 48th and Hoover with a monster sign running the length of the ridge, "The Olympic Tabernacle," with giant Olympic interlocking rings painted on the roof. He began his second series on July 24, preaching to 1,000 people on "Red or White: Will the Red Flag Wave Over the Entire World?" Assisting him were Henry de Fluiter leading the music, Reuben Nightingale as his assistant minister, and Lona Brosi and V. Hamilton as his Bible instructors.

One night during this series, Richards was striding back and forth across the platform, preaching about "How Near Are We to the Judgment Day," when a suspender button popped. It left his trousers so insecure that he had to stand in one place for the rest of the sermon, holding up his trousers with his left hand. "It spoiled my flow of thought," he confessed.

During the 1930s Dr. Louis Talbot of the Church of the Open Door began an aggressive program against Seventh-day Adventists. Richards made it a habit of attending his advertised lectures whenever he spoke on the subject of Adventists or the Sabbath. On December 4, 1932, Richards listened to him preach on the Sabbath, and again on February 5, 1933, on "Why Christians Keep the First Day of the Week." September 10 when Talbot lectured on Seventh-day Adventists, Richards had a stenographer present, and on September 19, Richards replied to Talbot's charges. People always seem to love a fight, and whenever Richards advertised such a reply, he could count on a standing-room-only crowd.

Dr. Talbot and Richards were well acquainted with one another. Sometimes when he would show up at Talbot's meetings, Talbot would spot him in the balcony or wherever he was sitting and give him a little verbal jab.

Once they met at the wailing wall in Jerusalem. Talbot said, "Well, Richards are you wailing here today?"

"No," Richards replied, "since Jesus died for me, I can't find anything to wail about."

In the February 24, 1960, issue of the Los Angeles *Times* Richards read of the death of Audrey Lucille Talbot, wife of his old antagonist, Louis Talbot, and wrote him a letter expressing his sympathy:

"This morning the Los Angeles *Times* brought to us the sad news of the death of Mrs. Talbot. Mrs. Richards and I wish to express our deepest sympathy to you in this your great loss.

"I have never forgotten our friendly meeting in Jerusalem many years ago. And while we have not always agreed in our interpretation of certain parts of the Holy Scripture, we do have common sorrows, and also the hope of eternal life through our Lord and Saviour, Jesus Christ, to all those who believe in Him.

"So at this time we wish you to know that we do pray that our Lord in heaven may sustain you through this affliction, and that the

Holy Spirit may make more real than ever to you the wonderful promises of immortal life revealed in the Word of God, which you have so ably preached for many years.

"I wish you to know also that our entire radio group join in this expression of sympathy and good will.

"Most sincerely yours in the Blessed Hope,

"H.M.S. Richards."

A few days later Richards received a reply from Talbot:

> "Dear Dr. Richards:
>
> "In going through the many hundreds of letters that came to me in connection with the long illness and death of my wife, I found your gracious letter. I am sending these few lines to thank you for it. It was very kind of you to take time out of your busy life to write me.
>
> "Mrs. Talbot was a great sufferer. Why these things should be in the providence of God is one of the great mysteries. She had suffered from cancer of the bone for two years and literally died 'by inches.' The pain she had to undergo was almost unbearable. However, the Lord has now given her a blessed release and her homegoing was indeed a triumphant one.
>
> "Since her death and burial, I have been taking time to recuperate because I spent many nights by her bedside, and oftentimes got no sleep at all. But I counted it a great privilege to so minister to her who had been so faithful to the Lord and to me as a life partner, for we had been married for over forty years.
>
> "I am now thanking the Lord for all my kind friends whose sympathy and prayer went out to me and my family, and again I thank you for your gracious expression.
>
> > "Ever yours in the Coming One,
> > "Louis T. Talbot"

Several years later Dr. Talbot was driving by the Glendale Adventist Hospital when he suddenly became ill. He was rushed into the hospital emergency room. Winona Crane, wife of one of the original Lone Star Four/King's Heralds quartet, phoned Richards from the hospital that Dr. Talbot was in room 117 and would like Richards to call. At 6:30 p.m. Richards was in his room. Talbot confessed that he regretted that he had done so much work of controversial nature and said that Jesus' death and resurrection were all important, to which Richards agreed. Then Talbot asked that he pray with him.

The day before Talbot's surgery, Richards took the quartet with him up to Talbot's room. We sang some songs for him there, and he prayed for us and for the *Voice of Prophecy*. After Talbot's surgery, Richards took his son, H.M.S. Richards, Jr., with him to visit once again.

In 1974 Talbot had a stroke and lived in a rest home in Long Beach. H.M.S. and Mabel drove down there to see him. By now H.M.S. was almost 80 years old. As the two old religious warriors met, Talbot recognized him, threw his arms around him, and kissed him. Richards often commented that God works in mysterious ways to bring healing between men and women who have sincerely held theological differences.

On December 12, 1932, Richards preached his final sermon in the Great Olympic Tabernacle. The meetings had been going for almost a year in the same location—two five-month campaigns with only about a week or more pause between them. By the end the baptisms totaled 164. Richards was disappointed when the conference, in a fit of economizing, sold the Olympic Tabernacle for $1,000.

On December 22, 1932, Richards received a summons to the office of the president of the conference, who informed him that six or seven people had come to them with reports concerning Richards and "a certain blond lady in the choir." Richards denied the rumors and demanded to be told who his accusers were so he could confront them. The president refused to divulge the names of the informants, but assured Richards that they would come forth. Of course, they never did.

The next several weeks were a source of continued pain for

Richards. To him it was like flailing in the dark against unseen foes. In his diary for December 28, Richards wrote: "This campaign of slander is new to me and keeps me in worry and discouragement. There are always bitter people or foolish people who are glad to cast a dart at one who is being criticized, especially when they are protected with the mantle of anonymity. May God deliver us. I trust in Him alone!"

On January 1 Richards wrote in his diary, "Happy New Year, but it's not very happy. The plague of slander still rages."

Two days later the conference office called in Uncle Henry and Richards together for further quizzing. During the session Uncle Henry fainted in the conference office. "Uncle Henry denied all rumors, he says, but he ought to for the evidence shows he could have stopped the start of most of it. But I must not allow bitterness a place in my heart."

A couple days later Uncle Henry said to Richards, "I have good news—I have thought of something. When they speak to you, just deny all and I can clear it all up." Richards to his diary replied, "No doubt he could, for he knows he started this whole thing by a little fib."

Soon after that all the rumors seemed to fizzle away to nothing, since they had no foundation in the first place.

As the old year ticked away, plans were already set in motion for a new series. The conference urged that Richards rent a hall, but they could find nothing suitable so the conference agreed they could build a new tabernacle if they raised the money for it. The evangelistic team delegated Elder Roy Cottrell, a fellow minister, to work out the details of financing and building the structure. He had visited lumber yards and determined that for about $500 they could buy the lumber for a new building 90' by 60'.

In the end it turned out that Cottrell's estimate was low. The new South Gate Tabernacle, 97' by 60', was completed and dedicated on 9000 Long Beach Boulevard in South Gate, Sabbath, February 18. The actual materials cost $700 though the labor was donated. Everyone worked feverishly on the building all day Sunday, but it was almost ready by meeting time. The meetings opened on February 19 to a full house of 800 crammed in to hear Richards preach on heaven.

The meetings had been going for less than two weeks when the devil decided things were getting out of hand. He began to lash out with three quick blows, one after another. First those who lived around the tabernacle began to complain to city hall about the people parking for the meeting. Next, on March 2, Governor Rolf of California declared a three-day bank holiday. By March 9 the banks were still closed. Even though people had paychecks, they couldn't get them cashed. On Friday morning, March 10, Richards took his check to the conference office, but cash was so scarce that the office would only give each employee $15 cash apiece to tide them over. Offerings at the meetings were pitifully small, because people were afraid to let go of any of their cash. During the bleak days of the depression that followed, Richards would send a truck down to the Los Angeles farmers' wholesale vegetable market and pick up day-old produce to distribute among the people attending his meetings, some of whom were destitute.

The third blow landed on Friday afternoon March 10 when Richards was sitting in his new tabernacle, studying for his evening sermon. All at once he heard what sounded like a freight train rumbling up Long Beach Boulevard. At 5:55 p.m. the earthquake struck with terrible power. In one violent shudder all the windows went out. As the tabernacle continued to jiggle and shake, Richards testified that he had to lie down in the sawdust to keep from falling. As the ground continued to rumble around him, he secretly thanked the Lord that Elder Grauer had put the tabernacle together with bolts instead of nails. It shook and trembled, but held together.

When the initial shock trembled into silence, his first thought was for his little family in the house to which they had just moved on 2647 Cudahy Street. He had visions of his children crushed by the upright piano toppling over onto them. As he ran up the middle of Long Beach Boulevard, bricks from collapsed buildings littered the sidewalks and edges of the street on both sides.

Automobiles lay crushed under the rubble of masonry. He silently prayed for the safety of his family as he carefully wended his way through the debris. With a great sigh of relief he saw them all safely camped in the front yard where Mabel had herded them during the first shock.

A few minutes later Halbert Richards raced up the street with the news that the radio had just announced that a tidal wave a half mile high was rolling up the coast. It had already struck San Diego and was rushing toward Long Beach.

"What shall we do?" the older Richards asked nervously. Up and down the street they could already hear automobiles starting up as people headed for the mountains.

"We'll do nothing," his son said. "If it's a half mile high it's the end of the world, and I'd just as soon meet Jesus here as in the mountains. If it's not a half-mile high it'll never reach us here, so let's just stay put."

That night the tabernacle had no electricity, but by the light of auto headlamps, flashlights, and a gas torch Uncle Henry de Fluiter held at the end of a garden hose, Richards preached to 300 faithful on earthquakes. All during the meeting the earth would tremble and shake from time to time. Sometimes a fearful individual would utter a little shriek of terror, but Richards would calm them down, assuring them that the tabernacle was bolted together and they would be safe. His audience stayed through to the end.

As the financial depression began to tighten its coils around the nation, Richards adapted his sermons to the times. March 22 he preached on "Banks and Golden Hoards."

Even though Richards had been broadcasting several times a week on KNX for three and a half years and had recently begun on KMPC, his broadcasts had been more devotional in nature. He longed to begin to present regular evangelistic topics over radio. In true Richards fashion, once he got "a bee in his bonnet" he didn't let it rest. To friends and foes alike and everyone in between, he drove the point home so persistently that he thought God wanted him to be on radio that some of them began to feel a little irritated with him.

One time between evangelistic meetings he was camping with three of his friends—Harold Young, Glen Luther, and Jack Irwin—at Jack's cabin in the San Bernardino mountains. When Richards began to saw on his one-stringed fiddle, Harold Young stopped him.

"Richards, I don't think you really believe God wants you to go on radio. I think it's all just talk."

"No, I really believe God wants me to preach on radio, and I want to do it."

"No, you don't."

"Yes, I do."

"No, you don't."

Now Richards was getting a little irritated. "What do you mean when you say you don't think I want to really go on radio?"

"Let me put it this way, Harold. If you really think God wants you to be on radio, and you're really willing to go on radio, you'd be on radio!"

For once in his life, Richards had nothing to say. Harold Young had stopped his mouth. Ever after that, he admitted that what Harold Young had said had a lot of truth in it. From that time on he said little about the topic, but his friend's challenge had "stuck in his craw."

One night at the meeting in the South Gate Tabernacle, Richards threw out the challenge to his audience.

"I know you all are doing all you can to help us keep the meetings going here. I know things are hard. Money is scarce. The country is facing an uncertain future, but I believe with all my heart that God wants His message of salvation to go every way possible, and radio is a way it can go faster and to more people. Tomorrow night we're going to have a table up here just below the platform. I want you dear people to look in all your dresser drawers at home and find all the old jewelry you have stashed away there. Bring that and put it on the table here tomorrow night, and we'll use it to get started with radio."

The next night the people began to pile up on that table all the things they had found in little boxes and drawers around their homes. To Richards' amazement he saw them put watches, rings, earrings, necklaces, bracelets, even gold teeth onto the table. He felt like Moses must have when he asked Israel to bring their ornaments to build the tabernacle in the wilderness. By the time Richards began to preach, the table contained a great mound of gold, silver, and jewels.

The next day Uncle Henry took all that old jewelry to a Christian jeweler who was able to sell the whole lot for $130. That $130 served as seed money that got H.M.S. started with regular commercial broadcasting.

The first broadcast went out over radio station KGER Long Beach on April 9, 1933, at 5:30 p.m. His subject was the prophecy of the great image of Daniel 2. It was a special day also for daughter, Virginia. She was having her eighth birthday.

At first the KGER radio programs broadcast only once a week, but later in the year they began to be released several times a week, and by early 1934 every day.

Though radio was taking more and more time, the evangelistic meetings went on without a pause. In the middle of May 1933 Richards attended a meeting by L. A. Meade, pastor of the Methodist Episcopal Church, to hear his attack on Seventh-day Adventists for their view of death. When Richards walked in, Meade called him out by name.

A few days later Richards advertised a response to Meade's attack under the subject title "Exposer Exposed." Every time Richards responded to attacks he spoke to a full house.

On June 18, 1933, Richards preached "God's Last Message to the World" in the South Gate Tabernacle, and a week later "Heaven's Last Call" as the final meeting of the series to an overflow crowd. The evangelistic team baptized 36 that night, bringing the total for the five month series to 191 baptisms.

Richards once told our quartet about a time when he was in the baptismal tank at the close of a big meeting. At the conclusion of the sermon he had invited those who were to be baptized to come behind the stage to change into their baptismal robes. In the tank as he was carefully leading the baptismal candidates by the hand down the steps into the water, he suddenly looked into the face of a man he had never seen before. How he had slipped by the deacons into the group to be baptized Richards couldn't guess. Apparently he had come forward when Richards had invited those to be baptized, thinking it was a call for decision. Now what could he do? Should he make the man go back up the stairs and out of the tank?

With a silent prayer for the Lord's guidance he began to quietly question the man. "Have you ever been to our meetings before tonight?"

"No."

"This is your first time?"

"Yes."

"Do you promise to accept as truth everything I can show you from the Bible?"

"Yes, I do."

Then grabbing the man's hand on which was a big lodge ring, Richards asked, "Would you give up that ring for Jesus?"

"Yes, I would."

With that Richards proceeded to baptize the man who later proved to be a strong believer and active in the church.

The team was proud that they were able to break even financially after the meetings. They had raised the money for their own tabernacle without conference help, and Richards and Uncle Henry de Fluiter went to the conference treasurer to present a check of several hundred dollars to him, expecting his surprise and warm congratulations. The treasurer sat at his desk, looking at it dourly for a few moments, then said, "Well, brethren, I hope you can be a little more careful with your expenses next time." Uncle Henry, once outside the office, broke down and cried.

Though Richards enjoyed the support and encouragement of

many good conference and Voice of Prophecy treasurers, he also had several experiences that led him to wryly comment in later years that he thought the Lord would have to make a special dispensation to get some treasurers into the kingdom. From sad experience he found that it seemed that some men were more eager to protect the "Lord's money" than they were to help the Lord's men and women.

Just two weeks after the close of the South Gate meetings, Richards invited his audience back to the tabernacle for a special occasion. His young assistant, Reuben Nightingale, was to be married to Pauline Woodyard, and Richards thought the crowd that had been attending the meetings for months would love to see it. Seven-year-old Virginia and her friend Bernice were flower girls. As they walked up the aisle in their pastel dresses with matching socks and white shoes, they were, as Virginia remembers, "an eyeful." They heard "oohs and ahs" as they passed by each aisle on their way to the front; praise enough to make a little girl's heart flutter. The tabernacle was packed, and Reuben and Pauline received a flood of wedding gifts from the delighted audience.

At the conclusion of the meetings in the big South Gate Tabernacle, Richards begged the conference to let him hold another series there, as he was sure they could get another 100 baptisms if they did. But the conference president wouldn't have it, insisting they move on to Long Beach.

Originally, the conference had promised that they could put up a tabernacle for their meetings in Long Beach, but the president and treasurer of the conference later reversed their position and advised them to put up a tent, which, said Richards, was "against my views for that big city."

On July 29 Richard baptized another 16 in the South Gate Tabernacle, including the daughter-in-law of his old friend, Elder Broderson, who had committed suicide a few months before. It brought their total baptisms in the South Gate Tabernacle to more than 200.

On August 6, 1933, they had the opening meeting in the 120' by

80' tent in Long Beach at the corner of Willow and Pine, virtually in the middle of a big field of oil wells. They had good attendance, sometimes cramming more than 1,000 people into the little tent. On November 28, just a few days before the close of the meetings, a big windstorm tore the tent to shreds. The meetings closed on December 10 when he preached his final sermon. They baptized 116.

It was during this meeting that the Richards family finally got the use of an automobile. Dan Kaplin loaned them an old Starr coupe which Mabel began to learn to drive. The rumble seat in the back was a novelty, especially to the boys. The car was a wonderful help, especially since Richards was not only preaching at the tabernacle every night, but was on radio station KGER several times a week.

He arranged to have a phone line run to the Long Beach tent so that he could broadcast the meetings right from the tent over KGER. The arrangement had an unhappy side effect. On the nights when the meetings were broadcast, the crowds were small. People stayed home and listened on their radios. When they weren't on radio, the crowds returned.

On February 9, 1934, Richards received a letter from Glenn Calkins, the Pacific Union Conference president. Calkins asked H.M.S. to be one of a committee of 12 who were to hear Victor Houteff, the leader of a Seventh-day Adventist offshoot movement called the "Shepherd's Rod," a name later changed to the "Davidian Seventh-day Adventists." Houteff had started his speculative theories in 1929 while a Sabbath school teacher at the Exposition Park Seventh-day Adventist Church on 54th Street in Los Angeles.

Richards unsuccessfully tried to beg off serving on the committee, reporting truthfully that he was too busy with his evangelistic meetings. The committee met in his old Olympic Auditorium on 48th and Hoover. Elder A. G. Daniels, former president of the General Conference, served as the chairman. Other members of the committee included Elders F. C. Gilbert, Fred Burden, Glenn Calkins, H.M.S. Richards, and William Wirth.

In his diary for February 19, Richards wrote: "At 9:30 a.m. went to the Olympic Tabernacle to hear V. T. Houteff explain his views on the 'Harvest.' He talked about two hours—proving he had studied hard, but his views are not influenced by common sense or historical or philological knowledge."

Later Richards remembered that as it neared noon, Elder Daniels moved that the committee all go to lunch then return. Houteff declined, saying that whatever we concluded about this one subject would decide the whole thing—that it was the heart of his message. Daniels continued to urge that he go on, that the denomination looked upon the hearing as a serious thing. He promised that the committee would stay there two days, three days, a week or 10 days, if necessary, to hear everything he had to say, but Houteff absolutely and positively refused to go any further.

He received an impartial hearing, no one interrupting him, yet he refused the additional time offered him. "What more could a man wish for a fair hearing," Richards explained later to those who were avowing that Houteff had not had a chance to explain and defend his views.

Later in 1935 Houteff with 11 of his followers moved from California to Waco, Texas, and established a colony on a farm called Mount Carmel Center. After Houteff's death in 1955, leadership of the group passed through several hands, finally coming to David Koresh, who with nearly 100 followers died in the conflagration there that made headline news all over the world.

At the conclusion of the Long Beach tent meetings Richards held a short series at the Ditman Street church, then on February 2 opened a three-month campaign in Belvedere Gardens on the corner of Hafner and Hubbard, the site of the East Los Angeles church that originated as a result of the meetings. The team consisted of Richards, Uncle Henry de Fluiter, Lona Brosi, Ben F. Allen at the book stand, and two volunteers not on the payroll. They baptized 94 by the close of the meetings on May 13, 1934.

At the conclusion of the Belvedere Garden meetings, the family took a short break in a borrowed cabin in the San Bernardino

Mountains. Son Kenneth remembers something that happened on that occasion that frightened the whole family. Kenneth, at the time only 4 years old, said that his father decided to hike to the top of the mountain behind the cabin late one afternoon. When sunset came Dad still hadn't returned. As Mother began to get nervous, the three children, of course, became jittery. It was long past dark and Dad still hadn't returned. The whole family by then was in a nervous state.

Richards later confessed that he had made it to the top without any trouble, but decided to come back another way. In his diary that night he acknowledged it to be the worst climb of his life. Time after time he ventured into dead-end box canyons in which he could find no way down in the dark, only to have to climb back up to where he had left his trail. He began to be afraid he'd have to spend the night in the dark wilds of the San Bernardino mountains. It was quite early in the spring, so he knew it could still turn very cold at that altitude. Finally after multiple ventures down false trails, he reached the cabin late at night, much to the grateful relief of his by-now-terrified family.

While they were there, a close friend came from her own vacation lodge in a nearby canyon to tell them she had traded in her Lincoln automobile for two Fords and was giving one of them to the Richards family. "This car gift was about too good to be true," Richards wrote in his diary for May 19. "Mabel is very excited about it, and of course I am, too."

Even though they now had their own car, it was about like giving up a member of the family to take the old Starr coupster back to Dan Kaplin.

In May of 1934 Richards began negotiations to broadcast on KFI and KNX radio stations. The two big stations demanded that he provide them with scripts 72 hours before broadcast time. Richards was now being heard on four radio stations in the Los Angeles metropolitan area—KGER six days a week, KTM with a question and answer program on Thursday nights, plus KNX and KFI several times a week.

During the summer of 1934 Richards held a three-month series in Huntington Park with a total baptism of 49 by its close in August.

In October they built the Grace Tabernacle at 123 N. Lake Street in Los Angeles. The meetings there were a disappointment almost from the start. Six hundred attended the opening meeting, but immediately the crowds dropped off to about 100 or sometimes less. It was a great disappointment to Richards. Personally beginning to suffer what we now call burnout, he didn't feel the old power in his preaching, and began to wonder if people were beginning to get tired of hearing him.

It's no wonder that he was suffering from fatigue as he coped with radio programs on four stations many times a week, preached six nights a week, as well as answered the hundreds of letters beginning to flood in from listeners. A crisis was coming.

TABERNACLE OF THE AIR

In January 1935 Richards and Mabel attended an evangelistic council in Philadelphia, and on the way back took the train to Detroit to pick up a new Plymouth for a friend. It was a wonderful opportunity for Mabel to practice her driving on the way back across the country. She didn't know it then, but she would end up being the family chauffeur. H.M.S. would never learn to drive. On the way home they stopped to visit family in Oklahoma, arriving back in Los Angeles on January 27.

While they had been gone, H.M.J. Richards had filled in for his son on all his radio programs.

In February Richards received a request to conduct the funeral of G. W. Rowan, husband of the self-styled "holy flesh" prophetess of the middle 1920s delusion. Mrs. Rowan was present with her sons.

Beginning in 1916 Mrs. Margaret W. Rowan issued messages in which she claimed that God had chosen her to be a prophetess to the church. Denominational leaders examined her testimonies and found them to be in error. In late 1919 she stated that she had seen a vision of a document in the manuscript files of Ellen G. White dated August 10, 1911. This document, she said, had been signed by Mrs. White stating that God would use Mrs. Rowen to present messages from Him to the church. A search of the files found a loose sheet with the message Mrs. Rowen claimed would be there. Though many suspected the document to be a forgery, it wasn't until 1926 that a Doctor B. E. Fullmer, a physician and one of Mrs. Rowen's disciples, admitted to slipping the document into the files while he visited the Ellen G. White Estate in St. Helena, California, in 1919.

On February 27, 1927, Dr. Fullmer received a summons to an auto court in Los Angeles, ostensibly to give medical aid. As he entered, someone hit him on the head with a pipe, and he lost consciousness. Suspicious neighbors called the police, and they caught Mrs. Rowen and two accomplices in the room with the unconscious Fullmer. The three had a shovel, a rope, and a burlap bag, apparently to use in disposing the body. Dr. Fullmer later recovered and was able to testify against the accused. They received sentences of from one to 10 years in San Quenten for "assault with a deadly weapon." Mrs. Rowen served one year.

Even though attendance at the meetings in the Grace Tabernacle was disappointing, the radio evangelism grew rapidly. Richards found himself bogged down trying to answer letters and preaching six or seven nights a week, in addition to guest appearances almost every Sabbath at some church in southern California. At first he and Mabel tried to take care of all the radio mail, writing answers in long hand, but it was soon clear they would have to have help. At times a Mrs. Knight or Verna Dutcher would help, but Richards needed someone they could depend on regularly. A phone call in October 1934 from Betty Canon, a public stenographer, proved to be a marvelous answer to prayer, and a friendship began that lasted for the rest of Richards' life.

Betty had heard Richards offer a free subscription to the *Signs of the Times* to any listener who wrote in. She had some family members she wanted to receive the *Signs,* so offered to do some part-time stenographic work to help pay for the subscriptions.

Richards had his first radio office in a little chicken coop shed in the backyard of their home on Cudahy street in Walnut Park. It was rough. The ceiling was so low he had to bend over to get in, and never could stand up straight in his own office. Some of the floorboards were so loose one had to be careful not to trip over them. The desk at which Betty worked consisted of boards laid across apple boxes. Her typewriter was a vintage model, but it did the job. Richards put his library books on 1 by 12 planks across cement blocks which stretched from floor to ceiling along all available walls. His desk, like Betty Canon's, consisted of boards across apple boxes.

Betty worked in the chicken coop part time, splitting her hours between Richards' radio correspondence and her job as a public stenographer. At the end of the day, Richards would always pay her if any money had come in the mail. It got to be a standing joke between them. "Betty, can you come back tomorrow? I'll pay you if there's any money in the mail." And Betty always returned the next day and almost always got paid. Eventually, Betty received her check from the conference office when they began to recognize the importance of the radio work Richards was conducting.

In February Richards visited Elder Arthur G. Daniels in the White Memorial hospital and had prayer for him. He was dying of stomach cancer. A few weeks later the old warrior was dead, the man who had encouraged the young preacher and counseled him to begin his career in Canada. Now the beloved man who had served from 1901 to 1922 as president of the General Conference of Seventh-day Adventists was laid to his rest. On March 27 in Paulsen Hall near the White Memorial Hospital, Richards took part in the services for "the Old General," as he had come to be known among his friends. "When I passed by his coffin after the service," Richards wrote, "it broke me all up to see him there." Daniels had been like a spiritual father in Richards' student days at Washington Missionary College.

On April 5, 1935, Richards announced to his KGER radio audience that it was his last regular broadcast on that station. He urged his listeners to pledge to send $1 a month for six months so that they could get back on the air. It was like abandoning a familiar home to leave KGER, he said. Listeners had heard his voice from that station for almost six years. Within a month he would be broadcasting for 30 minutes a night, six nights a week on another station, KMPC, of Beverly Hills.

April 14, 1935, Richards and his team opened their meetings at Avalon and J Streets in the area of Los Angeles once known as Wilmington, and broadcast them from the tabernacle. They called the program the *Tabernacle of the Air*. During the series Richards often had as guest singers a group called the Harmony Four. One of its members, Lon Metcalfe, would some years later become a coach for the King's Heralds quartet. The other members were B. Watts, Harold Graham, and A. Westerhout. And it was during the Wilmington meetings that his two little sons, Harold and Kenneth, made their first public appearance singing a duet together. Ages 6 and 5, the boys sang "The Old Rugged Cross."

It was also during the Wilmington meetings that Richards rigged up a remote line from the tabernacle to his new radio station KMPC, so that he didn't have to drive or take the street car to Beverly Hills for every broadcast. He could sit at the microphone behind the stage in the tabernacle, wait for the announcer in Beverly Hills to introduce the program, then throw his own microphone switch and begin to speak. Sometimes he would be speaking in Wilmington or Long Beach at the tabernacle, and his singer or singers would be in the studio at Beverly Hills. Occasionally it was a little tricky tossing the ball back and forth, especially when he had to exercise faith that his singer was at the microphone.

On May 8 his little staff of workers mailed out 5,000 letters announcing his new KMPC broadcast. For the July 4 program he, for the first time, made a recording and was able to relax at the beach and listen to himself preach by radio.

While the Wilmington meetings progressed, plans went forward to move the tabernacle to 4th and Loma in Long Beach and commence meetings there later in the year after the Wilmington series closed.

In August church leaders summoned Richards to Washington, D.C. A committee at church headquarters was toying with the possibility of starting a radio program on several big radio stations around the country. If he accepted the arrangement, Richards would have to break up his evangelistic team, and since he was not yet willing to do so, he declined the invitation to move to Washington at least for the time being.

In addition to all the other things he was doing, Richards prepared a series of Bible study guides, and made arrangements with S. N. Brown of the Collins Bible Publishers in Glasgow, Scotland, to bind them in the back of a special edition of the Bible. It seemed to Richards to be an ideal arrangement for lay members to give Bible studies. To his surprise, the project would encounter severe and continuing criticism from many Adventist church leaders.

On September 29, 1935, Richards opened his evangelistic meetings at the Long Beach Tabernacle on the corner of 4th and Loma. The family moved from their house on Cudahy in Walnut Park to 619 Euclid in Long Beach, just a few blocks from the tabernacle. His radio office became instantly more stylish, moving from the chicken coop to a garage. Betty Canon, his diminutive secretary, thought she had been translated to heaven, though the cold concrete garage floor on winter mornings reminded her that she was not yet in the celestial abode. To keep her feet warm, she nested them in a cardboard box.

In late October Richards attended the Autumn Council of Seventh-day Adventists which met in Louisville, Kentucky. It was one of the rare occasions when Mabel could tag along. They left the children with relatives in southern California. The General Conference had set up a radio commission, since a number of Adventist ministers were beginning to be involved in broadcasting. Pastor Herbert A. Vandeman of Pennsylvania (father of George Vandeman who later became the founder and speaker of the *It Is Written* Adventist international telecast) began to preach on the radio in the late 1920s. John Ford was on the air in Boston. Richards broadcast on several stations in California. Church leaders were beginning to explore the idea of supporting a national Adventist radio program.

At the Autumn Council meeting Richards heard the first rumblings of objections to what would be labeled the "H.M.S. Richards Bible," and which was now off the press. In November someone told him that the pastor of the Glendale Seventh-day Adventist Church had spoken out publicly against this Bible, and the same month Elder Glenn Calkins, president of the Pacific Union Conference, called a committee to discuss it. The "H.M.S. Richards Bible" would be a continuing burr under his saddle for years to come. He received a letter the following March from a conference president stating that some member was worried that he was going to get the colporteurs to sell it. "What falsehood," Richards remonstrated in his diary. "My heart just aches with the suspicion and stories about this Bible that keep starting up." It was especially painful to Richards when he later heard that his old friend, Elder E. L. Neff, president of the Oregon Conference, opposed the sale of the H.M.S. Richards Bible. Richards was never able to figure out why people objected to the Bible.

On Sunday night, December 22, 1935, Richards held the last meeting of his first evangelistic series at the Long Beach Tabernacle, but opened again at the same location on January 26, 1936. The meeting hall bore the name the Belmont Tabernacle. Richards preached six nights a week, in addition to his half hour radio broadcast on KMPC every day at 4:30 p.m., plus a Sunday broadcast on KFOX. The week before the Long Beach meetings started, King George V of England died, and his son, Edward VIII became king. Richards' opening sermon title at Long Beach was "King George V—His Kingdom in Prophecy." Eager listeners took nearly every seat in his tabernacle that night.

February 10, 1936, he for the first time invited the "Lone Star Four" to sing on his KMPC broadcast. A male quartet from Texas, the "Lone Star" state, had been so determined to stay together and sing that the men and the wives of the two married members of the group had all taken training to become registered nurses. They reasoned that this profession would give them time flexibility to practice and perform, but still enable them to make a living. Richards' father, now a chaplain at the Glendale Adventist Sanitarium, had invited them to sing for the patients, and their talent so impressed him that he recommended them to his son.

"About the best four I ever heard," Richards wrote in his diary for that date. The quartet consisted of three brothers, Louis, Waldo, and Wesley Crane, with bass Ray Turner. None of them knew at that time that their fellowship with Richards would continue for years and ultimately the quartet would be renamed "The King's Heralds."

The four first sang on the KMPC broadcast February 10, then that night for his meetings in the Belmont Tabernacle, and again on the broadcast the following Wednesday. On March 2 Richards invited the well-known "Goose Creek Quartet" of the Country Church of Hollywood to sing at his Tabernacle meetings. "They are very good," he wrote, "but not better than my 'Lone Star Four.'" He was already beginning to call them "my quartet."

Later that month the dream began to form in both his mind and the minds of the quartet that they might become a full time fixture on his broadcast and in his meetings. It was a shocking innovation for some. "Hire four men just to sing?" queried some doubters. "It's never been done before." Richards advanced the young men $40 from radio funds and helped find a place for them and their families to live near the tabernacle. Attendance had been flagging at the meetings, but when the quartet began to be a regular part of each night's meetings, the crowds immediately began to pick up.

Richards and the quartet would later remember that to survive those first few weeks, the men and their wives would forage on the hills around Long Beach and pick dandelion greens to keep from starving.

By April Richards confided in his diary: "Attendance better since the quartet has been with us." He was always generous in his praise of "his quartet." I have many times heard him credit the quartet for bringing big crowds to his meetings. He and minister friend

F. D. Nichol had a running but friendly feud about the crowds Richards always had at camp meeting.

"It's not fair, Richards," Nichol would complain. "I work hard to get a good sermon up for the people and you come along with your quartet and take all the crowds."

Richards would laugh and say, "Well, go out and get your own quartet." We knew he was the one who drew people to hear him, but it was always gratifying to hear his praise.

In April Richards and the quartet went to Elder J. E. Fulton to see if the conference would consider putting the men on salary. They could provide music for the different churches in the conference from Sabbath to Sabbath, and then be available for the KMPC broadcast every day. Fulton expressed himself as in favor of it.

Also that month Richards noted in his diary that his young 6-year-old son, Harold, was busy building boats, one four-foot boat and another seven feet long. "Driving more nails than I ever saw for a youngster his age," he wrote. Young Harold's fascination with boats would continue into his adulthood, when he taught his own boys to sail and fish and participate in all kinds of water sports.

April 9, 1936, was a special day for daughter Virginia. It was her eleventh birthday, and on that day she had a birthday party. Without her parents' knowledge, Virginia had sent an invitation to the little movie actress, Shirley Temple.

Several weeks later Virginia's father was out watering the front lawn at 619 Euclid, Long Beach, when Virginia came home from school. With a sly smile he told her she had received a letter in the mail that day. Virginia danced with excitement when she saw the return address. It was from Shirley Temple. The actress had sent regrets that she could not attend Virginia's birthday party because she had other conflicting engagements. A little cousin visiting at the time was impressed.

"Do you know Shirley Temple?" she asked.

Virginia later learned that Shirley Temple had received threatening mail from crank fans, and her parents were taking extra precautions for

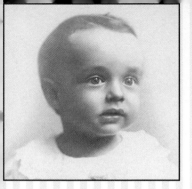

HMSR (age 10 months)

H.M.J. Richards
and Bertie
Richards with
HMSR (above) and
Kenneth (c.1898)

Home in Davis City, Iowa, where HMSR was born in 1894

William Jenkin Richards,
grandfather of HMSR

Margaret Thomas Richards,
grandmother of HMSR

Jasper Newton Sylvester, "Twopops," maternal grandfather of HMSR

Elizabeth Sylvester, "Twomoms," maternal grandmother of HMSR

HMSR, just before graduating
from Campion Academy
(his favorite picture of himself)

Handbill, tent meeting with R. E. Harter, Philadelphia, 1913

Henry de Fluiter's choir, Harter Philadelphia meetings, 1914

Campion Academy, 1914

HMSR, Mansfield,
Pennsylvania, 1915

Pennsylvania Campmeeting, 1916 (left to right: Elder Schradrot, Fred Harter, H.M.J. Richards, J. S. Washburn, Brother Fried)

Professor Lacey's Pastoral Training class, HMS front row, Kenneth Gant behind him

D. A. Rees, partner in evangelism during Washington Missionary College days

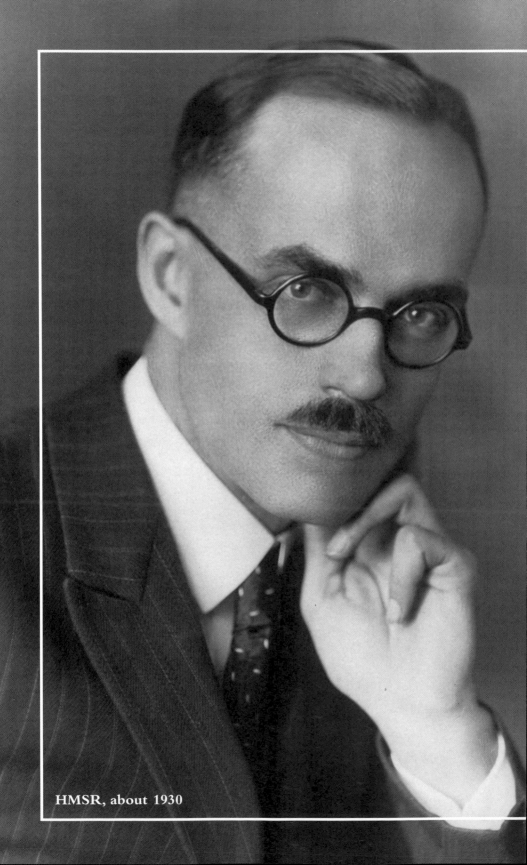

HMSR, about 1930

Ottawa SDA Church, 1920

Young preacher at his pulpit,
Ottawa SDA Church, 1919

Newly married

New bridegroom chopping wood at Harmony Corners

New bride and groom coming back from Oshawa after wedding

HMSR preaching in tent, 1921, Ottawa.; D.J.C. Barret and E. D. Lamont seated

Fresno Tabernacle, 1927–1929

Hanford, California, Tabernacle, 1928-1929

South Gate Tabernacle under construction, 1933

Tent in Long Beach before
the big wind, 1933

Tent in Long Beach after
the big wind, 1933

HMSR and Lone Star Four

Radio group in
studio, early 1942

Voice of Prophecy broadcast group, 1942: Elmer Digneo, organist, second from left

Broadcast picture, 1937: Irving Steinel at organ; H. M. Blunden, far right

HMSR at microphone, August 1934

HMSR, 1967

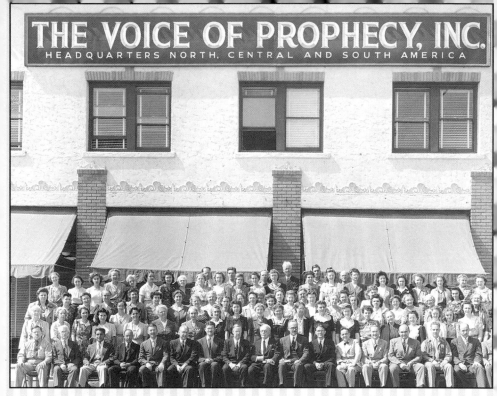

Second Voice of Prophecy office, 811 East Broadway, Glendale, California, 1943-1950

Voice of Prophecy General Board, 1955, in front of third VOP office, 1500 E. Chevy Chase

HMSR and three sons: Jan,
Kenneth, HMSR, Harold, 1966

King's Heralds,
1962–1967

The entire Richards tribe, about 1970

her safety. Virginia kept that letter from Shirley Temple for years, and only lost it when a big flood destroyed many of her treasured keepsakes while she and her husband lived in Yuba City, California.

On April 22, 1936, the Pacific Union Conference invited Richards to be a member of a small committee to make plans to start a radio broadcast sponsored by the Union.

May 17 was the closing meeting in the Long Beach Belmont Tabernacle. The hall was packed. Richards was overjoyed to see friends and family there. His old pal from Campion Academy days, Kenneth Gant, was present with his wife; also Albert and Rita Millner, whom he had married when they were all young church employees together in Canada; Roy Anderson from London was there. Roy would become a devoted lifelong friend. Father and mother and Twomoms had also come.

At the end of May Richards and family attended the General Conference of Seventh-day Adventists session in San Francisco. "What a feast of fellowship," he wrote in his diary for Sabbath May 30. "Old friends meeting in halls. I notice so many leaders absent who were big men when I attended my first two or three General Conferences." The session would elect Elder James L. McElhany as president, a position he would hold for 14 years.

On July 19, after General Conference, Richards opened another tent meeting series in North Long Beach on the corner of South and Orange.

A week later, on Sabbath morning at 7:15 a.m., the first broadcast went out from KNX under the title *The Voice of Prophecy*. Richards had chosen the name from the subtitle of one of the early editions of the book *Daniel and the Revelation* by Uriah Smith. The flyleaf contained the statement, "The Response of History to the Voice of Prophecy." He was now being heard on a religion in the news program on KFOX on Sunday night at 10:15 p.m., a half hour a day on KMPC Monday through Friday with *Tabernacle of the Air,* and a half hour on KNX Sabbath morning at 7:30 a.m. with *The Voice of Prophecy*. Beginning in September of the same year, Richards agreed to preach every Sunday morning at the county General Hospital. Is it any wonder he wrote in his diary on a Sunday evening after the 10:15 p.m. broadcast, "So tired!"

In September Richards was excited when two young sailors, who had first heard about the meetings while on board the battleship *Mississippi,* visited the Long Beach tent. That same month the family had a small "tragedy." Little Kenneth, almost six years old, got his first haircut. "Our baby is gone. We have a boy now!" Richards wrote.

To encourage listener interest and mail, Richards started a Bible Treasure Hunt on KMPC—find Old Testament quotations in the New Testament. And he invited listeners to write in finishing the sentence, "I read the Bible because . . ."

At the church Autumn Council in Ft. Worth, Texas, Richards encountered more opposition to his H.M.S. Richards Bible. A conference presidents' council came out strongly opposed to it. When Richards asked one of them what they had against the Bible, he answered, "We consider it unethical to print our doctrines in the same volume with the Holy Scriptures." Richards asked, "What about the Bible they printed with the *Bible Readings* helps in the back? And what about the Thompson Chain Reference Bible?" His critic seemed to think that too was a mistake, but was called away, and Richards didn't get to pursue the dialogue. A committee at this Fall Council actually voted to oppose the publishing of this Bible. Richards sensed that the opposition had come from the publishing department, though he couldn't imagine why, since it didn't cut into their sales.

As they drove home from Fall Council, Richards and the Lone Star Quartet heard word that Franklin D. Roosevelt had been reelected as president of the United States for four more years. He betrayed his own political sentiments as he wrote in his diary in the auto court on the evening of November 4, 1936, "I guess America has decided not to shoot Santa Claus."

That November Richards experimented with a little drama on

KMPC by getting a talented woman to portray the part of "Mammy Jane," and GeGe (Virginia) as "Little Abbie" in a radio skit. Richards was never afraid to try new ideas to keep his program from becoming stodgy and stilted—from getting in a rut.

On December 3, 1936, a committee took the final step that would change the direction of Richards' life and ministry.

RADIO TAKES
A NEW TURN

"The Conference Committee voted to unite with the Union Conference in putting our broadcast on the West Coast Mutual Network on Sundays from 5:30 to 6:00 p.m. starting January 10, 1937," Richards wrote in his diary. "They want me to give my whole time to radio and this grieves me. My tabernacle and company have been together for years. How can I break it up? I was born for the 'sawdust trail,' and I live for it."

Even though Richards' loyalty to his evangelistic team and his own yearning for "sawdust trail" evangelism narrowed his vision, God's providence overruled.

On Wednesday evening at 5:00 p.m. the new West Coast broadcast on the Don Lee Network chain first went on the air. Ten radio stations in California initially carried the program: KHJ Los Angeles; KFRC San Francisco; KGB San Diego; KXO El Centro; KFXM San Bernardino; KVOE Santa Ana; KDB Santa Barbara; KPMC Bakersfield; KGDM Stockton; and KDON Monterey. The program would be called *The Voice of Prophecy,* and would be heard

165

on Sundays at 9:30 a.m. and Wednesdays at 5:00 p.m. The title of Richards' first sermon on the network was "God, a Personal Being." The Pacific Union assigned Elder H. M. Blunden as an associate.

The daily program five afternoons a week on KMPC would continue in addition to a show every Sunday evening at 10:15 on KFOX.

In spite of his heavy radio workload, Richards was still unrealistically insisting that he continue with evangelism. He met with the committee and urged permission to begin a series of meetings in Redondo Beach, though Calkins, Pacific Union president, was opposed, suggesting that he be content to devote his time to the radio programs.

Against his advice, Richards began a series of meetings on February 7, 1937, in the Redondo Beach Women's Club on Pearl and Broadway. That day Mabel had driven him to Hollywood for the 9:30 a.m. broadcast, to the General Hospital for his sermon at the hospital chapel, back home for lunch, back up to Beverly Hills for the 5:00 p.m. broadcast on KMPC, to Redondo Beach for his opening night at the women's club at 8:00 p.m., then to KFOX at 10:15 p.m. for his *Prophetic News* broadcast. "I am tired!" he confessed to his diary that night. It was an unrealistic schedule, not only for Richards but also for Mabel. But it was a lesson that he could learn only by sad experience.

During the early days of their network programs Richards and his team decided that the quartet name should be changed. The name "Lone Star Four" identified it with Texas, not with California, so they initiated a contest to come up with a new name. The winning entry was "King's Heralds." Beginning in March 1937 that became the new title of the Voice of Prophecy singing men.

For all his busyness, Richards still delighted in his family. On April 7, 1937, he wrote, "God has so blessed me—such a good sweet loving wife and dear children. I want to be with them more. Kenneth [6 years old] said to me today, 'Daddy, do you know how I get out of spankings?' 'No, how?' 'By using my brains.'"

If the new radio adventure was to succeed, the Voice of Prophecy group would have to visit the cities and surrounding areas where it was being broadcast. On Thursday morning, April 15,

Richards, Blunden, and the King's Heralds left Glendale for their first radio promotion trip. They arrived in Salinas, California, about 5:00 p.m. and gave a program at the women's club where Elder Paul Wickman had been holding meetings.

"Paul Wickman gave us a wonderful reception," Richards confided in his diary that night after the meeting. "His personality will carry him a long way."

Richards was right in his evaluation of Wickman. A talented and able minister and administrator, he would later do evangelism in South Africa, then come back to the United States after a term of duty overseas to serve as director of the Seventh-day Adventist General Conference Radio Commission.

Friday they were up early and on the road to San Francisco; where they appeared that night in the Sage Brothers Tabernacle. Sabbath morning they were guests on the Sage Brothers radiobroadcast at 8:30 a.m., then hurried down the peninsula to Mountain View, where they held church services at the Pacific Press Publishing Association chapel. In the afternoon they drove around the bay to San Jose for a 3:00 p.m. meeting, then returned to San Francisco, spending the night at the YMCA.

Sunday morning they released the network program from San Francisco station KFRC, then headed to Lodi in the central valley for a night meeting, where 900 turned out at the local high school auditorium. Monday and Tuesday they went to Sacramento, Roseville, Auburn, Nevada City, and Fresno for personal appearances, then back to Los Angeles on Wednesday night just in time to put on their network broadcast at 5:00 p.m.

By the summer of 1937 church leaders persuaded Richards to give up his *Tabernacle of the Air* broadcast on KMPC, plus his radio questions broadcast on KFOX. The pressures of the network programs, public appearances, evangelistic meetings, and promotion tours made the extra radiobroadcasts too much to handle. He had too many irons in the fire, none of them getting hot.

But Richards couldn't give up KMPC without some anguish of

heart. "Terribly hard to give up KMPC after all these years," he wrote, "but I hardly have time to see my family—working out in garage day and night on talks for the VOICE."

Richards was becoming recognized as an authority on radio-broadcasting. The Oregon Conference of Seventh-day Adventists sent one of their ministers to spend some time with him learning the ropes. Julius L. Tucker would later become a well-known radio preacher, founder and speaker of the *Quiet Hour,* a charming devotional program still heard on many stations in the United States and now under the direction of J. L. Tucker's grandson.

In June Richards' landlord notified him they wanted to move back into the house in Long Beach. This put the family into a desperate house-hunting fever. Since their Voice of Prophecy office was now in the Pacific Union Conference headquarters, they zeroed in on the Glendale/Eagle Rock area, finally finding a place on 2164 Eagledale in Eagle Rock. After a hard day of packing and moving, they moved into their new place, only to find the house too small and not suitable at all. Before nightfall they had moved again, this time to an unfurnished house in Sleepy Hollow Canyon in Glendale. It would be a house that would become home to H.M.S. and family for almost a half century.

Richards was still not content just to do only radio. On August 29 he and the quartet began a series of meetings in Lodi, California. He had requested that his faithful Bible instructor, Lona Brosi, accompany them to Lodi. When the conference refused to let her come, Richards was more than a little upset. He had learned to depend on Brosi to bring the people into the church with her special Bible study meetings after they had heard the main points from the pulpit. He couldn't see how the union conference could expect him to have success in a "new effort with *all* new workers." But he was about to see how God, who can see the end from the beginning, had a Bible instructor waiting for him in Lodi that would be a faithful and successful helper for many future evangelistic meetings.

In Lodi the conference had brought in Ellen and Howard

Curran. Ellen was wonderful. She would run her little projector in the Pictured Truth tent, and regularly bring many individuals to the baptismal tank. By the end of the Lodi meetings 166 had accepted the Lord and received the rite of baptism. Richards gave much of the credit to Ellen Curran and her "Pictured Truth" meetings.

Lodi was a rewarding series for the Voice of Prophecy evangelistic team. In that luxurious grape country south of Sacramento lived hundreds of honest, hardworking German families. The Lodi gossip mill whispered that some of them still liked to sip a little German beer and wine on occasion, but they grew to love and respect H.M.S. Richards. The friends he made there were true and loyal, and revered him for the rest of their lives and his.

Henry de Fluiter led the singing, and young Kingsley Minifie and his bride were there, just beginning their ministerial service. Everything went well except that he had to be away from his little family back in Glendale who could come up only occasionally on weekends.

Opening night was a test of the power of radio. They had done most of their advertising over the Voice of Prophecy radio network. When Richards and the quartet walked on stage in the big tent at Lodi, they were gratified to see a crowd of about 1,000. Richards preached on heaven. For the next four months meetings convened every night, seven nights a week. They released the radio program from the local station for the network, though on occasion Richards and the quartet would drive over to San Francisco to put on their network broadcast.

As summer turned into fall in the San Joaquin Valley, the weather turned cold. To keep the chill out of the air, the evangelists installed a stove in the tent, but it was ineffective. On the night they put in a new stove, Richards reported to his diary that "the old stove seemed to resent it," and sent up a haze of choking blue smoke through which he had to preach.

During the meetings that stove caught the tent on fire three different times. It was only through the mercy of God that the results weren't tragic. One night a big storm almost tore the tent down.

169

The tent top came sagging down on the bookstand, ruining some of the merchandise. That night Richards had to preach in overalls, but the crowd of farmers didn't mind at all. It only endeared the preacher to these hardworking men and women of the soil.

On October 25, 1937, the Voice of Prophecy invited Frank F. Merriam, governor of California, to a big banquet at the Lodi Hotel. Richards sat at the governor's left and confessed he "didn't know how to act so just didn't act." He said the governor was "as friendly and common as could be." The King's Heralds sang, and the governor and staff seemed impressed. After the banquet the entire entourage went down to the tent at the corner of Oak and Hutchins. They had pitched an extra tent out toward the road to serve as an overflow for the crowds. That night about 3,000—some said 4,000—showed up for the meeting. Both the governor and Richards spoke. Governor Merriam asked for some radio logs and said he would listen to all *Voice of Prophecy* broadcasts from then on. Either he was impressed or a very good politician—maybe both.

December 9 President L. K. Dixon of the Northern California Conference brought a young man to Richards' tent. His name was Elmer R. Walde. Elmer led the music that night, sang a solo, and Richards said "he did well." At the close of the meeting the committee met in the parking lot and voted to take young Walde on as a conference employee. After two years in California, Walde went on to become a radio musician on a religious broadcast in Portland, Oregon, with Julius L. Tucker, then to Hawaii as an evangelist and pastor, and finally in 1947 as a member of Richards' own staff at the Voice of Prophecy, where he stayed for several years. Richards came to lean heavily on Walde, not only when they would sit in board meetings together, but later when Walde accepted a position in Washington, D.C., in the Radio Department of the General Conference.

A final baptism of 32 for the campaign took place December 18, bringing the total for the entire series to 166. Richards' sermon title was "The World's Last Saturday Night."

On Friday, January 7, 1938, Richards and the quartet started another three-week series of meetings in Lodi at the Lodi High School auditorium, where 1,000 showed up for the opening night meeting. During this short series 81 more accepted baptism. The closing meetings were to overflow crowds, and many shed tears as Richards and the quartet said goodbye to the friends they had made during the preceding six months.

In March Richards began another series of meetings in Shafter in the southern part of the San Joaquin Valley. Richards was again in the company of old friends. He had conducted two big campaigns in nearby Bakersfield 11 years before. On opening night at the tent all the seats were filled and some of the children had to sit up on the platform. The attendance was 959 by actual count! By the end of the series they had baptized 90. For his closing meeting on June 19 at Shafter Richards preached from the passage in Acts 20 in which the apostle Paul said farewell to the church members from Ephesus. "Now, brethren, I commend you to God." As his Shafter and Bakersfield friends said goodbye to Richards with tears at the end of the meetings, they must have thought about Paul's words to the believers from Ephesus—that some of them might see his face no more.

That September Richards started a series of meetings in San Diego, six nights a week for four months in the Big Tent Studio, and for the next four years he would conduct two and sometimes three evangelistic campaigns a year, all the while continuing his radiobroadcasts.

Early in 1939 Richards and his team went to Phoenix for five months. It was a challenging task to preach five nights a week, visit interested people, write radio scripts, and sometimes referee personality clashes between staff members.

Early in the Phoenix campaign, Louis Crane, first tenor of the King's Heralds, began to hint that he desired out. Louis had decided he wanted to take medicine and become a doctor. His disenchantment with singing for a living spread like an infection, and soon his brother Waldo, who sang second tenor, caught it, though both men agreed to stay on with the quartet until the team could find replacements for them.

Some who have not lived there might think that Phoenix is hot. It is in the summer, but in winter it can be uncomfortably cold. One night in February the temperature dropped. Richards walked to the meeting tent in freezing wind, rain, and sleet. He vowed he would never forget that walk through the mud and darkness. About 200 valiant survivors were present, and the evangelist preached the entire sermon with his overcoat on.

It was in Phoenix that Richards became friends with Jerry Pettis, who later became a U.S. congressman. Jerry was a young minister in Arizona, and Richards could see he had great promise. He had a beautiful speaking voice and was a pleasant-sounding bass singer who on more than one occasion filled in at bass in the quartet when Ray Turner was sick or absent from Phoenix.

On March 6, 1939, just as he was leaving with the other team members for a conference picnic, Richards received a telegram from Mabel. She had just given birth to Justus Alfred Norman Richards, who weighed in at 5:50 a.m. at 7 lbs. 7 oz.

It left Richards in a twitter, because he had sermons six nights a week, and just the evening before he had introduced the subject "The Change of the Sabbath." His friends the Nightingales were just leaving for Los Angeles, but he could not get back to the meetings in time by the next night if he rode with them in their car. He felt he would have to postpone his trip home to see his wife and new baby for a week, since the interest in the meetings had reached a high pitch.

If Richards had a failing, this decision exposed it. Everyone in the Phoenix meetings would have understood if he had passed the preaching off to one of his associates for a few days and rushed home to see his wife and new son. It didn't help when he received a letter from Mabel in which she told him that the Southern California Conference president had criticized him for not coming home. As it turned out, his new son was 2 weeks old before Richards was able to take a night train to Los Angeles from Phoenix. He climbed aboard after his sermon on March 19, 1939, arriving in Los Angeles the next morning. Since Monday was a day off in the Phoenix meetings, by getting his young minister friend Jerry Pettis to preach at the Tuesday meeting Richards did not have to catch a return train until 8:05 p.m. Tuesday. "How lonely I felt on that train," he wrote.

Richards was a single-minded man. God had called him to the ministry, and the ministry was his first love. Without doubt he loved his family deeply, but he could never quite bring himself to make them first in his list of priorities. He was never unfaithful to Mabel, but all of her life she had to play second fiddle to another kind of mistress—Richards' ministry. I know that some will say that was what he should have done—that he had his priorities straight—but I'm not sure that in his saner moments he would agree with them. Years later he would often preach to denominational workers' meetings on a text in Song of Solomon 1:6: "They made me a keeper of the vineyards; but mine own vineyard have I not kept." I think I could detect in those sermons the sorrow he felt as he took a backward look at his own life and perceived his own failure to devote more of his energy to his family.

His feeling of guilt cropped out in his anxiety to try to make amends for his past shortcomings, and he did it by lavishing affection on his newest son. I think Jan (Justus Alfred Norman's initials became his name tag for the rest of his life) will admit that he never suffered the same feelings of benign neglect that at least some of the other children may have at times felt. Any time Jan wanted to talk with his father, Dad was ready and willing to devote an hour, two hours, or half a day to sharing thoughts with his youngest son. It continued even after Jan's marriage many years later.

Ray Turner remembers a comical episode that happened back in Phoenix while Richards was away to see his new son. Jerry Pettis preached that evening on the moral decline in the world, of husbands and wives being unfaithful to their vows to one another. That evening, since he and his wife, Rachelle, were visiting in Phoenix, Ray invited them to stay in Richards' room at his place, since the Chief wouldn't be back for a couple days.

Rachelle and Ouida retired early, while Jerry and Ray stayed up talking until late. Just before the men were getting ready to call it a day, Ray noticed that Ouida had offered Rachelle their room, leaving her and Ray to sleep in Richards' bed. Jerry wasn't aware of the change of plans, so when he donned his pajamas he made a flying leap over the foot of the bed into Richards' bed. Ouida turned over to see what all the flurry was about and let out a scream. "Why, Jerry! What are you doing here?"

Poor Pettis, shocked to find himself in bed with the wrong wife, leaped out faster than he had jumped in. Ray stood in the background, his sides splitting with laughter. "Jerry, wait until our evangelistic crowd hears about this," he said. "How are you going to explain when I tell them I caught you in bed with my wife?"

After the close of the Phoenix meetings in May of 1939, Richards launched another series in North Hollywood that continued almost to the end of the year. During it Louis and Waldo Crane left the quartet and Bob Johnson, first tenor, and Vernon Stewart, second tenor, took their places.

It was also during these meetings that Virginia made a decision that brought joy to her father's heart. As Richards stood beside his 14-year-old in the baptistry he broke down for a moment. "How long have I looked forward to this!" he confessed to his diary. "May the heavenly Father keep her always true to Him!"

On the last Sabbath at the close of the North Hollywood meetings the evangelistic team had a beautiful baptism in the big tent. One of those baptized was a woman who wept because she was afraid her husband was going to kill her. The night before he had pressed a pistol against her forehead and pulled the trigger. It merely snapped, but he threatened her life if she went ahead with the baptism.

As 1939 came to a close, Richards preached for his last sermon of the year on radio, "When God Writes 30 for Tonight."

At the end of his diary for 1939 he listed 10 "often misspelled words: inoculate, embarrass, harass, supersede, innuendo, rarefy, vilify, plague, picnicking, desiccate." He was always trying to improve himself, but sometimes his sense of the ridiculous came out. At the end of one diary he quoted two nonsensical limericks.

"For beauty I am not a star;
There are others more handsome by far
But my face I don't mind it,
For I am behind it:
It's the people in front that I jar."
                                    —*Richard Burton*

And another by "Anonymous."

"There was a young lady named Banker
Who slept while the ship lay at anchor,
She awoke in dismay
When she heard the mate say,
'Now hoist up the top sheet and spanker.'"

A second four-month campaign in Phoenix that opened in January and closed in June of 1940 followed the series in North Hollywood. While they were going on, Hitler invaded the low countries of Holland and Belgium. Richards' sermons reflected the news as almost everyone wondered if the approaching unavoidable war would turn out to be the battle of Armageddon.

As the meetings began in Phoenix, the choir director reported to Richards that he was having trouble getting a choir started. Some prospective members were angry and wouldn't come to choir anymore because when they arrived someone else had already gotten there before them, taken "their robe," and wouldn't give it back. "The choir," wrote Richards in his diary, "if it's big enough to amount to much, is often the 'war department.'" It would not be his last experience with a musical "war department."

Soon Bob Johnson discovered that his voice could not hold up singing first tenor night after night. For a while Johnson and Stewart would trade parts—Johnson singing the lower second tenor part while Stewart tried to carry the first. But that didn't work out either, and it threw the quartet and the whole team into confusion, wondering what to do.

At the close of the Phoenix meetings, Richards had a brief vacation with his family. As they often did, they went by the home of his friend Bev McCulloch. The children—especially the boys—loved it when Dad could go hiking with them, and this time they drove up into the great Sequoia National Park and King's River canyons with their new Ford. Kenneth was only 9 years old at the time, but still vividly remembers them venturing across a bridge and up into the dark recesses of a cave. The boy was stepping timidly into the increasingly dark shadows when Dad strode bravely by, only to stop suddenly at the alarming whir of a rattlesnake. Both father and son shot out of the cave.

During the last months of 1940 and the first of 1941 Richards and his team conducted meetings in the Veteran's Memorial Auditorium in Sacramento. During the series Richards received word that Bev McCulloch in Visalia had suffered a stroke and his left side was paralyzed. What sorrow it brought him to see this beloved man laid low. Here was a man who all of his life had gotten up at 3:00 a.m. to milk cows and take care of the chickens. Now he was completely helpless. Richards sat at his bedside and wept with him. "I love him as no other man outside my own family!" Richards wrote in his diary.

Richards also loved his little family, and was depressed that his work kept them apart so often. In those days evangelism had not yet discovered the three-week meetings. Richards' series sometimes went as long as six months. Often Mabel would bundle the four children into the Ford and drive for a weekend to where her husband was holding meetings. It wasn't easy when his meetings were 400 or 500 miles away.

One day in the spring of 1941 she loaded the four children into the Ford and drove from Glendale to Sacramento. When Richards was too busy getting ready for the night meetings on Friday, she took the boys fishing. Even though they caught nothing but nibbles, it was an exciting time for them, and it was good to be near their father.

On one occasion that weekend Dad was hiking with the three boys near Sandy Gulch Creek. As they walked along, something he saw when the boys didn't know he was looking warmed Richards' heart. "Junior is so good to Jan," he wrote. "I saw him stoop and kiss Jan today when he thought no one saw it." Dad might not have been so rhapsodic had he also witnessed times when Harold and Kenneth delighted in tormenting Jan, or for that matter, each other.

The quartet struggled for the rest of the year, both Bob Johnson and Vernon Stewart finally asking to be relieved of their singing responsibilities. Stewart was the first to leave. Ralph Simpson replaced him. Bob Johnson hung on through the Sacramento meetings and the evangelistic campaign that followed in the city of Chico, California, but then he, too, resigned, and accepted work less demanding vocally.

In Chico Richards rented the Empire Theater, recently purchased by the owner of the only other theater in town in order to suppress competition. After Richards had been preaching there only a week, the anguished theater owner complained that "I'm competing against myself here. I let these preachers in here, and they're getting all the crowds."

The quartet struggled on that spring, but by May, Ralph Simpson found by hard experience that his voice could not take the heavy demand placed on it by singing day after day. On the May 25 broadcast his voice completely gave out on the last song. It meant that they would not only have to continue looking for a first tenor, but would also need to find another second tenor.

That June Richards was summoned to assist in the funeral of his friend W. B. Lindsay. Lindsay had been a coworker and companion 20 years before in Canada.

In August 1941 the Voice of Prophecy team began holding meetings in Portland, Oregon. During that period new voices replaced both Ralph Simpson and Bob Johnson. George Casebeer assumed first tenor and Bob Seamount the second tenor positions.

Before the end of the Portland campaign and the close of 1941, significant changes would come both to Richards and the Voice of Prophecy—and to the world.

COAST TO COAST
BY RADIO

August 26, 1941, at 8:05 p.m., Mabel took her husband down to the train in Los Angeles for Portland. As he pulled away from his little family standing on the dark station platform, 2-year-old Jan reached out and clung to him, "Da-da, bye-bye! Da-da, bye-bye."

"My, I can't stand it much longer," he confessed a little later to his diary as the train clickety-clacked up the coast. "Mabel trying to keep her tears in. It's not fair to her and it's just too hard for me." Yet even though it was hard to leave his family again and again, he had a strong pull to duty that kept him going in spite of his inward feelings.

Opening night at the Portland Civic Auditorium was Sunday, August 31, 1941. Elmer Walde, who had gotten his start as a young singing evangelist four years before at the Lodi meetings, led the singing. J. L. Tucker, who had spent some time with Richards learning radio a few years before, now pastored the Portland Tabernacle Seventh-day Adventist Church and operated his own *Quiet Hour* broadcast. He would be a great help during the series. A crowd of 2,300 showed up that opening Sunday night.

The next night 1,200 were present even though it was pouring rain. Richards soon learned that rain didn't keep Portland crowds away. They had meetings seven nights a week, and throughout the campaign they enjoyed an attendance of about 2,000 on the weekends and about 1,000 on weeknights.

On September 22 the city pre-preempted the Civic Auditorium for a giant rally by the "America First" committee, with Senator Burton K. Wheeler as the featured speaker. "America First" was a fiercely isolationist faction of the Republican Party organized by General Robert E. Wood of Sears, Roebuck, and Company to keep America out of the European war. Richards feared the rally would be divisive to America, but he could do little about such an interruption of his Voice of Prophecy evangelistic meetings on September 22. He signed off on the contract he had with the city of Portland for that date, since the city leaders told him the city desired it.

On Tuesday night, September 30, 3,000 crowded into the Civic Auditorium to hear Richards' lecture on spiritism and the San Jose Winchester House. For the past few days most of his coworkers had noticed that Richards had been moping around more than usual. He was homesick for his family. That night Tucker told the audience that since the auditorium would not be available for a few days, Richards planned to take a short trip to see his little family in California. In a matter of a few minutes they raised $90 to pay for a round-trip plane ticket.

At 10:05 p.m., after he had preached his evening sermon, Richards boarded a plane for Los Angeles. "It was my very first trip by air (aside from a 30-minute ride in a two seater with Jerry Pettis two years ago in Phoenix). What a ride! Portland from the air was beautiful, its thousands of lights glittering. Then later, over a sea of silver clouds, the moon flooded a strange new world. To the east an island covered with snow rose 2,000 feet above the shimmering sea—Mount Shasta in ermine robes."

Since his family did not expect him, he took a taxi when the plane landed at 5:30 a.m. What a glad surprise to Mabel and the children to have Daddy home, even if for only a few days.

A week later his family got up early to see Daddy off on an airplane at 7:00 a.m. No doubt big brothers Harold and Kenneth had coached 2-year-old Jan. "Daddy go zoozz!" he said excitedly as they pulled up to the airport.

A week later a wire came from Washington, D.C., that Richards would be needed at the big Seventh-day Adventist Church Autumn Council meeting in Battle Creek, Michigan. Richards' first thought was that he couldn't take a break from the meetings in Portland, even though he knew the Radio Commission meeting would be discussing a national church broadcast. Ray Turner and the other members of the quartet urged him to go, but Richards still held back. "I don't even have the money to buy a ticket, and I'd never get there in time on the train," he remonstrated. "Besides, who'd take the meetings here while I'm gone?"

"But Chief," Ray urged, "this meeting is too important to miss. You've got to go. The train is too slow. Take a plane. And the Pacific Union will advance the money for the ticket. Send them a wire, and Reeves from just over the border in Canada can preach for you."

After more urging, Richards at last agreed to at least send a night letter to the Pacific Union Conference office in Glendale. Early the next morning a money wire came from Glendale.

The meeting would certainly have a great impact on the *Voice of Prophecy's* future. Just two months before W. H. Branson, North American Division president, had whispered to Richards one morning as he visited the broadcast studio in Los Angeles, "I hope it will not be long till we hear you all over the U.S."

So on Tuesday morning, October 14, after the fog lifted from the Portland airport, Richards boarded a United Airlines Chicago-bound plane. His plane was a local, landing in Pendleton, Oregon; Boise, Idaho; Salt Lake City, Utah; Denver, Colorado; Omaha, Nebraska; and finally Chicago. At almost every stop he had well-wishers out to meet him at the plane. It was like Elijah and Elisha meeting the young men at the schools of the prophets on their way to Elijah's appointment with a fiery chariot. H.M.S. arrived at Chicago at 1:30 a.m. and took a train to Battle Creek.

On October 15 and 16, 1941, the committee voted for a national broadcast, choosing Richards and the *Voice of Prophecy* to be the church's official broadcast. Elder Branson leaned over and whispered to Richards after the committee vote, "Dreams do come true sometimes, don't they?"

But even then the devil threw an obstacle in the way. When the church contacted the network, it told the denomination that it had already sold the time slot. "You were too late making your decision," the network executive explained. "My own church has given word that they want the time, and we've promised it to them."

"Have you got the money in hand?" the Adventist representative asked.

"No, but they've promised to get it to me," he answered. "They said they'd get the money to me by tomorrow morning. If they don't show up by then, the time is yours."

That night a lot of praying went on in Battle Creek. The next morning the Adventists knocked at the network's door.

"I don't know what happened," the network representative said. "I told my church to get the money to me by this morning. They haven't come, and I've given my word to you. If you've got the money, the time is yours."

As Richards sailed over the North American continent on his way back to Portland, he knew in his heart that life would from then forward be very different. Too excited to sleep, he sat looking out of the window all night, wondering what things would be like now. Fog had delayed his planes, causing him to arrive Sabbath morning. Two hours after landing he was preaching in the Vancouver, Washington, Seventh-day Adventist Church.

Wes Crane, the quartet baritone, had been hinting that he wanted to get out of the quartet and enter singing evangelism. Now the prospect of the *Voice of Prophecy* becoming a national program changed his views, and he decided to stay.

Though Richards continued with the Portland meetings, he had to fly to Los Angeles in late November to take part in making plans for the coast-to-coast broadcast that would start on the first Sunday of the new year.

A few days after his return to Portland the sneak attack of the Japanese navy and air force on Pearl Harbor, Hawaii, stunned the whole nation. When he first heard the news, Richards could hardly believe it. It was inconceivable. "The Japanese have accomplished what the president could not do. They have unified the nation. And if America wins the war (God forbid any other end) it may well mean the end of the empire of Japan."

In his evangelism sermons Richards had long predicted that Japan would attack the United States, mistakenly applying the prophecies of Daniel to the Asian nations of Japan and possibly China. Now events seemed to be fulfilling his predictions. "Is this Armageddon?" he and many other sincere students of Bible prophecy wondered.

The immediate effect of the Japanese attack brought about blackouts in the big coastal cities. Portland ordered blackouts from 1:30 a.m. to 8:00 a.m., and all local radio stations went off the air during those night hours. The airlines canceled all night planes to Los Angeles.

Richards received word from young evangelist and radio preacher Fordyce Detamore that he would accept the Voice of Prophecy invitation to serve as associate speaker. H.M.S. also learned that he would need to submit his radio scripts to a reading committee. "This deflates my enthusiasm a lot," he confided to his diary. Though it was an irritation, he would later recognize that it was a wonderful protection for him. It would insulate him from the criticisms of self-styled theological experts.

On December 21 the big Portland meetings closed, and Richards and his team returned home in time for Christmas, but it wouldn't be a relaxing vacation. They had hundreds of details to begin to iron out, involving finances, hiring staff, buying typewriters, desks, chairs, filing cabinets, finding office space. January 4 was now only days away. As 1941 came to a close, Richards worried a little about young fireball Fordyce Detamore blending in with the others assigned to manage the new organization. He wrote in his diary for December 31: "May God help us to make 1942 better than 1941. Romans 8:28."

New Year's Day dawned with Mabel sick in bed with severe lung congestion. "She is almost never sick," Richards said, "and when she is our whole family is at sea." Fordyce Detamore left for Kansas City on New Year's night to wind up his affairs there.

Sunday, January 4, 1942, was a busy day. Richards and the quartet put on a music and poetry program for their Don Lee stations at 8:45 a.m. At 4:00 p.m. they all stood in their places for the first broadcast to the Eastern and Central time zones, Richards at his microphone, the quartet ready for the opening theme song, Elmer Digneo at the organ. At 9:15 p.m. they would repeat the broadcast for the West Coast.

Detamore listened at his radio in Kansas City. Richards' first sermon on the coast-to-coast broadcast was "March of Dictators." A network of 89 stations carried that first broadcast. As soon as the last sounds died away, telegrams and telephone calls of congratulation began to arrive from all across the country.

Within a week 5,000 letters had arrived, along with $5,000 in donations. It would be a stream of income that continues to this very day. Richards saw it as a work of faith. "When God wants us to go off the air, He will simply shut off the supply of funds. If He wants us to continue, He will impress the hearts of our listeners to send in their sacrificial offerings." Again and again, during times of financial drought, Richards and his staff would find themselves driven to their knees to literally pray down the heavenly blessings needed to continue the program.

On January 8 the Voice of Prophecy office moved from the Pacific Union Conference offices to 700 W. Broadway, Glendale, California, in a residence converted into office space.

January 20 the Voice of Prophecy operating board voted to have 2,000,000 radio logs printed and then scattered around the country to make America aware of the new radio ministry. They also authorized sending two automobiles out on trips to rally support for the broadcast. It was not going to be easy because of wartime restrictions on travel. The government rationed gasoline, and tires were almost impossible to get, even if you had permission from the newly authorized ration boards around the country.

Friday, February 6, Fordyce Detamore arrived from Kansas City. On Sunday the 8th he made his first appearance on the air as announcer. His exciting style of speaking was a perfect contrast to Richards' lower pitched, more soothing voice for the sermons.

Detamore had been with the Voice of Prophecy only a few weeks before he launched the Bible Correspondence School. Within a month 2,000 had enrolled in this new way to study the Bible. By June the Bible course appeared in Braille for the blind, and by the first of July enrollments had ballooned to 27,000. Voice of Prophecy staff numbered 30.

On February 16, Richards, Detamore, and the quartet made a quick promotional trip to Kansas. The quartet sang as they clickety-clacked along the rails, and Detamore moved among the young soldiers that jammed the chair car on the train, signing them up for the Bible correspondence course that would soon be ready. The trains were so crowded with soldiers and other travelers that sometimes the quartet would have to sit on their own suitcases in the aisles of the chair car. They were back in Los Angeles for the Sunday broadcast on February 22. The next week they left for Chattanooga, Cincinnati, Washington, D.C., Philadelphia, New York, Boston, Pittsburgh, Cleveland, Battle Creek, Kansas City, Wichita, and Oklahoma City. Richards and Detamore had gone by train, with the quartet driving by car. When they all finally dragged back into Glendale, California, on Friday, March 27, 25 days later, Bob Seamount had broken out with the measles. Now it was clear why he had been struggling to keep singing during the past week or more. He had no doubt left a generous trail of measles patients from coast to coast.

In May the board voted a young man in as Voice of Prophecy treasurer. Ithiel E. Gillis had been born to missionary parents, and he and his wife had served in overseas mission assignments. Gillis would continue as a faithful and loyal Voice of Prophecy treasurer and eventual manager of the Voice of Prophecy until he retired many years later. Even then he continued to work in the Trust Department until shortly before his death.

On Sabbath May 23, Richards was overjoyed to witness the baptism of his oldest son, Harold, Jr., who joined 47 of his fellow classmates from Glendale Academy in the rite at the Glendale Seventh-day Adventist Church. The entire family attended the important occasion.

As the radio group traveled north on a West Coast promotion tour in June, they saw evidence of the war's nearness. A wrecked oil tanker lay on its side just offshore from Crescent City, California, torpedoed by the Japanese.

The trip took them to Lodi, San Francisco, Eureka, and Crescent City in California, then on north to Portland, Walla Walla, Bozeman, and Salt Lake City. When he reached home on June 26 Richards learned of the death of his faithful Bible instructor, Lona Brosi. The next day he conducted her funeral.

June 10 Ray Turner drove to Tijuana, Mexico, to buy tires. The Voice of Prophecy had been using Ray's Buick for their official travels. He was buying tires so that there would be rubber on the wheels for future trips. No doubt he should have known better, but others had told him it was perfectly legal to buy tires in Mexico. When he came back across the border into the United States, U.S. Customs officials stopped him and under a recently passed law charged him with smuggling, seizing his car and the new tires. It would take months before he would get his car back, the tires never.

In the middle of July 1942 the Voice of Prophecy and many other Christian broadcasters reacted in alarm to a law proposed by the Federal Council of Churches, Catholics, and Jews to limit religious broadcasts on radio. An attorney was hired to fight the new threat to Christian broadcasting. Fortunately, the law never passed.

Since government authorities were still holding Ray Turner's car, the Voice of Prophecy was desperate to find transportation for their summer camp meeting promotion tour. Bob Seamount had somehow learned of a Cadillac limousine for sale owned by the movie star Dolores del Rio. The word was that Miss Del Rio was planning to return to Mexico. Enlisting the help of Fordyce Detamore, Bob managed to get the 3-year-old Cadillac for $600. A seven-passenger limousine, it was equipped with all the latest gadgets, including a glass partition between the driver and passenger compartment. The Dolores del Rio limo made its maiden voyage as a Voice of Prophecy car on a camp meeting tour up the West Coast to Portland, Seattle, Spokane, and Caldwell, Idaho. The "movie star car" served as Voice of Prophecy transportation for several years, and was always the center of attraction at camp meetings and other public appearances.

By September enrollments in the Bible correspondence course numbered 60,000, and by the beginning of October 225 stations carried the broadcast in North America. During that month 22,711 letters came in. The letters were wonderfully encouraging. One came from a woman in Philadelphia who had been planning to commit suicide. "I cannot begin to express to you my appreciation for your wonderful explanation of the Scriptures," she wrote to Richards. "Your work means much to me, and I can't thank God enough for the help I have received. I think I shall tell you my experience, so you can understand why it means so much to me.

"War conditions and home troubles had become more than I could bear, and I had decided to end it all. Someone had told me there was no hell, so I decided to take a chance. I felt that I could not stand the nerve strain any longer; then just in time, a young man handed me one of your radio logs. Out of curiosity, I tuned in, and thanks be to God, He sent you to me, even though you are thousands of miles away. You spoke the very words I needed for comfort and reassurance. Now the coming of Jesus means much to me. These Bible lessons are priceless. I can hardly wait to get the next lesson. May God help you to bring to many others the same hope you have brought to me."

The ministry soon discovered that a number of the students enrolling in the Bible correspondence lessons were children, inspiring Fordyce Detamore to write a course especially for them. Printed in varied colors, it became an immediate success. Over a span of 19 years more than one quarter of a million youngsters enrolled and finished the Voice of Prophecy Junior Bible Course.

By April 1942 the *Voice of Prophecy* went on the air in South America in Spanish and Portuguese with national speakers Braulio Perez and Roberto Rabello respectively. The King's Heralds learned to provide music for the foreign broadcasts as well as for the English programs.

In October Richards, Detamore, and the quartet set out on another cross-country tour by train and car. It was my first exposure to the *Voice of Prophecy*. I as well as my fellow students and teachers at Union College in Lincoln, Nebraska, found ourselves entranced when they made one of their appearances at our college campus in October. Jerry Pettis, Richards' old friend from Phoenix days, was my Bible teacher at the college at the time. He gave the Voice of Prophecy group a big welcome, and we were all delighted when Ray Turner asked Jerry to sing bass with the quartet on one song. I was especially captivated by the first tenor singing of George Casebeer. Little did I know that in five years I would be with the King's Heralds.

Richards was still getting static about the Collins Bible that had his Bible studies printed and bound in the back. This time it had started when someone wrote to one of the Seventh-day Adventist publishing houses asking for the Seventh-day Adventist Bible. The incident prompted General Conference president J. L. McElhany to send out a circular letter warning everyone against Richards' Bible with the special Bible lessons.

As 1942 wound down Richards could look back on an eventful year. The broadcast was thriving, his family was growing up, and in many ways all was right with the world. Virginia, his 18-year-old, had a boyfriend. She told her mother that Walter had kissed her Saturday night. Father wrote: "I'm glad she has confidence in her mother, but I wish she would wait a year or better two. This boy seems manly, but is too young to start a family. I am praying." It was a typical father's worries about his daughter.

The family in late 1942 owned a quacking duck, and Harold, Jr., came home one day with three bantam hens he had adopted. One morning the loud quacking of their duck awakened Richards. Afraid it would disturb the neighbors, he got up and ventured out in his bathrobe. It so startled the poor duck that she ran pell-mell into the fence and back behind the chicken coop, but she gave no more quacks all day.

Even though Richards was only 48 years old, he was beginning to feel his mortality. On New Year's Eve he wrote in his diary: "Another year has come to its end! How many dear friends have reached the end of the story this year. I notice it more and more. As a family we thank God for life and many blessings. May the Lord help us to serve Him faithfully in 1943!" Then the next day he recorded: "Another year starts in the calendar of earth—just a tick in the clock of eternity. The war is still raging. Russia making bloody progress against her invader—the United Nations seem in slow motion in North Africa and the Southwest Pacific."

In March of 1943 a telegram came from Paul Bradley of the Radio Commission of the General Conference that the commission had appointed Professor George Greer as a quartet coach. Though Richards was apprehensive about appointing a choir teacher to direct the quartet, he had no idea of the hornets' nest that this seemingly trivial bit of news would stir up.

TROUBLE IN THE WAR DEPARTMENT

As 1942 wound down to a close, the *Voice of Prophecy* picked up steam. The broadcast expanded to more and more stations, and the Bible school grew.

On the military front, the pinch of war needs made the rationing of many items necessary. Gasoline, tires, eggs, butter, sugar, coffee, soap, cooking oil—all were becoming scarce and in many cases unavailable to the civilian population. The shortage of tires and gasoline made it difficult for the Voice of Prophecy to travel to promote the newly instituted broadcast among listeners across North America.

The war interfered with the *Voice of Prophecy* broadcast in other ways. On April 25, 1943, Richards rode to the broadcast. At 8:37 p.m. the air-raid sirens signaled a blackout. An officious over-eager air-raid warden flagged down their car and held them up until the all clear sounded at 9:30. It caused them to miss their 9:00 p.m. live broadcast, and the station had to use a pre-recorded transcription.

In the West, home base for the Voice of Prophecy, the Southern California Conference sought to use Richards in their 1943 evangelistic plans for the city of Los Angeles. The committee concocted a plan for evangelism that involved holding meetings in the downtown Biltmore Hotel three times each Sunday. It was a novel idea, but the plan to have three different speakers conducting three different meetings each Sunday didn't seem to Richards to make a lot of sense. His experience in evangelism had taught him that as people become interested, they naturally bond with the evangelist. As their interest grows, the evangelist can help them expand the sphere of their affections to include the pastors and church members where they will be joining. To fragment the audience by throwing three different preachers at them each Sunday, in Richards' eyes, only caused confusion.

All the preachers were successful evangelists. Elder Philip Knox would have a meeting at 2:30 p.m. in the Biltmore Theater every Sunday afternoon, Elder B. R. Spears was to be on at 4:30 p.m., and H.M.S. Richards at 6:30 p.m. All the follow-up of the names to bring about a baptismal harvest would go through a minister coordinator, Elder Louis E. Folkenberg. Richards loved evangelism, but thought this particular plan was doomed only to succeed feebly or to fail, and was, as he put it, "an outrage on common sense."

On Richards' opening night at the Biltmore in January 900 were in attendance, and his opening sermon title was "The Divinity of Christ." When he wanted to bring in Ellen Curran and her Pictured Truth premeeting for the next Sunday night meeting, the evangelism committee vetoed his plan as unnecessary "entertainment." They didn't understand that Ellen's Pictured Truth lectures reinforced what Richards had said in his sermons, filling in for the more deeply interested individuals details of doctrinal truth that Richards had wisely touched on only briefly. By the fourth Sunday Richards' pleadings had prevailed, and Ellen Curran proceeded with her premeeting Pictured Truth sessions.

By mid-March Richards' part of the Biltmore meetings had shifted from 6:30 p.m. to 2:00 p.m. to attempt to resolve some interpersonal problems that had arisen. What they were we can only guess. In his diary Richards wrote: "I want to get away from the envy and heartbreaking misunderstandings of these unified meetings." Perhaps there should be a question mark after the word "unified." Was it that the crowds attending the three different sessions were greater for some of the evangelists than for others? At this date it's hard to know. It hardly matters since on April 9 the Radio Commission voted that the Biltmore meetings were draining too much of Richards' time and energy, and he should phase out of them as soon as possible. His last meeting in the Biltmore three-headed evangelistic campaign occurred at 2:00 p.m. May 9.

Not all of the church's leaders were happy with the format of the *Voice of Prophecy* programs. In early 1943 at a meeting of church leaders some strongly recommended that the program carry the name of the church. Richards felt that unwise since much prejudice still existed in North America against Seventh-day Adventists. It was his firm belief that if the program identified itself as a Seventh-day Adventist program, it would cause many to tune out without listening to the truths he was trying to give.

During March of 1943 the first dark storm clouds began to rise over what Richards came to refer to as the "war department." I have often heard him say, tongue-in-cheek, that war started in the heavenly choir, and that the devil continues to have great success in church choirs here on earth. The Radio Commission in Washington, D.C., voted on March 3 to send Professor George Greer to be the full-time coach of the King's Heralds quartet. The quartet had already been employing a local musician to coach them on a part-time basis. An individual named Folette helped the men with their voice production and ensemble blend. Richards and Detamore had nothing personally against Professor George Greer. He was an outstanding choir leader, but Richards thought it was a vast mistake to employ a choir leader who had little experience in evangelism to plan music for an evangelistic broadcast and to coach his quartet.

Word began to drift from east to west that Greer was planning to make major changes in the membership of the quartet. One rumor stated that when he arrived in September he was going to sing baritone in Wesley Crane's spot and replace George Casebeer and Ray Turner with Jimmy Eaton and Don Hamilton.

Richards was able to forget the broadcast problems for an evening when his daughter, Virginia, graduated from Glendale Union Academy. It was such an important occasion that he had the network radio program for the West Coast released that evening by transcription. "As she marched up the aisle in her blue cap and gown to get her diploma," Richards wrote, "I was thinking of that crying red baby the nurse showed me to be kissed before she was fixed up in Ottawa, Canada, in 1925."

During the summer of 1943, even though the music storm was still in progress, Richards, Detamore, and the quartet went to as many camp meetings as possible, scrounging scarce tires and gasoline as they could. Sometimes they went by train, waiting in line at stations for hours, hoping for a seat or a berth on a cross-country train. Bob Seamount remembered sitting on suitcases in the aisles as hundreds of soldiers crowded the passenger cars.

On an August trip to the East Coast they had radiator trouble with the old Dolores del Rio Cadillac. In New York state they could get only 2½ gallons of gasoline at one stop, and on their way out of Canada after a camp meeting appointment, they had just enough gasoline to get back across the border. During one trip up the Chinook Pass in the state of Washington the gas gauge read empty for seven miles before they reached the top. Road crew workers refused to give them any gas, but agreed to push them over the hump if they didn't quite make it to the top. The engine sputtered to a stop just after they reached the crest, and they coasted 10 miles down the other side before they reached a station and could obtain a few more gallons.

On September 1 Professor Greer arrived. He made a point to come up to Richards' office at once to assure him that he did not plan to make any changes without his counsel. Richards urged the need for music to appeal to the average radio listener. Greer countered that it must not turn away the musicians. In turn, Richards pointed out that most of our listeners weren't musicians, and that common people supported the program. The battle lines were drawn in the sand.

Despite the continuing conflict over music, Richards and Greer never became enemies. Years later, long after Greer had left the Voice of Prophecy and was teaching at Avondale College in Australia, he and his wife eagerly invited Richards to come to their home, "treating me like a king," Richards testified at the time. Their conflict was not personal, but ideological. Something about music makes its conflicts extremely visceral. I'm quite sure that a number of readers will still choose sides in the conflict, some coming down on the side of Greer, others supporting Richards and the quartet.

Professor George Greer was a dedicated man, extremely conscientious. His views about music appropriate for church and for the *Voice of Prophecy* radiobroadcast were deeply felt. It was almost impossible for him to compromise, for he sincerely thought compromise in this area was morally wrong. He often quoted Ellen White's statement in *Fundamentals of Christian Education* about the young men in the schools of the prophets. "The art of sacred melody was diligently cultivated," she wrote. "No frivolous waltz was heard, nor flippant song that should extol man and divert the attention from God; but sacred, solemn psalms of praise to the Creator, exalting His name and recounting His wondrous works." It caused him to wince at any religious song sung in three-beat time, because to him it represented a "frivolous waltz." He had such a serious nature that it even seemed to pain him that Richards and the quartet would sometimes tease one another and laugh together.

Greer insisted on traveling to public meetings with Richards and the quartet so that he could keep watch over his charges, monitoring their music choices and singing styles. Richards found him an amiable traveling companion, but his interpersonal human relations with the quartet in their practice sessions became increasingly

195

strained. As he sat on the platform behind them, Richards could see that it inhibited their ability to express themselves in their music.

But quartet problems weren't Richards' only Voice of Prophecy worry. In September of 1943 the Mutual Broadcasting System sent through a dictum that the Voice of Prophecy would lose their time slot in the afternoon and evening to Charles E. Fuller of the *Old Fashioned Revival Hour.* The *Voice of Prophecy* would move to early Sunday morning.

Richards thought it unfair to be without warning suddenly shifted to a morning time slot, but even though J. W. Turner and Paul Bradley from the General Conference offices in Washington, D.C., went to the Mutual headquarters in New York to make a special plea to network officials, they were unsuccessful.

In late 1943 Wesley Crane, baritone of the King's Heralds, began having physical problems that seriously interfered with his singing. By November Harold Hare tried out for Wesley's part. Some of the quartet felt he would do all right, but Ray Turner disagreed. Harvey Miller of La Sierra sang temporarily with the quartet on a trip to the East. When the Voice of Prophecy group stopped in St. Louis on this tour, they auditioned Wayne Hooper for baritone and Ben Glanzer for George Casebeer's first tenor part. Greer was ecstatic with both new voices. He exclaimed that with them the Voice of Prophecy could have the best quartet in the country.

A Radio Commission meeting in December 1943 voted Wayne Hooper to take Wes Crane's place. Richards' confession in his diary for December 17 reflects his tender feelings for the men who worked with and for him. "I held back from calling Wayne Hooper a long time," he said, "not because I don't like him. I do, much, but it hurts me to see Wes Crane dropped after our long and intimate work together. Poor boy. I know he will be heartbroken because his health has forced this change." At the same meeting the Radio Commission summoned Ben Glanzer from Canada to take over for George Casebeer.

On January 15, 1944, at the Hollywood Seventh-day Adventist

Church, "Wayne Hooper sang with the quartet for the first time and it was good," confessed Richards. "He has life and puts into our quartet what it has always lacked."

Bereavement struck Richards on February 1, 1944. He wrote this sad commentary in his diary: "At 8:10 p.m. our dear Twomoms fell asleep in Christ! Her life of hard work and earnest prayer is over. She rests from her labors and her works follow her (Revelation 14:13) . . . She knew us within an hour of her life's end. She prayed this morning when she suffered so much, but we are so glad she had no hard pain apparently the last few hours. 'Now is Christ risen from the dead and become the firstfruits of them that slept' (1 Corinthians 15:20)."

Twomoms, his mother's mother, had been his close companion all through his life. She had moved up to northeastern Colorado to cook for him and Kenneth Gant when they were young evangelists still in high school. Then she had sold the little cabin in the Rocky Mountains to help pay his college bills at Washington Missionary College, and had come to keep house for the young bachelor during his school years there. Finally she had gone with him to his first pastoral assignment in Ottawa, Canada, and had left him only when he married Mabel Eastman in 1920. Now she was gone.

On Thursday afternoon at the Utter-McKinley Mortuary they held her last service. The quartet sang "Abide With Me," and Twomoms' hands held two little daisies that 5-year-old Jan had picked from his grandma's lawn.

A few days later Richards boarded a Union Pacific train taking Twomoms back to Loveland, Colorado, to lay her to rest by Twopops' side. "It was hard to ride out of town past the burial park and leave Twomoms and Twopops alone there under the cold wind," Richards confessed. "It seemed I should stay and watch over them as they did so long for me."

He remembered a letter she had written him when he was holding meetings in Phoenix four years before. She had closed it with these words: "Be a good boy so that everybody that knows you will want to know Jesus, because they know you."

The stress continued between Professor Greer and the quartet. "I hear the quartet and Greer do not get along at all," he noted in his diary. "He seems to grate on the nerves of each one, though he tries so hard. . . . He tries so hard to make a success of his work with the quartet, but all four all the time seem in a state of unrest and irritation."

Ben Glanzer arrived in Glendale and sang with the quartet for the first time on a broadcast May 14, 1944. "He is good," noted Richards in his diary, "but as yet does not blend as well as George Casebeer, and also flats a little at times, as do other human beings."

In July 1944 Fordyce Detamore said goodbye to the Voice of Prophecy. A hyperactive personality, it frustrated him to be stymied at every turn by reluctant and sometimes truculent committees. December of the previous year the Radio Commission in Washington had appointed H. H. Hix as manager of the Voice of Prophecy, a position Detamore had held with enthusiasm for two years. Unfortunately, Detamore's management style ruffled the commission. He made decisions that got things done, then waited expectantly to be spanked by the committee later. Fordyce wasn't a man you could put in a mold and squeeze into shape. Instead, he enjoyed the freedom and autonomy of active evangelism.

On July 9 Elder D. A. Delafield, a man who soon won the hearts of all who worked with him, became associate speaker. Several years later Del (as he came to be called) with his warm and winning way was instrumental in giving the last tug that would bring Richards' brother Kenneth with his family back into the church from which he had strayed for so many years. But that is another story.

Richards loved Delafield and his manner. Once when they were in Abilene, Kansas, they took a taxi over to the home of the mother of General Dwight D. Eisenhower. They found her in the back yard with a big knife digging dandelions. "She was kind and friendly," wrote Richards in his diary, "just a dear old American mother and was glad to take our Bible correspondence course."

Another time for which "Del" (Delafield) will always be remembered was the day the group drove north on the highway near

Susanville, California. On a long stretch of open road they came upon a flock of chickens that decided to cross just at the wrong time. Richards always said that Del had shouted "Whee" as they tunneled through a cloud of white feathers. For the next mile or so H.M.S. laid such a heavy guilt trip on Del that he finally turned the car around and knocked at the door of the farmhouse where they had slaughtered the chickens. After apologizing to the farmer's wife he enrolled her in the Voice of Prophecy Bible course.

While H.M.S. wrestled with office problems, Mabel struggled with her own war department at home—raising a girl and three boys. Virginia remembers one little episode Dad probably never even heard about, but the rest of the family would just as soon forget.

"When Harold Junior was a high school student at Glendale Union Academy, he formed a band with Kenneth and several of his academy friends. Some members of the band would later become pastors, doctors, and at least one a conference president. At the time, however, they were simply teenage boys who enjoyed belting out popular music, very little of which was approved of at Glendale Union Academy.

"Adventist schools produce first class musicians and my brother and his group were no exception. When they performed, they dressed formally and played behind a set of bandstands with the initials HR on them. They were really professional, and were paid quite well for playing at wedding receptions and other perhaps more questionable functions, although they would not play where liquor was served. In Adventist circles HR stood for Harold Richards, but professionally they were known as 'Hal Ross and His Band.' Few of their clients suspected they were just high school boys.

"On Sunday afternoon Daddy was out in his study in the garage and the band was rehearsing in the front room. The music was blaring with a vigorous beat and the house seemed to be jumping up and down on its foundation in time with the music. Mother and I were working in the kitchen when I heard her give a gasp. Standing on the front steps, with his hand reaching for the doorbell, was the conference president, Elder David Voth.

"My recollection of Elder Voth is probably skewed as he was in my teenage eyes an older man in a position of authority, but I recall him as a stern, serious little man who was not at all given to humor. I always thought that if he smiled or laughed his face would probably shatter like a plate dropped on the sidewalk. You get the picture.

"Mother regained her composure and hastened to answer the doorbell. She had to step outside and shut the door in order to hear and be heard above the music, which continued unabated. Elder Voth was obviously very embarrassed and was looking down at the ground. He said, 'Sister Richards, is your husband here?' 'Oh, yes, Elder Voth, he's out in his study. Just go up the driveway and it's the door on the right side of the garage.' Voth kept looking down at the ground as he walked away. When he had gone two or three steps Mother called after him, 'Oh, one other thing, Elder Voth. We're raising a family here.' 'Yes, I understand, Sister,' he answered.

"We always wondered how much he really did understand."

Harold recalls coming home early one morning from one of his "gigs" and seeing a light on in the garage study. Quietly he sneaked up the driveway, on the way picking up a baseball bat leaning against the house, thinking it might be a burglar making off with some of Dad's valuable books. As he came closer he heard the low murmur of a voice. Peeking around the corner, he saw Dad kneeling by his office chair. He was praying for his boys and his girl. Harold never did tell Dad, but neither did he ever forget the picture he saw that night.

On January 27, 1945, Richards passed a family milestone that was both joyful and painful to a father. He walked down the aisle with his beloved daughter, Virginia, to give her to another man. As they reached the front of the church, young medical student and groom Walter Cason stepped up and took her arm, while H.M.S. walked up the steps to his place as the minister. Instead of saying, "Who giveth this woman to be the husband of this man?" he said, "Walter, I now place Virginia's hand in yours." "She was beautiful and both seem supremely happy," he confessed. The new couple left for Palm Springs after the wedding, as Walt had to be in medical school the next morning.

The trouble between the quartet and Professor Greer continued to wax and wane. From the vantage point of time it seems that both sides attempted to work out their differences. On September 11, 1944, Richards and Mabel, the quartet, and their wives all went over to surprise Professor Greer on his birthday. "We had a good time, and a fine spirit and fellowship," Richards wrote that evening in his diary. But the differences in philosophy and temperament were just too great to smooth over.

In order to satisfy his own longings for the kind of music he enjoyed, Professor Greer organized other musical groups, hoping to sometimes use them on the broadcast. Unfortunately it made his interactions with the quartet even more stressed, as they interpreted it as a threat to them and their singing. Maybe that's what he intended.

By early February 1945 Greer was so exhausted from haggling with the quartet that he sometimes could not even bring himself to go to the broadcast. One Friday afternoon as the quartet polished up their music in their practice studio for the upcoming Sunday broadcast, Greer came in. After listening a few minutes, he suddenly asked, "That's not a song for the broadcast, is it?"

"Yes."

"You're not singing that song on the broadcast."

"Oh, yes, we are," they responded.

"No, you're not."

"Yes, we are!"

They became more heated and irrational with every exchange. Finally Greer, in foolish desperation, said, "It's over my dead body you'll sing that song on the broadcast Sunday."

That was like putting the ball on the tee and asking one of the quartet to hit it. It was the kind of challenge Ray Turner couldn't pass up. Ray doesn't take kindly to threats.

"Yes, we're singing it on the broadcast," he responded, "and I suppose that would be as good a way as any."

Richards found himself in the middle of the continuing confrontation. In his diary he wrote: "Ray came over and told me there's trouble again over what songs to sing. Professor Greer and Ben Glanzer on one side, the three others on the other side. Greer and Glanzer say it is principle with them not to use the gospel songs others want. You can't argue or vote against another Christian's principles," Richards admitted, "therefore Professor Greer will have to decide which songs they sing, it seems to me." Even though he didn't agree with Greer's choice of music, Richards supported him as long as he was doing the job assigned him.

It was a battle no one was likely to win.

In May of 1946 Professor George Greer scheduled his newly formed Symphonic Choir of 60 voices to perform on the *Voice of Prophecy* broadcast. Greer always had a magnificent choir, but to a radio audience accustomed to the more intimate sound of a male quartet, the new sound invited immediate considerable audience protest. When the choir sang again the next Sunday, the letters began to flow in, about half in favor of the choir, and the other half opposed.

The on-again off-again truce continued all through 1945 and 1946 and finally in December 1946 it came to a head. Some thought that Professor Greer's wife had shared her husband's hurt feelings with her uncle, Elder J. L. McElhany, the General Conference president. Maybe so, maybe no. Whether true or not, all the quartet except Ben Glanzer were now suspect among those who had authority to make big waves for the quartet and the Voice of Prophecy.

Ray, despite his open Texas nature, was not one to let anyone cow him, even those in a position to hurt him. Wayne Hooper, by his outspokenness, got into trouble with Paul Wickman, secretary of the Radio Commission. Paul, who was not a vegetarian, made fun of Wayne who is. Wayne, who in his early years sometimes displayed a chip on his shoulder, went to Paul and called him on it. Wickman didn't take kindly to what he perceived as Wayne's impertinent insolence. And Bob Seamount faced accusations of lacking spirituality.

Elders Blunden, Wickman, and Williams called Seamount and Hooper on the carpet December 9, 1946, and told them that their attitude toward Professor Greer and others made them unsuitable for a place in the quartet.

Richards was devastated. Bob Seamount didn't seem to be much grieved—at least he didn't show it. From later conversations with Bob I discovered that the uncalled-for and unexpected attack deeply hurt him. Here is Richards' report in his diary for that day: "Wayne is a fine Christian, quick on the trigger, but good as gold. He was told to take a call to other conference work, but said he would go on with his education."

His experience with the "star chamber" proceedings against the three of them also wounded Ray Turner. He received a brief reprieve, but was sacked a few months later, much to the sorrow of H.M.S.

Richards defended "his boys" like a tiger. He correctly sensed that the big problem was a total difference in philosophy about what it takes to make a good quartet, and what music it required to please and move the program's listening audience.

H.M.S. correctly recognized a big difference between leading a choir and coaching a quartet. A choir needs a director. The singers must respond to the musical intuition of their leader. They succeed best by slavishly following his every musical nuance. A quartet must perform as a single unit without a director. They must learn to feel the music together—to breathe, to think, to perform as one. At times under the inspiration of the moment they will perform in ways they never planned or thought of before.

In January Elmer Walde, Richards' old friend from Lodi days, returned to the mainland from his time as pastor of the Central church in Honolulu. The Radio Commission auditioned him, not only to take Delafield's place as associate speaker, but also to sing baritone in the quartet. Maybe it was their thought to get two for the price of one. Elmer accepted the invitation to be associate speaker and announcer for the broadcast, but declined to be a member of the quartet. Richards concurred, saying that if he tried to do both jobs he would not be able to do justice to either.

Walde fit in beautifully. He had a jovial personality, and both Richards and the quartet loved him. Many years later he remembered a time when the radio group was traveling. For some inexplicable reason, Ray stopped for a hitchhiker on a lonely stretch of highway. The fellow was somewhat awed as he climbed into the seven-passenger Cadillac limousine, and as he looked from face to face of the six stern-faced men in their dark glasses, he became more and more nervous. At that time several of the radio group were big men—Richards, Ray Turner, Bob Seamount, and Elmer Walde all were more than six feet tall. The fellows noticed that he was ill-at-ease and decided to have a little fun by giving him the silent treatment. He thought for sure he had fallen in with a gang of the Mafia until they finally broke down and told him they were a bunch of Adventist ministers.

Richards used to tell about another time the group was driving in the Cadillac on the way to a broadcast in Hollywood. A driver became angry when he perceived that Ray had cut him off in traffic. Coming up beside our limo, he gestured angrily that he wanted Ray to pull over. As Ray eased over to the curb, the angry driver stopped behind him. One by one our fellows got out of the car and walked back to see what the problem was. As he sized up the six big men he had challenged, the driver had a change of heart.

"It's all a mistake, fellows," he stammered as he climbed back into his car. "Have a nice day."

In the midst of all the quartet turmoil, Walde, who had just accepted the position as Voice of Prophecy associate speaker, found himself called out of a committee meeting one day by Elder McElhany, president of the General Conference and a member of the Radio Commission. Some of the committee members had made some flawed value judgments based on their perceptions of the actions and attitude of the three members of the quartet. Apparently they thought Richards was out of line for his dogged defense of "his boys."

They were good men, sincere leaders, but they were also human beings, and at this time seem to have made judgments (as we all may do) based on faulty, or at least incomplete, information.

McElhany, inviting Walde to sit down, began by saying that some of the leaders were deeply concerned about what was happening to the Voice of Prophecy. They felt that changing quartet members was not enough—that the time had come to make a clean sweep. Would Walde be willing to accept the role as speaker of the *Voice of Prophecy* broadcast?

The question stunned Walde. What he was hearing was to him incomprehensible. For a moment he was mute, then almost reflexively he clutched the knee of the president of the General Conference who had just made what to Walde seemed a disastrous proposal.

"Don't do this to me, Elder McElhany!" Elmer blurted out. "Don't do this! This would destroy the work of the Voice of Prophecy! Elder Richards is highly revered by the people. If the men make this kind of change, the funds that now come in to support this great radio-broadcast would dry up. It would be a tragedy for this church!"

McElhany looked at young Walde quietly for a moment, then without another word walked out the door, Walde following. To my knowledge nothing further was ever said about it.

In most cases, older experienced leaders point out the wisest and safest course of action to follow. At other times God uses courageous young individuals such as Elmer Walde to stop an ill-advised action by older leaders. In the afterlight of history, I'm quite sure that Elder McElhany and the men of the Radio Commission were grateful to Elmer Walde for stopping what would have been a tragic decision.

Richards' anguish over the sacking of his boys didn't end that day. During the next two years H.M.S. Richards and the committee in Washington would watch as the new quartet who succeeded Ben, Bob, Wayne, and Ray would struggle to make beautiful music. They were thrust into a difficult position. Greer was gone, but the committee in Washington had not given up on the idea of having a full-time coach. The Radio Commission would again saddle the new young men with another choir director. One of the new boys was not yet 20 years old, two were in their early 20s, and they would try with Ben Glanzer to forge a quartet that would sound good and that would win the affection and confidence not only of Richards but of the listening public. For reasons not yet understood, it would prove to be an impossible task.

QUARTET IN TRANSITION

While the little tempest simmered in the Music Department at the Voice of Prophecy in California, a hurricane tore the world apart in Europe and Asia. On Tuesday morning, June 6, 1944, D–Day, the Allies, under the command of General Dwight D. Eisenhower, struck across the channel onto the Normandy beaches with an initial strike force of 176,000 men, a number that would increase by August to 2,086,000. In August 1944 General Patch landed in southern France and drove up the Rhône valley, and all the while the Soviets advanced relentlessly from the east. In less than 11 months the provisional German government under Admiral Doenitz would announce the death of Adolf Hitler, and on June 5, one year lacking one day after D–Day, the victorious forces would place Germany under an Allied Control Council. Before an armistice could be signed, President Franklin Delano Roosevelt, one of the big three leaders of the Free World, would die of a massive stroke on April 12, 1945.

With the end of the war in Europe, the Allies shifted their efforts to Japan. On August 6,

1945, the first atom bomb dropped on Hiroshima, and a few days later a second one on Nagasaki, bringing to an end a horrible war that had lasted six years and cost millions of lives.

But the war hadn't stopped the Voice of Prophecy. If anything, the unsettled political international scene caused unrest among the people and made them more open to the message of peace that alone could bring comfort to their hearts. On the Sunday after D-Day, Richards preached on "Prayer." Two weeks later his sermon title for the broadcast was "The Seven Blunders of the World."

On his fiftieth birthday H.M.S. Richards reminisced in his diary. "Yesterday my brother Kenneth and I were playing together in Loveland, Colorado. I was baptized at 13 in the lake there by Father. Then Campion Academy—only a few days ago Mabel and I met in the railroad station in Ottawa, Canada. Virginia was a baby just a few days ago. It's all a dream—I'm still a boy, and have just imagined that 50 years have gone by. But others say it's real—that I'm 50 years old. One wish today would be that Mabel and I could live together 50 years more at least before we get old! God has given me just the wife I needed—far better than I deserve."

In February 1946 his friend Jerry Pettis came by the house with the sad news that he and his wife, Rachelle, were splitting up. Devastated, Jerry poured out his heart to Richards, who had been almost a father to him since their Phoenix days nine years before.

Later on in the year, his divorce in process, Jerry Pettis left pastoral and evangelistic work and received a job offer from the president of United Airlines. He was to be the president's personal pilot. Turning the job down, he accepted a position as field representative for the Loma Linda University (at that time the College of Medical Evangelists) Alumni Association.

Early in 1946 a request came for Richards to hold a series of meetings in the Washington, D.C., area. He didn't want to go. Busy with the *Voice of Prophecy* radio program, he felt more and more reluctant to be away from home and family. In the midst of his indecision, he received a visit from his mother. Their conversation went something like this:

"Harold, I hear you've been invited to go to Washington, D.C., and hold meetings."

"Yes, Mother, that's right, but I don't think I can accept it. We're just too busy here right now."

"For years you've been praying for your brother, Kenneth [who lived in that area]. Now the Lord is making it possible for you to help answer your own prayers, yet are you telling me you're saying no?"

That was the kind of loving logic Richards couldn't resist. At any rate, he never was able to ignore an appeal of any kind from his mother.

On September 25, 1945, Richards, the quartet, Professor Greer, and Delafield piled into the old Dolores del Rio Cadillac and headed east. With a heavy load of seven men and all their luggage, the old war-era tires couldn't stand the strain. One tire blew before they left California, another one in Chandler, Arizona. Tires were still scarce, and they could find only two old ones. Two more tires failed before they reached Amarillo, Texas. In Amarillo a local Christian friend helped them get more tires, but a fifth tire failed west of Oklahoma City and a sixth one just west of Little Rock, Arkansas.

Enough was enough. Delafield and Greer took the bus on into Washington, D.C. With the lighter load, the old car with its frayed tires held out the rest of the way.

On Sunday night, October 7, 1945, Richards and the quartet began their series of meetings in the Sligo church in Takoma Park as 2,300 crowded in. His opening topic was "The World's Greatest Character." It was like old times with Ellen Curran holding her Pictured Truth meetings.

On the first Thursday Richards made an appeal for all to stand who would surrender to the Lord. His brother, Kenneth, with his wife, Gertrude, and their son, David, were there. Though they did not stand, someone told H.M.S. that his brother seemed deeply moved.

On Friday evening at 6:00 p.m. he had an evening worship at his brother's house, and Kenneth prayed for the first time in years. That evening Richards preached on "The Man Who Tried Again." The Sligo church was crowded with the biggest audience since the beginning of the meetings. On his appeal at the end of the sermon, nearly half the audience surged into the aisles, but not Kenneth. While H.M.S. went downstairs to the prayer room with all those who had come forward after his public appeal, "Del" Delafield sought out Kenneth and Trudy Richards, and they responded to his urgent request for them to come back to Jesus. When Kenneth phoned his brother with the news, H.M.S. hurried right over to their home to rejoice with them. It was a high day for him. In his diary entry that night he wrote: "We had a *wonderful time!*" It was not only a joyful time for H.M.S. and his brother's family, but also for Mother and Father back in California.

During the meetings three of the King's Heralds took flying lessons at a little airport near Washington. Ray Turner, Bob Seamount, and Wayne Hooper earned their solo licenses. Two more quartet members would catch the flying bug several years later, but that's another story for another time.

On their drive home from Washington, D.C., after the series, Richards and the quartet stopped to see George Miller, the old undertaker in Millerton, Pennsylvania, who had challenged the young Richards to a fight. The man was alone now. His wife had died some years before, but that evening he and Richards had many memories to share together. Before they parted Richards prayed with him. H.M.S. saw him again only once before Miller died, but they kept in touch for years through Miller's daughter, who lived in California.

On November 6 the Voice of Prophecy group had a public meeting at Emmanuel Missionary College in Berrien Springs, Michigan. I was a junior theology student there at the time. As I listened to Ben Glanzer sing his special song, "Keep Looking Up," I was really impressed. That night I think I had the first glimmer of hope that I might some day be able to sing with the King's Heralds. I longed to be able to talk to the quartet afterward, but they had to rush off to their night accommodations in Battle Creek, so I didn't get to speak with any of them.

In December 1945 the Radio Commission elected J. Berger

Johnson to be the new manager of the Voice of Prophecy, replacing H. H. Hix, who was not well.

Richards always liked to keep in personal contact with the leaders of other denominations, especially evangelists. After leaving the Michigan camp meeting in the summer of 1946, the radio team drove to Homer Rodeheaver's camp in Winona Lake, Indiana. Rodeheaver had been the song leader for Billy Sunday years before. He entertained Richards and the quartet all day, telling them stories about his work with Sunday.

It was also the same summer trip when the group visited Saskatoon, Saskatchewan, during a persistent windstorm that H.M.S. picked up a quote I have often heard him repeat. Richards asked the manager of the campground, "Does this wind ever stop?"

"I don't know," the man responded. "I've only been here 37 years."

Also that summer they visited W. K. Kellogg of cornflakes fame. He was an avid fan of Richards, and always invited him and the quartet to stop by his summer estate on Gull Lake, Michigan. They were able to stay only a few minutes, but the blind old man was pleased when the quartet sang for him.

That October Ray Turner and Bob Seamount of the quartet decided they were going to fly a small private plane to the Seventh-day Adventist Autumn Council meeting in Grand Rapids, Michigan. Richards opposed the idea, but didn't forbid it. Wayne Hooper, Delafield, and Richards took the train to Grand Rapids, and they were relieved to see Bob and Ray grinning like Cheshire cats at the gate when they arrived on Tuesday evening, October 15. It was just the first of quite a number of times the quartet would manage to sandwich a little personal flying time into the Voice of Prophecy trips.

I'm not sure Richards ever found out that the flight home in their little plane almost ended in tragedy for Seamount and Turner. They flew from Battle Creek to Louisiana to see Ray's folks. As they were landing in a pasture just beyond some flooded rice fields, the engine quit. Bob was flying and had forgotten to transfer fuel tanks.

Quickly switched over to the full tank, the engine caught again just as they were about to ditch the plane in the rice paddy.

Richards never visited Grand Rapids, Michigan, without stopping at Kregel's Bookstore. Kregel's is probably the biggest religious used-book store in the world. The owner and Richards became fast friends. Bob Kregel would offer his friend Richards unlimited credit any time he came into the store. One night when I was with him, it came closing time, but Richards wasn't finished roaming through the stacks. Bob Kregel showed him a cot, and allowed him to stay in the store all night. The next morning, when the store opened up, Richards had his big pile of books alongside my little pile, ready for Bob Kregel to mail them all back to Glendale, California, to be paid off $1, $5, or maybe $10 a month—however Richards wished to pay—without interest. On that particular trip to Kregel's, Richards picked out $53 worth of used books—quite a lot of money as prices went in 1946. The Radio Commission voted him $100 for books per year at that Autumn Council session.

As Richards entered the difficult time when his quartet was under the gun, it was a relief to him to spend time with his old friend Bev McCulloch near Visalia, California. Bev had been his head usher at the big Visalia evangelistic meetings when Richards first came to California in 1926. For the next 25 years the McCulloch ranch served as Richards' haven of rest.

One time his stay there almost ended in tragedy. In the morning, after the fog lifted, Richards wandered out into the grape vineyards to just get away from everything and everyone. One of the McCulloch boys decided to go out hunting for quail. As he tramped through the vineyards he noticed a movement among the leaves of the grape vines. Just as he raised his shotgun to let go a blast at "the quail," Richards stood up. He never knew how close he came to being filled with bird shot.

Richards performed the weddings for most of the McCulloch girls. In November of 1944 he had finally married off the youngest, Chrystelle, to Raymond H. Cothell. "I told Brother McCulloch at the wedding," Richards wrote in his diary, "that when I go up to the farm again I shall feel that the house ought to be full of boys and girls as it used to be! How fast the face of the world and of life passes."

On January 17, 1947, at 6:15 p.m. Elder Berger Johnson, the manager, died suddenly. "He was only 57—too young!" Richards said in his diary for the day. In February the Radio Commission voted a new manager for the Voice of Prophecy, Walter E. Atkin. Atkin was a good man, but it would not be a happy association. He would preside over a number of wrenching changes in the Program Department in the course of the next few years.

That same month D. A. Delafield requested release from his position as the associate speaker at the Voice of Prophecy. His replacement would be Elmer Walde, Richards' friend of years past.

Another blow to Richards came from H. M. Blunden, chairman of the Radio Commission. Blunden said the "brethren" of the Radio Commission wished H.M.S. to drop his father, H.M.J. Richards, from his prayer spot on the broadcast. Their complaint was that his voice was too old and his prayer too formal sounding. Blunden named McElhany, president of the General Conference, as the one requesting the change. Richards was incensed. "It may be politick," Richards complained to his diary, "but it goes against the heart to have big plans put on the low plane of action pleasing to Elder McElhany rather than on what is right and just. I can't believe Elder McElhany is back of half the things done in his name!

"I want Father with me in the work as long as both of us can work—and I don't want him hurt. He is loyal and true and faithful. But why do I write here? Possibly no one will ever read this when I am gone. We plan and work, but when we depart, our plans fade into nothingness, except that which is wrought of God."

In March Richards received a long semi-apologetic letter from Paul Wickman, showing that he expected Richards to be troubled by the actions of the Radio Commission. "They have done four things to take peace from the earth," H.M.S. commented to his diary. "One, they have broken the quartet; two, they have given

213

control of the quartet to the manager; three, they have changed the format of my broadcast; and four, they have put Father off the air. What next!" On Sunday, March 23, for the first time "we did not stop for Father to go along and offer prayer on the broadcast. I missed him and I know others will, too. What shall I say when asked why he is not on the broadcast? Shall I tell the truth—that a few members of the Radio Commission ordered him off?"

In 1947 the General Conference voted to expand the *Voice of Prophecy* to Europe. A large station in Luxembourg would carry the program, beaming it across the channel to the British Isles. To promote the broadcast, they asked Richards to visit Europe and the British Isles during the summer of 1947. I think he must have sensed that there was a move afoot to replace him as the broadcast speaker. Rather than fight it, he suggested to Blunden that while he was away on his proposed two-month trip, they invite guest speakers to take the microphone. Blunden "seems pleased" Richards wrote in his diary on March 18, 1947. The guest speakers ultimately chosen were Elmer Walde, Alger Johns, Arthur Bietz, William Fagal, J. L. Tucker, Robert Thomas (the man who fought his way into the church in Richards' Santa Barbara meetings), and Paul Wickman.

With the impending change in the quartet, the program had to find new voices. Some considered Richard Lange to be a promising young man who could take Wayne Hooper's place as baritone. The committee named Albert Mays of San Jose as a candidate for first tenor. Jim Stevens was suggested as a possible replacement for Ray Turner. The Radio Commission chose Lon Metcalfe of Oakland, California, to be the coach who would replace Professor George Greer. Richards had nothing personal against the choice of Metcalfe, except that he still didn't think the quartet needed a full-time coach, especially a choir director. Paul Wickman told Wayne Hooper the men were as good as hired, though they would be auditioned to forestall criticism that the committee had made their choices on too limited a basis. Blunden and Wickman, no doubt following Metcalfe's suggestion, were now thinking of creating a larger Music

Department, perhaps hiring six or more staff members instead of only four. The idea was that the quartet could then change from time to time for variety, using first one combination of voices, then another. No matter how grand the plan sounded, it would ultimately prove to be more grandiose than grand.

The new administrative chart authorized a program committee. Paul Wickman would be chairman, Walter Atkin the secretary, with Elmer Walde, C. L. Bauer, and Metcalfe filling out the list as members. Metcalfe as the music director would be placed administratively over the quartet.

April 1947 the Radio Commission decided it was time for the Voice of Prophecy to move to new quarters. It chose a large lot on Colorado Boulevard in Glendale that cost $51,000.

As they started out on their summer camp meeting travels in 1947, the team traveled in a new Cadillac limousine. The old Dolores del Rio Cadillac had finally died. All the Voice of Prophecy workers gathered outside as the group planned to leave. They sang "God Be With You," had prayer, and sent Richards, Walde, and the old quartet (Ben, Bob, Wayne, and Ray) on their way.

In those days automobiles did not have air-conditioning, so the quartet had a bright idea. They bought a cooler in Indio just before they headed out across the desert. It was supposed to fit in the car window and keep everyone comfortable. Richards wrote of it: "It couldn't handle so big a car and I nearly roasted in the front seat. We had all the windows closed to make that $15.00 wonder work." But it didn't! They got as far as Benson, Arizona, the first night, then were up again at 5:30 the next morning. At midnight they arrived at Ray Turner's parents' home in Texas, 1,075 miles later.

On Friday, May 23, the group arrived at the campus of Forest Lake Academy, the site of the Florida camp meeting. It was a red-letter weekend for me. I was a newly hired young minister in the conference and ached to hear the King's Heralds quartet. That weekend, as I mentioned previously, I made myself an absolute nuisance to them, though I did learn that they were looking for a first tenor to take Ben's place. After standing in line with them at the cafeteria, I pestered them while they ate.

I'm sure that it must have been to get rid of me that they asked me to try out in a miniaudition before the afternoon meeting. I eagerly accepted. We went to a little ministers' room backstage at the camp meeting auditorium and sang a cappella a quartet arrangement of John Newton's hymn "Glorious Things of Thee Are Spoken." Wayne blew the pitch pipe to give us the key. After each stanza he blew the pitch pipe a half-step higher, testing me to check my vocal range. Of course, I knew nothing of the trauma that had taken place in the Music Department back in California. This was my big moment, and I was as proud as a peacock.

The next morning I followed them down to radio station WLOH in Orlando and reluctantly watched them go on their way to their next camp meeting appointment up the line in North Carolina.

Later that summer Earl Hackman, Southern Union Conference president, personally urged Wayne Hooper to write a letter to the Radio Commission and send a copy to each individual member, asking them to reverse their decision to break up the quartet. Wayne didn't do it, but Richards noted in his diary, "What a stir that would cause!"

Within days I received a formal invitation to come to California in July to audition for the King's Heralds. Three other prospective first tenors were also there to try out. Unknown to me, of course, Richards was attempting to head off the audition, hoping to rescind the quartet firing. The commission did grant Richards his request that the old quartet be allowed to stay with him through the big youth congress that would meet in San Francisco in September.

With his Music Department in shambles, Richards left for his Europe trip on July 8. All night long he flew over an unbroken overcast in a United Airlines DC-6. Early in the morning, through a sudden break in the clouds, he saw a vivid flash of green— Ireland—and the winding river Shannon.

The trip proved to be a wonderful shot in the arm for him. Even though he had never before seen it, he loved London. "Paris is a feminine city," I've heard him often exclaim, "but London is a man's city." He not only was able to stir up the interest of the Adventists in the British Isles for the Voice of Prophecy, but would visit the great sites of London, then went on to Stonehenge and to his old family haunts in Cornwell—Redruth, Exeter—all the way to "Land's End" at the tip of the peninsula.

He visited John Wesley's chapel and prayer room and prayed there silently. Then he explored Bunhill Fields and saw the graves of John Bunyan, Daniel Defoe, and Isaac Watts. Soaking up the history of old London, he toured St. Paul's Cathedral, the Tower of London, and Westminster Abbey. "In the Abbey and St. Paul's I prayed for the dear ones and friends by name. It is humbling to stand by the stone tomb of a king who has been in silent rest for over 1,000 years—to walk quietly in a House of God where His worship has not ceased for centuries."

Journeying to Wales, he reveled in the singing of the Welsh as they went about their tasks in the hotel kitchens and dining rooms, or while picking up the garbage in the streets early in the morning. Their voices "sounded to me like the singing of the angels," he said.

In Scotland he stopped by Greyfriar's Church and the graves of the dog "Greyfriar's Bobby" and of his master. Besides the home of John Knox, he managed to visit the Island of Iona, where the spiritual descendants of St. Patrick trained to be missionaries throughout all Europe. Going to Glasgow, Bobby Burns's country, he found the grave of David Livingstone.

But all good things (and bad) come to an end. Late in August Richards returned to the cauldron of confusion still brewing at the Voice of Prophecy. His manager advised him that the ministry would hire several singers in addition to the quartet. "Where will the money come from?" he asked.

"Oh, these extra singers will work in the Bible School."

At the same time the General Conference treasurer threatened to cut 65 radio stations because of the lack of funds. To Richards it seemed they were forgetting that 2 and 2 don't make 5.

That September the Radio Commission with musical coach Lon Metcalfe settled on a quartet composed of Frank Dietrich, first tenor; Ben Glanzer, second tenor; Richard Lange, baritone; and Jerry Dill, bass. Another tenor, Don Carlson, and I waited in the wings as extras. The next month the VOP hired Del Delker, a young contralto singer from Oakland, California, to sing part-time and the rest of the time to work as an office secretary.

That first autumn, while the new quartet was trying to get started, Bob Seamount, young Harold Richards (17-year-old son of H.M.S.), and I decided to start a quartet of our own. We tried several basses, but finally settled on Jim Stevens. Our little quartet turned out to have a nice mellow blend, so we started taking appointments around southern California. Since the boss's son belonged to the quartet, we often practiced up at the Richards' home. On a December Sabbath after we had been singing in the Richards family living room, H.M.S. wrote in his diary: "This afternoon Junior had the other members of the quartet he is in—Seamount, Stevens and Edwards—at our place. They sounded like the dear old King's Heralds."

We became so popular we decided we should have a name. H.M.S. suggested the "Gleemen of Glendale," and before long we had more invitations to sing than we could fill. We practiced several evenings a week, and soon were getting more local appointments than the official King's Heralds. People seem to love competition. Our audiences and their audiences began to make comparisons and choose sides. The Gleemen of Glendale quartet had started out innocently enough, but the practical result was the buzzing of a new hornet's nest in the VOP Music Department.

Early Sunday morning, December 28, Frankie Dietrich phoned me that he had a bad throat and asked me if I could fill in for him at the broadcast that morning. In those days we had to get up at 4:00 a.m. to get warmed up to sing at a 6:30 a.m. broadcast released to the East Coast. I eagerly accepted even at that early hour.

The Voice of Prophecy put on the two Sunday morning programs at network studios in Hollywood, one at 6:30 a.m. for Eastern and Central time zones, and one at 9:30 a.m. for Mountain and Pacific time zones. Metcalfe insisted on coming and couldn't resist trying to direct the quartet from the engineers' control room. Since the quartet couldn't see very well from sound studio to control room (the group didn't try very hard), it not only didn't work, but made the quartet extremely uneasy during the broadcast. Milton Carlson, the broadcast producer, began to see what was happening, so urged that Metcalfe stay away.

Late in 1947 the Radio Commission once again suggested a significant change in the Voice of Prophecy format. For years, when it came time for the radio sermon, the announcer would simply say, "And now, the Voice of Prophecy." By his own choice, the program never gave Richards' name. He preferred to be known as just "The Voice." From 1947 on the announcer would introduce him as "H.M.S. Richards, the Voice of Prophecy." It turned out to be a positive thing with the radio audience.

During these late months in 1947 and early 1948 I worked part-time in the Bible school, part-time as a secretary assistant to H.M.S. in his garage office behind his home, and part-time practicing with the other six or seven musicians in the Music Department. In late January, because of the unsettled quartet condition, the Voice of Prophecy General Board listened to trial recordings of several quartet combinations, and voted to shuffle its membership once again. The new quartet combination would be Bob Edwards, first tenor; Ben Glanzer, second tenor; Dick Lange, baritone; and Jerry Dill, bass. This quartet continued to function for about 10 months before more agitation for change surfaced.

Metcalfe wanted to direct the quartet just as he would a choir. As I mentioned previously, a quartet doesn't work well that way. They need to learn to feel their expression and timings together without leaning on a director. It made for an uneasy 10 months.

Even though I was now in the King's Heralds, I continued to sing with our little Gleemen pickup quartet until Harold, Jr., went to college in the fall of 1948. We began to negotiate with the Spanish language Voice of Prophecy to make recordings for them for their South and Central American broadcasts.

In May 1948 we had an interesting and embarrassing experience during an appointment at the Loma Linda Hill Seventh-day Adventist Church. Here's what Richards said about it in his diary entry for May 22. "The quartet came in our new VOP Chrysler car. They sang very poorly. On one song there was a completely sour mixture. I am told Ben was singing in another key. The place was packed."

We were presenting a song that Ben had sung dozens of times as first tenor. For those who understand musical terms, the piece had a duet in thirds between first tenor and second tenor. When we started singing, Ben, who was supposed to be doing the second tenor, sang his first tenor part a third low. On some chords it sounded fine, but then we would come to a chord that would absolutely clash. We tried starting the song three times, but finally had to give up and sit down. It was mortifying.

That summer we made some long camp meeting trips and had some high adventure with Richards and Walde. We rode on top of a stage coach in a Washington, D.C., Fourth of July parade. Later we visited the first Seventh-day Adventist church in Washington, New Hampshire, and with Richards wandered among the white grave-stones waiting in lonely silence for the great day that seems so long delayed. Then we spent a few days of rest in the shadow of Mount St. Helens in Washington State at Spirit Lake Lodge, the vacation spot belonging to the father of our baritone, Richard Lange. After being away from home and families for six weeks, we started out from Redmond, Washington, at 5:00 a.m. in order to make it home by evening. We were only about three hours from home when Elmer Walde became so sick he fainted. Even though everyone was terribly disappointed (including Walde), we decided to get a little motel cabin at Mono Lake and wait until morning to continue on.

When we arrived home, we discovered that Metcalfe had contrived to restructure the quartet once more. He proposed two options:

(1) Edwards, Dietrich, Dill, Melashenko; (2) Edwards, Dietrich, Lange, and Dill. Richards' diary of that day says: "The latter was fine. Number one was bad, but it was clear that the coach wanted number one. I expressed my policy as this—whatever the musical director wants I will vote for! What a tragedy this whole thing is!"

Since Melashenko couldn't come for several months, we had to use a substitute for a big autumn appointment at a youth congress in Des Moines. We drafted teenager Harold Richards to sing baritone for that one trip. A freshman at La Sierra College, he brought his school books along and studied Greek and his other subjects from day to day as we drove across country and back.

Although the beginning of another short period of trauma in the Music Department, at least it was the last thrashings of the musical serpent until it finally died and was replaced by a King's Heralds group that won the hearts of the Voice of Prophecy world for the next 12 years.

TRANQUILLITY—FOR A LITTLE WHILE

That first summer I sang in the quartet it wasn't an easy schedule. We left on May 31, 1948, in a new Chrysler limousine. Our first stop was Chattanooga, Tennessee, for a big Southern Youth Congress. The car contained six of us— Walde, Richards, and the quartet. H.M.S. summed up the feelings of the group pretty well in his diary entry after that first day's drive:

"Drove 800 miles. Stopped Las Cruces, New Mexico. We drove steadily 60-65 miles per hour—ate all meals in the car as we traveled. Easy group to be with. Walde is a prince. But what does the future hold for the singers? More changes—a poor morale? It does if we continue to have a coach on the present plan. May the Lord help us!"

As we drove along, the Chief asked some of us to read aloud from the Bible. Richards wrote in his diary: "Each day I ask Bob Edwards or Ben Glanzer to read two or three chapters from the book of John. As we ride along we discuss the Word and enjoy it. When another reads, I get new view of it."

On such car trips H.M.S. always took a big

box of books to read as we traveled along. He had his own little nest in the front seat beside the driver. At his side was his big leather satchel. A brown paper bag at his feet contained crackers or bread or fruit to nibble on. The rest of us were scattered through the car.

H.M.S. had never learned to drive, but the rest of us would religiously change drivers every 100 miles to keep any one individual from becoming tired or sleepy. The driver relinquishing the wheel had last choice of where he could sit in the car, the next driver first choice. The seating arrangement in the limo consisted of front seat, back seat, and two little fold-up jump seats in between.

After preaching his main sermon at the youth congress in Chattanooga, Richards took a flight home to preach the commencement sermon for Harold, his eldest son, at his graduation from high school. Even though we carried on a heavy traveling schedule, we always considered it vital to be allowed to attend such important family events. When Richards finished preaching his son's commencement address at Glendale Union Academy, he took the train back to meet us at a camp meeting appointment in Texas, then we all drove home together.

We made four long trips for the Voice of Prophecy by car that summer—one trip of two weeks, one of two-and-a-half weeks, one of four weeks, and the final one of six weeks. In order to make our appointment schedules that summer, several times we had to leave our car out on the road somewhere and take the train or a plane.

Once we left our car in El Paso, Texas, flying to Philadelphia. When we arrived, Philadelphia was hot and sweltering, the temperature still a scorching 100 degrees at midnight. Checking into the Penn Sheraton Hotel, we tried to sleep under the humming paddling of ceiling fans. In those days few hotels were air-conditioned. The next morning Richards preached to the assembled youth in the Philadelphia Convention Hall. The weather was the hottest it had been in 30 years. In June the Republicans had nominated Tom Dewey for president, and in July the Democrats had nominated Harry Truman in that same hall.

We crisscrossed back and forth across the continent that summer by car, plane, and train, singing and preaching in 30 states, arriving back home just in time to find our quartet had been changed yet again.

In November after our fall trip to Des Moines the new quartet bass arrived from Canada. Joe Melashenko was a great guy. He had a wonderful deep Russian bass voice, but it was too big to blend with those of the other members of the quartet. Ben Glanzer had dropped out of the singing group, Frank Dietrich took his place, and Jerry Dill had switched from bass to baritone. For the next three months we tried desperately hard to make the quartet work, but it was really hopeless. The blend was bad. Frankie wasn't really a second tenor and Jerry wasn't really a baritone. And to add to the confusing mix, the quartet still didn't get along well with Lon Metcalfe, the coach.

In the midst of all the conflict about the quartet, Richards faced some good and bad stress at home. Harold, Jr., had met a young woman at college, and he and Mary Margaret Gullet were mutually attracted to one another. Since it was Harold's freshman year, his father was both happy and apprehensive. "We pray he will find a godly girl to make his life happy and successful. Not too soon, or too late!" he confided in his diary on November 15, 1948. A few days later Harold brought Mary Margaret home for family approval. "I liked her modest simplicity," H.M.S. said in his diary about 18-year-old Mary. "She went out in the kitchen and helped with supper, was friendly and not silly. Our prayers are for God's special care over Junior now and her, too."

The next day son Kenneth sprained his ankle and had to hobble about on crutches.

A couple weeks later Mabel had to go in for emergency surgery. The day before the operation, H.M.S. wrote this in his diary: "Sweetheart, if you ever read this, know that I have been blessed far beyond my ability to ever show my appreciation to you. I love you, darling! You're God's gift to me! I pray we may go on together until the Lord Jesus comes—but we are in His hands."

Then next day Richards "awoke during the night thinking of Mabel and praying for her." With a heavy sigh of relief, he discovered later in the day that Mabel had a nonmalignant tumor removed and was relaxed and doing nicely. A few days afterward he learned she was ready to come home from the hospital. "We miss Mabel at home and hope tomorrow she will be with us. How terrible it would be if she were taken from us and we would know each night that she would not come. I begin to see a little how hard it has been for her to have to carry on here with me away all summer, months at a time. What little I have done I owe to her in more ways than one."

What a joy and relief it was when Jerry Dill drove with him to the hospital in the Voice of Prophecy Chrysler to take her home.

By February, a couple of months later, I confided to the Chief that I was going to drop out of the quartet. Bob Seamount, young Harold Richards, Jim Stevens, and I had continued with our Gleemen quartet singing. Richards entered in his diary one day that fall that Bob Seamount had phoned to say that Elder J. L. Tucker at Oakland, California, was about to ask our Gleemen quartet to sing on his radio *Quiet Hour* broadcasts. Harold, Jr., desperately wanted to go along with us, but Father used the same pressure on him that his father had employed 30 years before. Harold enrolled at La Sierra College, and the other three members of the quartet left for Oakland in February 1949. Our baritone would be Eugene Ericson, Tucker's son-in-law. A young predental student joined the King's Heralds as first tenor.

One good thing finally came out of all the confusion. The Radio Commission finally decided that Richards had been right all along—that we didn't need a quartet coach. They asked the manager to find a position for Metcalfe at a college or high school someplace.

Elwyn Ardourel, my first tenor replacement, had a great voice and was a fine musician. It didn't take him many weeks to realize that the current quartet wasn't going anywhere. By April he asked for an interview with Richards and advised him he could not go on with the quartet, explaining his reasons in great detail. Richards asked him to write it in a letter and present it to Atkin, the Voice of Prophecy manager.

On the way back to the Voice of Prophecy General Board meeting in April at Washington, D.C., Atkin drove by Union College to interview Wayne Hooper. Wayne told Atkin in detail what he thought needed to be done to fix the quartet problem. He suggested a quartet of Jerry Dill as bass, Wayne Hooper as baritone, Bob Seamount as second tenor, and me as first tenor.

On April 11 Elder M. V. Campbell, one of the Voice of Prophecy General Board members, introduced the quartet problem into the board agenda hopper. Atkin told the board of his visit with Wayne, but inferred Wayne would be willing to work with the men currently singing in the quartet—Ardourel, Dietrich, Dill, and Melashenko. Richards had just been on the phone with Wayne the evening before, and realized Atkin had misunderstood Wayne's intentions. Asking for a brief recess he invited another board member to get on a conference phone call with him to Wayne at Union College. They established what Wayne's conditions were for coming back to the Voice of Prophecy. In his diary for that night Richards wrote: "Voted to call Wayne Hooper, Bob Seamount and Bob Edwards to join Dill in the quartet. All I can say is 'Praise the Lord.' May His grace lead to wonderful blessings with this group." After the meeting Atkin wryly congratulated Richards on getting the men he wanted in the quartet.

Two days later Richards left on a whirlwind Voice of Prophecy trip to Australia and New Zealand. This time when the plane took off he had a light heart about his quartet for the first time in four years.

Six weeks into his tour Richards received a phone call from his Voice of Prophecy manager that arrangements had been worked out for the program to go on a new network in June. It disappointed him to cut his trip short, but on Thursday, June 9, 1949, Richards returned to the U.S. Two days later we put on a spectacular new broadcast in the fabulous Hollywood Bowl with 15,000 in attendance. We recorded it for release the next day. It was the first time Richards would appear with his new quartet.

When our quartet had first gotten together after returning to Glendale, California, we met around the kitchen table at Bob Seamount's home. There we reflected on the anguish the quartet and the Voice of Prophecy had suffered during the past four years and pledged we would stay together for at least five years. It turned out to be 12.

We had a good quartet. Bob Seamount had a bright, lively Swedish tenor voice. Jerry Dill, though not a deep bass, had a brilliance that gave a unique quality to the quartet sound. Wayne Hooper's warm baritone had the perfect quality to glue the parts together. I did my best to hold up my end of the quartet. All of us had a great time together. Things were looking up in the Voice of Prophecy Music Department for the first time in many years.

That initial summer was great. Richards was happy. We laughed and joked as we rode along in the car. Sometimes we would learn new songs. Wayne taught us a couple of new spirituals he had learned from a Black singing group that had been active on campus at Union College while he was there: "Now Don't You Let Nobody Turn You 'Round" and "If We Ever Needed the Lord Before, We Sure Do Need Him Now." They became favorites of our listeners everywhere.

Jerry Dill was the only unmarried member of the quartet, but he had met a young woman the summer before. Now they planned to be married. After a big meeting in the Aberdeen, South Dakota, Civic Theater on August 21, Walde, Richards, and the quartet piled into the car at 5:30 next morning and set out across country toward Amarillo, Texas. In those days the United States had no freeways across country, especially from north to south, but by nightfall we had covered 1,019 miles and delivered Jerry to his bride-to-be. The next evening at 8:30 Richards performed the wedding ceremony between Jerry Dill and Laura May Ross.

That summer H.M.S. became a grandfather for the first time. On September 19 Marshall Dean Cason was born to daughter, Virginia, at Loma Linda, California.

A few weeks later the Voice of Prophecy board voted to accept a bid of $210,000 to build the new Voice of Prophecy offices to be located at 1500 E. Chevy Chase, Glendale, California. When he had the building finally completed, contractor Emmet Jensen presented it to us for a figure below his bid.

In the fall of 1949 the board voted that H.M.S. Richards finish the trip he had been forced to abbreviate earlier in the year. On New Year's Day he was in the Middle East. The next day he received news that hit him like a hammer blow. His old friend of Visalia days, Bev McCulloch, was dead. How he wished he could have been by his friend's side during those last hours.

A few days later he was in Egypt visiting the great sites that brought Bible stories to life for him. He visited the Cairo museum and looked into the face of the mummy who might have been Pharaoh when Moses led the children of Israel from Egypt. After taking the train down to Luxor and the Valley of the Kings, he returned to Cairo the next day. That afternoon as he was enjoying the sights of the great pyramids across the Nile River from Cairo he reached into his pocket for his pocket watch and for the first time realized it was gone. Immediately he knew what had happened. The night before on the train from Luxor he had left his watch in the sleeping car berth.

The rest of the day was ruined for him. His beautiful gold Hamilton watch was gone—the watch that had been a gift from his friends and coworkers at the Voice of Prophecy. When he returned to his hotel in Cairo that evening, his friend and host Neal Wilson phoned the railroad company. To everyone's astonishment, the railroad ticket office reported that they had the watch. The Sudanese young man in charge of cleaning the cars had turned it in to the office. The railroad company had the watch hand-delivered by private messenger to Richards at his hotel. Richards left a generous reward for the honest young man who had returned the watch.

On April 18, 1950, the Voice of Prophecy held a special cornerstone laying ceremony at the site of the new building on Chevy Chase. The mayor of Glendale, George Wickam, was there. John

Burt of the *News Press* spoke as did Miss Alma Cook of the Los Angeles *Herald Express*. Alma Cook had been instrumental in first getting H.M.S. Richards on the radio regularly in Los Angeles in October 1929. As a bonus for advertising his meetings in the Los Angeles *Express,* she had arranged for him to broadcast several times a week on KNX, a Los Angeles radio station.

H.M.S. Richards always had faithful secretaries. One of the first had been little Betty Canon, who typed letters in the chicken coop office in Walnut Park. Many others followed her. During the early days of 1950 he had three wonderful young women working for him: Norma Beegle, Clara Haynes, and Clara Prehoda. When Voice of Prophecy offerings were down, they would get together in Richards' office and pray about it. One day in May Norma phoned Richards at home to tell him that she and the other girls had been praying for $5,000. That morning a phone call had come in with a gift of $4,736.75. A few days later they contacted him to say that another gift of $10,000 had arrived, and a few months after that they laughed and cried on the phone in their excitement to tell him that VOP had received another $10,000. H.M.S. was always grateful for his wonderful secretaries, whose devotion to the work and their boss did not end at 5:00 closing time.

In June of 1950 Richards received a Father's Day letter from oldest child, Virginia, that brought tears to his eyes.

"Dear Daddy," Virginia wrote, "I'm afraid it's been kind of a long time since I told you I loved you, so this being Father's Day—when daughters are supposed to write love letters to their fathers—I'll let you know what's down in my heart all the time.

"There are all kinds of things that I could thank you for: a Christian home, ditto education, food, clothing, etc., and tolerating my growing up pains. But I think I'll remember longer and deeper your sympathetic and understanding attitude that never varies from one day to the next, or ever is greater toward one of your children than another; the way you and Mother exercise faith in everyday things and pray for us children; your sensitive emotions that are so evident when you read us fine poetry or Bible passages; the gusto with which you sing; the way your eyes sparkle with mischief like a little boy's when you tell a joke or a funny story; the loyalty and love you show to your mother and father; your humble way; and so many, many other things! One very important item I can't keep from commending you on is the wonderful girl you picked out for my mother! If I can grow to be just half her spiritual stature I shall be happy!

"Daddy, I love you. All the qualities that people have wished for in their fathers down through the centuries seem to have been bundled up in you. With love always, from your only daughter, Virginia."

When she was little Virginia had certain poems she loved to hear him read. One that was special to her was "The Burial of Moses," by Cecil Francis Alexander. It starts out, "By Nebo's lonely mountain, . . . On this side Jordan's wave." "Read Nebo, Daddy, read Nebo," Virginia would cry. She loved the cadence of the rhythm and the sound of the words as her father read poetry in his own special way. His early love of poetry helped to make his sermons so powerful. Even his prose had the lovely balance of poetry.

In July of 1950 Richards sadly had to say goodbye to his faithful coworker, Elmer Walde, who accepted an invitation to be the associate secretary of the Radio Department of the General Conference. "Of course, Elmer Walde will go places in the General Conference," he wrote on July 20, 1950. "There is no position too high for him to receive eventually. But I will miss him so much!" It would be several months before we would be able to find someone to take Elmer's place as the associate speaker of the broadcast.

Late that summer, as the Voice of Prophecy radio team traveled through Oklahoma City, the quartet found a little 1946 Aeronca Champion airplane for sale. Bob and Wayne were already pilots, and Jerry and I were eager would-be pilots. The $300 price tag was too good to pass up, so, much to the dismay of H.M.S., we bought it and decided to fly it home.

Since the little "Champ" was only a two-seater, we had to take turns flying it. Bob and Jerry made the first leg of the journey home.

Wayne and I and the Chief were to meet them in Gallup, New Mexico, but when we arrived there, the little plane had not yet arrived. Richards was worried. We phoned the airport at the last big town, and found they had run into some "minor" problems that held them up. They had landed in Albuquerque and would stay there for the night.

The next morning at about daybreak they dropped into the Gallup airport, and we switched flight crews, Wayne and I to take the little plane on home. Well, almost all the way home.

We landed at Winslow, Arizona, for fuel, but on the hot summer afternoon as we took off from there, the little Aeronca was very slow gaining altitude. Since great threatening clouds hovered over the mountains west of Winslow, Wayne landed at a little dirt strip in Cottonwood, Arizona. Quickly we shoved our plane into a hanger until the storm blew by, then about an hour before sundown we took off for home again. By then we had discovered that the magnetic compass didn't work accurately, so we navigated by carefully watching check points along the way. It was getting dark as we approached Wickenburg, Arizona. When we landed our little yellow-and-red bird it was a quart low on oil.

We had been warned not to put detergent oil in the plane, but since that was the only kind the airport had, we put a quart in anyway. Big mistake! The next morning when we took off from Blythe, that detergent oil had loosened up some of the gunk in the engine. It started heating up, and the oil pressure began to rise dangerously. Wayne had no choice but to put it down in Desert Center. We left our little jewel tied to a fence in the desert and took a bus the rest of the way home.

Several weeks later the four of us drove back to Desert Center, removed the engine, and hauled it home where we put it in Wayne's garage and overhauled it completely. Jerry Dill and I got our private pilots' licenses, at least in part, in that little plane, before we sold it.

In November of 1950 our Voice of Prophecy manager, Walter E. Atkin, had to have emergency surgery that would incapacitate him for several months. The board asked Ithiel Gillis, our treasurer, to be acting manager. A few months later he had done such an admirable job the board asked him to take the position permanently. He managed the Voice of Prophecy with an even hand until he retired almost 20 years later.

During the spring of 1950 Seventh-day Adventist leaders voted to support an Adventist television program. On May 21 the first telecast of *Faith for Today* went out from a New York City TV station, with Elder William A. Fagal and his wife, Virginia, heading up the broadcast. In the late months of 1950 the Radio/TV Committee of the General Conference voted to expand the *Faith for Today* telecast to the West Coast, and asked the Voice of Prophecy to prepare the telecasts. The styles of the two telecasts were to be different. I suppose the goal was to see which format was the most successful. Fagal's East Coast program was a religious drama. The West Coast program was more like an evangelistic meeting, with preaching and singing.

The Voice of Prophecy continued to produce the West Coast *Faith for Today* telecast through most of 1951, but we found it impossible to do justice to both a radiobroadcast and telecast. In October the General Conference Autumn Council voted, much to our relief, to allow us to discontinue our responsibility for the West Coast telecast. Our last telecast was on November 25.

Though Walde had taken new responsibilities in the Radio Department of the General Conference in July 1950, we were not able to find a replacement for him at the Voice of Prophecy until December. Elder David Olsen phoned to tell us he and his wife had been praying and had agreed to accept our invitation to join us as associate speaker of the broadcast.

During our travels about the country, our group sometimes had unique experiences. The autumn of 1950 Richards and Olsen flew to Grand Rapids, Michigan, to attend the annual Autumn Council of Seventh-day Adventists. Newly elected President Branson of the General Conference and Paul Wickman, chairman of the Radio Commission, asked Richards to invite the quartet for the closing weekend of the Autumn Council. It was decided that our group would record our Sunday broadcast from the stage of the Battle Creek, Michigan, Civic Auditorium.

Back in California we hurriedly packed our bags and headed for Michigan in the Voice of Prophecy car. At the close of the Autumn Council our group headed out of town, stopping for meetings along the way.

After a meeting in Aurora, Illinois, near Chicago on Saturday night, we had to start out at 4:00 a.m. for a long drive the next day. It was still dark when we left town. I was driving and all the group had settled back, most of them already snoring, when I noticed flashing red lights in the rearview mirror. Automatically I checked the speedometer to see if I had been speeding, and sensing nothing amiss, continued to drive somewhat apprehensively down the road, all the time watching the approaching red lights. As the highway patrol pulled up behind our car, he flashed a spotlight into our back window. I pulled to the shoulder of the road.

An officer approached the driver's side, cautiously holding a flashlight, and peered into our Chrysler seven-passenger limousine. After shining the light in the faces of all six men, he muttered almost to himself, "A bunch of Seventh-day Adventist ministers."

"How did you know?" Richards asked him.

"My wife's an Adventist," he replied. "Why else would I find a car with six men and not smell tobacco smoke?"

He explained why he and his fellow officer had stopped us. "We saw this big black limo cruising through the last town early Sunday morning not far out of Chicago," he explained, "and we had a sneaky suspicion you were a bunch of hoods going to rob a bank. We just thought we'd better check you out."

It was with great relief that we drove on our way.

January of 1951 the Voice of Prophecy invited Elder Raymond Libby to come for three months to write scripts for our West Coast release of *Faith for Today*. When the television program fizzled, Libby received the task of writing a new Bible course for the Voice of Prophecy. In the process of creating the new "Faith Bible Course" Libby got into several doctrinal arguments with old Father Richards, who was one of a reading committee assigned to make suggestions and criticisms of Libby's drafts. Libby took the elder Richards' criticisms personally. In order to defend himself, Libby apparently wrote to several General Conference leaders, accusing the man of being unorthodox in his scriptural beliefs. It was not true, but rather involved a question of semantics. H.M.S. reported the conflict in his diary for January 29, 1952. "Father asked to retire. Three men, Bauer, Rice and Ochs, came to me with the story that Father was reported teaching some new doctrine about the state of the dead (his insistence, no doubt, that God in His mysterious providence, preserves our identity after death). Could a charge be more cruel or wicked to such a one as my dear faithful, honest, orthodox, old-time SDA like Father?"

At a January Voice of Prophecy board meeting the members asked Halbert Richards to retire, giving his age as reason. Even though he was 82 years old, his son had come to rely on him for help in writing letters to students of the Bible correspondence course, and it pained him greatly to see his father hurt.

About the same time something else happened that deeply chagrined Richards. He forgot to attend a funeral he had promised to conduct for the son of his old friend and former conference president, Elder P. E. Broderson. Ray as a boy had helped Richards in his Santa Barbara tent meetings 21 years before. The evening before the funeral his mother, Bertie Richards, had fallen and broken her wrist, apparently causing him to blank out the funeral appointment for the next day. He wrote a letter of apology to Ray's widow, but a few days later received an angry response from her. He couldn't blame her for being upset, but as sorry as he was, he couldn't do anything to change what had happened.

During the summer of 1951 Bob Seamount had a butane converter put in our big old Cadillac. Running on butane had its good and bad points. It was a marvelously clean burning fuel and it saved us a lot of money, but it was sometimes hard to find places where we could re-fuel. The butane tank took up all of the trunk space, so we had to have a luggage rack fabricated that would fit on the roof of the Cadillac limousine. It offered a rather strange sight, a Cadillac seven-passenger limousine with a huge aluminum luggage rack strapped to its top.

September 1951 was a month to remember. For the Richards family it was a triple header. On Thursday evening, September 6, H.M.S. conducted the wedding of his oldest son, Harold, to his bride, Mary Gullett. His brother Kenneth was best man.

Ten days later Kenneth married Jacqueline Mills, his father again presiding.

And on September 24, daughter, Virginia, presented her father with his first granddaughter, Laura Dale.

In January 1952 Elder Branson, president of the General Conference, urged Richards and the Voice of Prophecy to conduct a series of meetings across North America that would be called "Survival Through Faith" rallies. For the next number of months we crisscrossed the United States and Canada.

That June, while we were on a camp meeting tour, we received word that the *Voice of Prophecy* would be released in Japan. We laughed when they told us that our quartet would be recording songs for the Japanese broadcast. To our surprise we discovered that Japanese is not nearly as difficult to sing as some languages. Of course, we didn't understand what we were singing, but by using international phonetics, our quartet managed to record songs that we were told our Japanese listeners clearly understood.

When we returned from our first camp meeting tour in June 1952, H.M.S. attended the graduation exercises of his oldest son, H.M.S. Richards, Jr. Harold was now a minister, following in the footsteps of his father. He would soon be heading for Texas, his first assignment.

Almost immediately after Harold's graduation, the Voice of Prophecy radio team flew to Hawaii for a big youth congress. It was the first time we had traveled outside of continental United States, and for us it was a big adventure.

While there we visited the leper colony on the island of Molokai and saw the grave of Father Damien, the Roman Catholic priest who gave his life for the lepers residing in it. After serving as a pastor to the lepers, he himself became infected with the disease and died as a leper.

In Honolulu we conducted a Voice of Prophecy Bible school graduation in the territorial prison. One of the graduates was a young Japanese soldier condemned to die for the murder of two fellow Japanese. As a fiercely loyal soldier of the Japanese empire, he had been filled with hatred for two men whom he felt had been traitors to the emperor. His fanatical companions had given him the task of taking their lives.

Now as a prisoner he had at first been completely incorrigible, refusing to cooperate with the prison officials. When a group of Seventh-day Adventist Japanese Christians visited the prison, he tore up the Bible they gave him, but something about their Christian spirit touched his hard heart. He began to read the torn pages of the New Testament that lay scattered about his cell, and it changed his life. He enrolled in the Voice of Prophecy Bible course that someone had offered him in the prison.

The warden of the territorial prison gave him a wonderful testimonial at the graduation. He said he had never seen such a radical change in a young man's behavior. Later the warden helped in having his death sentence commuted to life imprisonment, and eventually the territorial governor pardoned the young man.

As he walked out of the prison doors, his Japanese fellow believers presented him with an airplane ticket to Japan, where he attended Japan Missionary College.

Sixteen years later, as the Voice of Prophecy quartet made a stop in Okinawa, a handsome young Japanese man came running up to me as I walked toward the air terminal and gave me a big hug. He asked me if I remembered him. As I looked at his face, I recalled the slim young prisoner in the territorial prison in Honolulu. He was the same man. Having graduated as a minister from Japan Missionary

College, Saburo Arakaki was now a pastor on the island of Okinawa.

The summer of 1952 our Voice of Prophecy group traveled into the far north Peace River country of northern Alberta. We left our car in Edmonton and took the train. It was a wet summer in northern Alberta, and we were lucky we didn't have our car. The roads were deep in mud, but we had the unique experience of discovering what it was like to live in a land where it never gets completely dark in the summer. At 11:00 at night you could still read a newspaper in the fading dusk, and by 1:00 a.m. it began to get light again.

That fall Richards learned of the death of his old friend Elder W. A. Spicer. Spicer, when he was General Conference president, had come by the Richards' humble little home in Ottawa and had admired his library. Now the old pioneer was dead. Richards had visited him a few weeks before in Washington, D.C. As he had said goodbye at the door, Spicer had waved, and his last words were, "Keep the bell ringing! Keep the bell ringing!" Richards' response was, "I hope I do as long as I live."

In the radio and telecasting business the customer must do all negotiating for radio and television time through a recognized advertising agency. The Radio Commission had voted early on to contract for the services of the Western Advertising Agency to do our time buying from the networks and from independent stations. An advertising agency acts between the customer and the radio network, purchasing radio time for the customer, and in almost all cases can fight for customers more effectively than they can do for themselves.

The Western Advertising Agency was a partnership between two men, Milton Carlson and Ed Kieler. Early in 1953 Kieler and Carlson decided to split up their partnership. Kieler, who bought out Carlson, retained the name Western Advertising Agency, and Carlson started his own agency.

Since Milton Carlson had been Western's customer representative for the Voice of Prophecy, he had earned the confidence of Richards and the other members of the local Voice of Prophecy board and broadcast team. Under normal circumstances Richards would have chosen to go with Carlson, but something happened to change the situation. Paul Wickman, head of the General Conference Radio Commission, had decided to resign his job and accept a position as vice president with Kieler's Western Advertising Agency. Wickman felt he needed more money than his position in the church could pay him. He had teenage youngsters about to enter college. Kieler offered him a job as vice president with the idea of holding onto the Voice of Prophecy account.

It put Richards, Kieler, Walde, and Carlson in an embarrassing position. Richards and his team wanted to go with Carlson, yet Wickman had been hired to keep the Voice of Prophecy account. Wickman had been Walde's immediate superior in the Radio Commission, and expected his old friend to work with him to keep the Voice of Prophecy account with the Western Advertising Agency.

The Voice of Prophecy stayed with Western until their contract expired, then the board voted to go with Carlson. Wickman for a long time felt that Walde had betrayed him by not twisting the arms of Richards and other Voice of Prophecy board members. That, along with other circumstances, caused Wickman to turn away from the church that had long nurtured him. It took many years for the wounds to heal, but before his death in 1996 Wickman at last became friend and confidant again with his old coworker, and spent many hours on the phone with Walde in the months just before he died of a malignant brain tumor.

In March of 1953 Richards had the joy of visiting and working for a few days with his oldest son, Harold, now a young preacher in Texas. Harold in his natural gregariousness, and Mary with her warmhearted loving ways, captured the hearts of the people, and that made Richards proud. He could see immediately how much the people loved Harold and his wife.

Then in June Kenneth, the second son, graduated from La Sierra College. The president of the Colorado Conference had already sent a request for Kenneth and Jackie to pastor in that conference. Anyone acquainted with the two sons will instantly recognize how different they are. Kenneth is quiet and retiring, Harold an open extrovert. H.M.S. summed up a lurking fear in his diary that spring: "Kenneth and I had good talks on the work of the ministry. He will be a good preacher IF he talks loud enough." He needn't have worried. Kenneth never would become a bombastic speaker, but his quiet dry humor and study habits endeared him to the people.

The young couple's first assignment was in Salida, Colorado, helping in evangelism in the Isis Theater with Elder Alexander Snyman. Dad was proud to visit with his son and daughter-in-law as we passed through Salida that summer and participated in one of their evangelistic meetings.

In August Richards went on a world trip to Africa, India, Australia, and the Pacific Islands to encourage and support our Voice of Prophecy overseas Bible schools and broadcasts. For the first time he was able to take his beloved Mabel along with him, but it pained him to drive away from home, leaving his teenage son Jan standing at the curb. "How I love my growing boy, Jan," he wrote on August 17. "I feel sometimes that I am not doing my duty, that I am deserting him. I pray it may prove to be a blessing. He is growing into young manhood. I am so proud of him! I love him as I think Jacob loved Joseph! May God keep him safe!"

Virginia had agreed to stay at their home and watch after Jan, but it was also hard for H.M.S. to leave his father and mother that summer. "Father fears he may not live until my return," he wrote, "but never suggested that I not go. It is God's work."

He and Mabel remained away on the trip during the rest of 1953, meeting the new year in Auckland, New Zealand. They arrived home on January 17, 1954, exactly five months from the day of their departure the preceding August.

Though Richards wasn't yet 60 years old, the trip took a greater toll on his health than he realized. When he returned, a medical checkup by a doctor in New York, plus his own family doctor's overreaction, caused Richards a physical and emotional setback that would seriously affect his work for years to come.

HEART TROUBLE

February 18, 1954, Thursday: "Roy and Freda Schultz at our house for evening—I told him the New York Life doctor had found eight premature beats a minute in my pulse—Roy ordered me to bed at once!"

The next day Richards went to the Glendale Sanitarium and Hospital to get an electrocardiogram from cardiologist Dr. Hoxie. Hoxie said there was no evident damage to the heart muscle, but it still didn't calm Richards' fears. He had always been health conscious, with a little tendency to be apprehensive about coming down with some disease about which he had been reading.

From childhood migraine headaches had troubled him, though he rarely allowed them to interrupt his preaching. In Carleton Place, Ontario, even though only 28 years of age, he came down with a severe headache one evening. "Severe headache," he wrote. "Spoke in Carleton Place in great pain, but Lord gave power." He complained about being extremely sick in Almonte, Ontario, but went ahead and carried out a baptism of four in a bathtub.

That same year he mentioned in his diary about being not well. He went home and vomited blood, confessing that he thought it might be an ulcer. The next year in California he had a recurrence of his problems with his eyes that the explosion had injured when he was a boy.

His migraines continued year after year. In 1926 he was so ill he could not preach at a ministerial convention in San Luis Obispo. Two nurses who were there from the Glendale Sanitarium and Hospital gave him a hydrotherapy treatment at the hospital tent, and his headache disappeared within 30 minutes.

Sometimes his self treatments were effective. Other times he just had to wait the headaches out until they went away after a day or two.

In 1934, after he had been preaching series after series of evangelistic meetings in California for the past eight years, Richards began to experience what has now come to be known as burnout. He commented to his diary, "Either I am very tired or my talks are not as interesting as formerly. I seem to be speaking in a sort of vacuum."

A few days later: "I find it very hard to speak and have very little enthusiasm. I feel I am about ready to cave in, and I have little fire." A few days' rest must have solved that problem, for he ceased mentioning it.

While helping to take down a tent in San Diego in 1936, he hurt his back pulling up a tent stake. For the next few days he felt a constant feeling of intense discomfort in the lower region of his back. It created recurring back problems for him for the rest of his life. Two years later (1938) he lifted a 75-lb. box of handbills and his back slipped out again. He could hardly move. That time Dr. Harmes of National City near San Diego was able to relieve the pain somewhat by heat and muscle massage.

The next year in Phoenix he again had an episode with his back. At that time he didn't know what caused it to happen, but the pain was just as uncomfortable. Mabel discovered certain things she could do to help him readjust his misaligned back, and later on, those of us in the quartet learned the same techniques that would give him relief.

Basically, Richards was health-conscious. He watched his diet, drank plenty of water, and was what some would call a fanatic about walking. Every day, every night, rain or shine, he would be out hiking. During his Phoenix meetings in 1939 he walked sometimes three miles, other times four miles a day. One day his walking almost got him into trouble. He was hiking along a country road near Phoenix when a huge dog came bounding out to attack him. A combination of his large walking stick and the loud voice of the farmer-owner of the dog saved him from being savagely mauled.

When we traveled from camp meeting to camp meeting in the car, every time we would stop for gasoline, Richards and one of the quartet would hike up the road in the direction the car would be going. Sometimes we would get a mile or two beyond before the car would catch up. On one occasion, the Texas highway patrol stopped him and me as we hiked along. They told us it was against the law to walk along their express highways. That curtailed our exercise, at least along interstates.

I can remember that when I lived on Glenoaks Boulevard about three fourths of a mile from the Voice of Prophecy office I would see "the Chief" heading down the street by my house, using his own peculiar high-stepping gait that would protect him from tripping on things as he walked along and read his book at the same time. He often hiked in the hills above his home in Scholl Canyon. From those hills he could look out over the whole panorama of the city below him.

His exercise time in the hills above his home was also a daily prayer time for him. In his sermon on the "Tears of Jesus" he told his audiences how the Bible describes Jesus weeping three times. Once He prayed at the grave of Lazarus for one man, once from the Mount of Olives He prayed for the city of Jerusalem, and in Gethsemane He prayed for the whole world—for one person, for one city, and for the whole world. Asking us if we ever prayed for the cities in which we live, he shared with us in this sermon that on his hikes up in the mountains above his home as he looked out over the Los Angeles basin with its millions of people, he often prayed to God for the city of Los Angeles.

When he and the quartet were holding meetings in Portland, Oregon, he and Ray Turner would go out into a grove of trees in Gladstone Park and cut wood. It not only gave them exercise, but warmed their house as well, echoing the adage that "he who cuts his own wood is warmed twice."

Between meetings he would take his family up to a cabin in the Sierra Madre mountains. The cabin in Ice House Canyon belonged to a Mr. Williams, and provided a wonderful place of relaxation for Richards and his family.

Though he sometimes worried about his health unnecessarily, the episode with Dr. Schultz triggered what some of us saw as an extreme reaction. He was terrified that he was on the brink of death. A few days later he was at home alone. Mabel and Jan had gone to a concert in Los Angeles. As he lay there by himself, he began to suffer some intense chest pain that he interpreted to be a heart attack. Concluding that he was dying, in his panic he phoned his 85-year-old father, who in turn contacted a cardiologist, Dr. Fisher, who came over and gave him a sedative that was supposed to calm him down. It didn't.

It turned out to have been just some discomfort from gas, but it brought him face-to-face with his own mortality in a way he had never before experienced. He imagined that in just a few moments he would be shutting his eyes for the last time, only to open them again in the presence of the Lord.

Even Dr. Schultz seems to have realized he had set in motion fears that needed to be calmed. A few days later he reassured Richards that his heart was better, and that he should get up and walk around. But what Schultz had triggered couldn't be stopped so easily. Richards began to obsessively check his own pulse every few minutes.

Two weeks later, at the end of February in 1954, Richards and the quartet were scheduled to hold a series of meetings in the Majestic Theater in Ft. Worth, Texas. Mabel made arrangements with the airline company that on the plane east he could breathe oxygen while aboard. That night at the theater he had them put a chair on the platform and sat down while speaking. While in Ft. Worth he had a cardiogram test by a Dr. King who found no heart fluctuation at all.

When Mabel notified the airline that he needed oxygen on the return flight home to Los Angeles, they very nearly refused him a seat, and only after some discussion did they allow him to travel without a doctor's permission.

When he would go with the quartet on an appointment, even though we felt that his illness was imagined, we loved him so much we would fix up the station wagon so that he could lie down as we drove along.

Mabel urged him to walk a little more. She told him she thought he was largely to blame because he was too nervous. Although probably right, she had common sense enough to recognize that she couldn't argue him out of it.

Dr. Roy Schultz owned the abandoned Golden Queen gold mine up in the Mojave Desert, and had a little clinic he operated there one or two days a week. Schultz invited H.M.S. to go up there with him. He no doubt thought the change and the higher altitude would do Richards good. It was a helpful move. He lay down in the back of the car on the way up, and found that as he got away from the smog of the lower elevations, he felt considerably better.

During this time of Richards' real or imagined illness, Dave Olsen, our associate speaker, accepted a call to pastor the church at Long Beach, and Orville Iversen came from the Illinois Conference to take his place. Iversen had been in charge of youth work in Illinois, and stayed with the Voice for several years before accepting an invitation to become Walde's assistant in the Radio Department of the General Conference.

Also during this time of Richards' incapacity the VOP asked me to act as a correspondence secretary to him, answering the many letters that came to him requesting answers to Bible questions. Also

Richards asked my help in preparing material for a book of daily devotions he had been asked to write.

He celebrated his sixtieth birthday on August 28, 1954, but his preoccupation with death caused a shadow to fall across even that celebration. In his diary he wrote: "60th birthday. Can it be possible? 60 years old. It's true. I'm really getting old. (Dickens died at 58.) Time is both kind and cruel. When we get ready to live, the time for living is gone. But God has been good to me." He had no way of knowing then that God would give him another 30 years of life and service.

A month later he recorded in his diary, "Feel better than I have for a long time, but I fear I have an ulcer."

In November he asked his diary, "Why do I feel so bad? I'm depressed and have a dull ache on the left side of my chest. Mabel thinks I'm worried, but I have no worries. God has forgiven my sins, and I have dear ones and friends and a part in God's work."

A couple of days later he commented: "I wrote a Voice of Prophecy talk today for September 11, 1955. I wonder whether I will be here to listen to it!"

During the next year the Voice of Prophecy urged him to fly to appointments. The quartet would go ahead with the car, and would be there to give him and Mabel transportation. It was probably a good thing, and made it possible for him to be effective for the Lord for many more years.

While at home in Los Angeles he would visit Dr. Schultz's Golden Queen mine whenever he could. The desert climate was good for him, and often Mabel and Jan would accompany him.

On one occasion his visit to the Golden Queen almost ended in tragedy. While they were sleeping one Friday night, the doctor's clinic and living quarters caught fire. He awoke to hear Mabel's voice calling amid the roar of the flames and choking smoke. Richards escaped through a window, then with a heavy flashlight smashed the window of the room where Jan was sleeping and pulled his youngest son to safety. "Oh, how good the Lord was to us—no terrible tragedy!" he told his diary.

On February 2, 1955, Mabel's Grandma Eastman died. A cheerful person, she'd lived with Mabel and H.M.S. in their home for a number of years after Grandpa Eastman died. "Oh," she'd say, "I want to live to be 100. I want to see what's going to happen next in the world." She reached past her goal to be 100 years old. When she died, she was just two months shy of reaching 102.

For the next year Richards continued to worry in his diary about his health. March 7, 1955: "Notice a tingling in my left hand and left foot." April 5, 1955: "I wonder if I will be allowed the health and life to go on through time till I am 65. I hope so! But God's will be done! He is my guide and my life is in His hands."

As 1955 progressed Richards began to forget to be sick. He was too healthy, both physically and mentally, to sustain a long-term bout of hypochondria. As we started to busily march through our camp meeting appointments, he began to act like the same old "Chief" we knew.

It would be a long hard summer and fall. We headed out in May. Our first appointment that summer was Texas. What a joy it was for the Chief to see his eldest son in action as a minister at the Texas camp meeting, leading the singing, preaching. We went on from Texas to Mississippi, Florida, North Carolina, West Virginia, Pennsylvania, New York, then took in a big Youth Congress in Cleveland, Ohio. On the way to a Laymen's Congress in Kansas City, we stopped for a little sightseeing at the old jail in Carthage, Illinois.

One of Richards' great interests was the history of Mormonism. He owned one of the most complete libraries on Mormonism outside of Salt Lake City. Carthage is famous as the place where Joseph Smith, founder of the Mormon religion, died as he leaped out of the jail window there. While in the area we stopped by the site of the Mormon temple at Nauvoo, Illinois.

From Kansas City we drove on to camp meetings and other appointments in California, Oregon, British Columbia, Washington, Colorado, Minnesota, Illinois, Michigan, Ontario, Quebec, New Brunswick, ending up with a wonderful visit for the first time to St. Johns, Newfoundland.

In Washington we stopped for a delightful meal at the home of Jerry Dill's parents. Richards always loved to spend time with the families of the quartet members. Whenever we stopped at Jerry's parents' place we always would be assured of a wonderful feast. Jerry's mother was a marvelous German cook.

In September Richards and the quartet held a 10-day series of evangelistic meetings in the Spokane, Washington, Civic Auditorium. It was an especially memorable time for me. I was worried about the coming birth of a child. As we were getting ready to leave for the meeting on the evening of September 12, I received word that my son, Charles Loren, had been born. The audience cheered when H.M.S. announced it to the crowd that night.

A few days later Richards and the quartet stopped by Cortez, Colorado, where Kenneth Richards was working as a young minister in his first solo assignment.

A few days later when we drove through Chicago, the Voice of Prophecy group had a big spaghetti feed at the home of my wife's parents, Mr. and Mrs. Sansonetti. They went all out and sewed up little red-and-white checkered bibs for us to wear while we slurped our spaghetti.

In Montreal we visited the old church where Virginia Richards as a baby had tried to sleep in the same room with the blower that ran the pipe organ. From there we flew to our appointment in St. Johns, Newfoundland.

In St. Johns the Chief persuaded me to drive him to the top of the hill to see Marconi's monument that stands as a memento of the very first transoceanic wireless radio message. Our stop at St. Johns was memorable because we were stranded there in the fog, causing us to miss an appointment. We had been scheduled for a night meeting in Augusta, Maine, but the fog canceled all flights out of St. Johns. We had to make a long-distance phone call to Pastor William Fagal, asking him and his quartet to take our meeting in Augusta. It was the only time I can remember when the Voice of Prophecy failed to make a scheduled appointment.

Though Richards had looked death in the face and now was more keenly aware of his own mortality, he was able to begin to take a healthier look at himself and life. As most of us do with the passing of time, he began to notice the youthfulness of his fellow workers. His old friend F. D. Nichol, editor of the *Review and Herald,* had confided in him that after age 50 he began to feel increasingly the urgency to do things quickly. Richards in his sermons often quoted the caption at the base of a famous statue in Chicago: "Time goes, you say?—Oh, no—time stays—we go!"

It had been a strenuous summer and fall, especially for a man who felt he had been so near to death's door. Instead of death's door, Richards would walk through a new door opening in his ministry. Some of his best days lay just ahead. And he would be able to leave his dilapidated, dangerous study that had been located alongside the family Ford in the garage. A new library would arise in the backyard that he would soon fill with the books he enjoyed so much.

READING AND PREACHING

On December 15, 1955, we started pouring the concrete slab that would be the foundation of the library in the Chief's backyard. When I say we, I mean the King's Heralds quartet. It had been our dream for years. Four years before a young doctor in Los Angeles had caught the spirit of that dream and pledged $1,000. By the time we started building, another $1,000 had accumulated in the kitty. We estimated that this, with our own free labor and 1,000 feet of two-by-fours donated by a mill in Vancouver, Washington, would build the structure.

Bob Seamount had, with his dad, done quite a bit of building as he was growing up, and Wayne Hooper, who had not long before finished his own home up Glenmore Canyon, acted as job supervisor. With the help of Bob Seamount's dad and Reuben Yeager, a licensed contractor and member of the Eagle Rock Seventh-day Adventist Church, where all the quartet were members, we began to pour concrete at 6:00 in the morning.

I clearly remember that morning. It was a gray December day. The big Redimix truck

251

backed up to the curb, and the quartet had lined up some volunteer wheelbarrow pushers, including Orville Iversen, the Voice of Prophecy associate speaker. As a quartet we loved to kid around and play tricks on one another, but we got even more fun out of tormenting Iversen. On this particular morning we negotiated with the operator of the cement truck to load Orville's wheelbarrow to the brim with sloppy, soupy concrete. Poor Orville struggled with that load. In case you're not aware of it, a wheelbarrow filled to the brim with sloppy concrete is *heavy!* As Orville staggered along the driveway toward the back of the lot, he had to push his wheelbarrow up a plank ramp before dumping his load into the forms for the slab floor of the new library. He didn't quite make it. Half way up the ramp he lost his load, dumping it onto the ground. Of course, the sadistic quartet was standing in the wings to give him the horse laugh. He had every reason to store up some credit for revenge, and I'm quite sure he found occasion more than once to get back at us for our miserable trick.

When I'd first come to the Voice in 1947, the ministry had assigned me to help the Chief in his garage library during the hours when we weren't practicing for the broadcast. It was kind of scary, not because it was a dangerous place to work, but because the Chief stored all his books in the south half of a two-car garage. Just one little carburetor fire and several thousand dollars' worth of irreplaceable books might have gone up in smoke.

All his life Richards loved books. When he was a young preacher in Canada, Elder Spicer, the General Conference president, had dropped into his little study and admired his collection of books. Now 32 years later the Chief's hunger for books and his love for reading had resulted in a library of more than 6,000 volumes, many of them extremely valuable and irreplaceable. His book collection would eventually swell to more than 8,000.

His reading habit started at an early age. The first book he is reported to have read was his mother's Bible. For that he received a dollar from his father, with the promise that it would be doubled each time thereafter. Of course, Dad had to repent of that promise, for by the time his young son had finished the Bible 21 times (and in his lifetime he more than tripled that), Dad would have been forced to fork over $1,048,576 for that twenty-first reading.

The next books the boy read were *Conquest of Granada* by Washington Irving and *Pilgrim's Progress* by John Bunyan. Those books launched an avid reading career that impelled his mother to hold him back from school until he was 8 years old. She was afraid he would read himself into an early grave.

As he grew older he developed a wide taste in literature. When we were traveling along in the car the quartet could not bring up a subject to argue about, from photography to ancient history to meteorology to ad infinitum, to which he couldn't make a valuable contribution. And when we'd start out on a trip, we'd always have to load his book box into the luggage rack on the top of the car. He would keep a few books tucked in his nest in the car to take care of his reading needs of the day as we drove along. From time to time we'd ship home the ones he'd read, and bring out a new supply from his "minilibrary" in the luggage rack.

Of course, if we stopped in Philadelphia or Grand Rapids, he would add to the collection at Leary's or Kregel's secondhand bookstores. And on Manhattan Island in New York he loved to browse in the used-book store section of the city.

Let me give you an illustration of the kind of books he would be reading in the course of a year. In 1955, the year we began to build his library in the backyard of his home, he went through the following titles:

He began the year with the *Complete Poems of Robert Frost,* then on to the *Prophetic Faith of Our Fathers,* Volumes I and IV, by L. E. Froom; the *Seventh-day Adventist Bible Commentary,* Volumes I, II, and III; the New Testament 11 times (he had planned to read it once a month, but didn't quite make it that year); a little storybook by his old friend R. E. Finney, Jr., entitled *Judy Steps Out; The Untold Story of Douglas MacArthur* by Frazier Hunt; *Triumph of the Crucified* by Erich Sauer; *Christian View of Science and Scripture* by Bernard Ramm; *History of the Crusades,* Volumes I, II, and III, by Stephen Runciman; *The Revised Standard Version: An Appraisal* by J. A. Huffman; *The Greatest of the Prophets* by George McCready Price; *God Speaks to Modern Man* by A. E. Lickey; *Parnassus on Wheels* by Christopher Morley; *The Haunted Bookshop* by Christopher Morley [you can see he sometimes let his hair down and relaxed with a good mystery story]; *Marie Antoinette* by Stefan Zweig; *Botany Bay* by Nordhoff and Hall; *Biographical Preaching* by Andrew W. Blackwood; *The Indescribable Christ* by Charles J. Rolls; *Peace With God* by Billy Graham; *The Archer of the Lord,* a biography of Darley P. Pratt; *The Divine Comedy* by Dante; *Looking Backward* by Bellamy; *American Notes* by Kipling; *The Light That Failed* by Kipling; *Mine Own People* by Kipling; *Wee Willie Winkle* by Kipling; *Kipling Stories I and II* [he sometimes got stuck in a groove with a particularly favorite author]; *The Eternal Galilean* by Shean; *Why I Accept the Genesis Record* by John Raymond Hand; *Unidentifiable Flying Objects* by M. K. Jessup; *The Black Donnellys* by T. P. Kelley; *Creation* by Theodore L. Handrich; *The Life of George Washington,* Volumes I, II, and III, by Douglas Southall Freeman; *Highlights of Archaeology in Bible Lands* by Fred H. Wight; *The War of the Revolution* by Christopher Ward; and he finished the year on December 31 with a book by A. W. Hewitt called *Highland Shepherds.* For the year 1955 he had read 54 books, some of them pretty heavy stuff as you can see for yourself.

His obsession with reading became a joke to family and friends. When his son, Harold, Jr., took him out for a ride in his new sailboat, Dad watched what was happening on deck for a little while, interesting himself in estimating how fast the boat was sailing in knots, then all at once when Harold looked away, Dad was gone. Where else? Much to Harold's chagrin, Dad was down below, reading a book.

His constant Bible reading so saturated his mind that in his sermons when he would hold the Bible up to read a text, we often noticed that the Bible was upside down. He wasn't reading—he was quoting the text by memory.

Richards loved to talk to young preachers. He had definite convictions about what it meant to be a minister. "A man should never go into preaching if he can conscientiously avoid it," I have often heard him say. "Preaching is not a profession, it's a calling."

His advice to young ministers was to never stop reading and studying. "Become experts with your Bibles," he would advise. "I wish each young minister in a conference would become an expert in some book of the Bible. Then when they get together at a workers' meeting they could share with one another their love of the Word."

"It's so easy," he would say, "for a pastor to be diverted by the mechanics of the ministry. Let your wives be lionesses protecting your time to study and pray each day. You need to read the Bible, become experts in the Word. I take the month of January every year and put aside the Los Angeles *Times, Time* magazine, *Ministry,* even the *Review and Herald*, every other book and magazine for the whole month. I finish the Bible in January, then leisurely go through it again between February and December.

"There will be times when the leader of the Dorcas Society will phone wanting you to come help her with something. That's important, but your wife should help you protect your time of prayer and study each day. If you allow your study time to be eroded away with good things, you'll stagnate as a preacher. Your wife doesn't have to lie and tell people you're not there, but she can take a number and promise that you'll call back later.

"Know your Bible," he would advise. "It should be your primary source for sermon material. Sometimes young men tell me they have a hard time finding sermon topics—knowing what to preach about. Read your Bibles."

In an interview with his friend Wilbur Alexander, he said, "The Bible is a vast and infinite source of sermons. If you become a Bible preacher, you are never out of sermon material. If you are merely a topical preacher you will run out of something to say and will have to move on and start again. But, when you start preaching the Bible you'll find it to be an exhaustless mine. As you keep probing into it, you get to be a better preacher and people will want to hear you.

Get on fire with the Bible, and people will come to see you burn!

"As you read your Bibles, sermons will jump out at you saying, 'Preach me! Preach me! Preach me.' As I read my Bible, when I come to such a text I write the letters 'SER' in the margin of my Bible. I won't begin to live long enough to preach all the sermons that are waiting to be preached." He was right! He lived to the age of 90 but still didn't have a chance to present all the sermons marked in his Bible.

Every member of the King's Heralds quartet who ever traveled with Richards can tell you about times when he would look up from his Bible reading in his special seat in the car beside the driver. With a light in his eye he would recite a text that had just impressed itself on his heart. We would look down, and sure enough, there in the margin of his Bible were the familiar letters SER marked in blue pencil.

I remember one day he was reading in Matthew about the soldiers assigned to guard Jesus' tomb. After the Resurrection, they rushed into the city of Jerusalem with the news that Jesus had risen. Finally they were ushered into the chambers of the high officers of the nation and given "large moneys" to change their story. Matthew 28:15 says: "So they took the money." "What a sermon that would be," Richards said with excitement in his eyes and voice. "So they took the money." Sure enough, it wasn't long before we began to hear the sermon "So They Took the Money" as he preached in churches or to camp meeting crowds.

H.M.S. Richards was fond of the King James Version of the Bible, but he recommended that a minister should have in his library as many versions and translations of the Bible as he could afford, including Greek and Hebrew. But he always recommended preaching from the King James Version, relying on the other translations and versions for his own mental and spiritual enrichment. He recognized that since the King James Version had been translated scholars had found thousands of manuscripts, and new discoveries in biblical archaeology had brought new knowledge of language meaning and the cultural background of Bible times. After the discovery of the Dead Sea scrolls he hungrily devoured just about every book he could find on the subject.

In addition to urging that a young minister immerse himself in Scripture, Richards suggested that he memorize great portions of the Bible. Since the King James Version was translated at a time when the English language had flowered to a peak of excellence and was itself an example of great literature, he recommended that should be the translation to memorize. He himself discovered that even though he had read a chapter a thousand times, when he memorized that same chapter, he suddenly saw new meaning that had before remained hidden to him.

"After the Bible, get acquainted with the other great literature of the English language," he would advise young ministers. "Some of the people in your congregation are intelligent and educated people. Memorize great poetry. It will help you in your preaching. I don't have time for good books—only the best books. There are thousands of good books published every year. You won't have time to read them all, but you need to take time to read the great books."

He told us how as a young student minister at Washington Missionary College he had often walked the halls of the Library of Congress. Looking hungrily at the towering shelves and stacks of books, he desired to read them all. When he asked the librarian how long it would take to read all the books in the Library of Congress, he was told that if he read all the books in one of the little alcoves surrounding the main rotunda it would take him 80 years. With that bit of trivial knowledge he gave up the idea of reading them all and usually settled for reading only the best and greatest.

An entry in his diary for March 1, 1952, illustrates both his thirst for knowledge and his appreciation of the great literature of the English language: "Reading Tennyson—what a master of words—it's thrilling. Want to read Milton next—re-read 'Paradise Lost.' Then John Donne. Then hope to gradually read the *Encyclopedia Britannica* from A-Z."

Richards loved biography. As he explored the lives of the men and women who changed history, he would see history come alive. He quoted Emerson who said, "There is no history, only biography."

To him the past was not just dates and facts. It was flesh and blood.

Richards never let the well of his mind run dry. He was forever replenishing it by devouring great books and literature. In the evening after a long drive in the car the quartet would settle down behind him for a sermon they had perhaps heard 100 times before, yet they invariably found that it was never the same. Richards always brought something new, some new flash of inspiration into that "old" sermon from what he had picked up in the day's reading. He was forever changing, growing, because he believed that as an individual takes new information into his mind, he becomes a different person than he was the day before.

The teachers of young ministerial students at La Sierra College soon discovered what a learning experience it was to bring their charges to visit Richards in his study. Roy Anderson, Horace Shaw, Edward Heppenstall, Norval Pease, Wilbur Alexander, and others would take their students to Richards' Glendale library, and H.M.S. always had something to say that would light a spark in the hearts of those young men and women whom God had touched to become preachers. Here's what he said in his diary for April 25, 1951: "Wednesday. Heppenstall and about 20 of his ministerial students came to see the Voice of Prophecy and to my study at home to see how I worked. I gave them a list of books suggested for Bible study."

Richards learned to preach by preaching. He often told the story of how Benjamin Franklin loved to go hear the preaching of George Whitefield. Even though Franklin was a deist, he went again and again, and learned that each time Whitefield would preach the same sermon, it would be better. Each new delivery would hone the sermon to a keener edge.

In preaching, Richards believed in putting his strongest arguments first. "If you begin with your weaker points, your listeners may recognize those weaknesses, and lose confidence in your presentation of your subject." In his book *Feed My Sheep* he said, "Make your strong points of truth right at the beginning of your talk. This is a restless age. Bring your listeners face-to-face with the mighty facts immediately. Show proof after proof, evidence after evidence, text after text, like successive hammer blows. Illustrate, make your points clear, and while the people are still interested, sit down."

From my own observation of the Chief's preaching, I saw how he gave his audience emotional relief during his sermons. Some preachers exhaust their audiences by keeping them tense and at a high pitch for 30 or 40 minutes. From time to time during his sermons Richards would provide his audience relief by inserting a story or an amusing personal illustration. I can never remember him telling a joke just for a laugh. His stories, even when humorous, made his sermon point easier to remember, and gave his listeners an opportunity to let their emotions down before he proceeded on to the next point.

Richards recognized that as he preached either to his radio audience or in public meetings, many of his listeners were spiritual and biblical illiterates. Not ignorant. Highly educated, but biblically illiterate. "We are living in a generation of spiritual illiterates," he would say, "millions of whom know as little about the gospel, the Bible, the story of the Old and New Testaments, the facts of the life of Christ, and the plan of salvation, as did the people of Asia Minor in the days of the apostle Paul." For this reason he kept his message simple. "Jesus said, 'Feed My sheep,' not 'Feed My giraffes,'" he explained. "I believe in putting the cookies on the lower shelf where even a child can get them." He wasn't one to employ big words, though he knew them and understood what they meant. Instead, he liked to use the strong one- and two-syllable Anglo-Saxon English in his sermons.

He deplored a practice common in the Seventh-day Adventist denomination for many years of too frequently moving young preachers from place to place. Richards felt that it tended to make them shallow preachers, tempting them to build up a sermon repertoire of 100 sermons or more that they would use again and again at each new pastorate. As a result he felt strongly that young ministers ought to stay in a place long enough to enable them to grow as preachers—to stretch their minds. As an example he would point out that Spurgeon, after becoming a young minister at New Park Street Chapel in London, continued for 38 years with a congregation that continued to outgrow their facilities. The great Metropolitan Tabernacle that held 6,000 people was built at Newington to hold his crowds. Spurgeon continued to preach there until his death, publishing a collection of 50 volumes of sermons.

Richards loved to needle his close minister friends who succumbed to the temptation to move from preaching into administration. "So I hear you've left the Lord's work and gone to be a conference president," he would chide with a twinkle in his eye. Walde, Nightingale, and others felt the sting of his good-natured little barbs.

He seriously felt that the church had accepted the misconception that moving to an administrative position somehow constituted a promotion. To correct it he had his own little formula—when people moved from a pastoral or evangelistic position to an administrative one they should take a modest cut in pay, if only a dollar a week. Richards felt that a preacher ought to be respected, and to demonstrate that respect should receive the highest salary scale in the church.

In 1957 the Columbia Union Conference of Seventh-day Adventists and Washington Missionary College, his alma mater, invited him to give a series of lectures on preaching, patterned after the famed Yale Lectureship on Preaching. Beginning Sunday, May 12, 1957, Richards, over the course of five days, delivered nine lectures at the college. The series sponsors invited young ministerial students as well as established pastors and evangelists to attend. By 1957 Richards had become known as "the preachers' preacher." Any young person who had the privilege of sitting at his feet in such a lecture series always came away a stronger preacher for it.

In his opening sermon Richards led off with "What Is Preaching?" One epigram in that sermon set the tone for the series: "God's message, from God's Book, by God's man, in God's house, on God's day—that's preaching!"

Richards stressed the urgency that should consume a preacher.

He told how a couple years before he and Mrs. Richards had visited New Zealand. The Queen had just landed in New Zealand and the whole country was in a good mood. It was Christmas Eve. The moon was bright and there wasn't a storm from one end of New Zealand to the other.

That night a train sped northward from Wellington, filled with Christmas travelers hurrying home for the holidays. About halfway up to Auckland, just to the west, is a high volcano. In its crater is a lake frozen most of the year. The outlet of that lake is blocked with ice—has been for centuries as far as anyone knows. That night the ice gave way and water from the lake burst through, carrying mud, ash, and great rocks weighing many tons. The avalanche swept the railroad bridge away in its rush to the sea. More than 140 people lost their lives that Christmas Eve as the train tumbled into the yawning chasm, among them a couple Seventh-day Adventist young men.

"Do you know the first thing that came to my mind when I heard the awful news in the morning?" Richards asked the young preachers at that first sermon of the first lectureship series. "I wondered whether anyone I had preached to during the previous three days was on that train. What had I said that would help him to meet eternity? That was what I was thinking about. Had any of those people been in my meetings? What had I said?"

That's what the urgency of being a preacher meant to H.M.S. Richards.

Richards continued to grow as a preacher. All his life he loved Uriah Smith's book *Daniel and the Revelation*. In his early evangelistic meetings he followed Smith's interpretation of prophecy quite closely, and sprinkled many prophetic topics from Daniel and Revelation throughout a series of meetings as did most Adventist preachers in those days. When he got to California in 1926 he learned that some of the church's Bible scholars were beginning to take a second look at prophecies that Adventists called "the Eastern Question." Who was the "king of the north"? Was Armageddon a physical battle, or was it a spiritual warfare, or both? What about the "kings of the east"? It troubled him at first. Though he continued to preach on the prophecies of Daniel and Revelation until the end of his life, he more and more focused on the high points that were irrefutable, and avoided the controversial minutia.

From time to time his old ministerial friends would come to him, deeply concerned about changes they saw occurring in the church. As early as 1937 one pioneer preacher voiced his concern to Richards about the theological seminary at Washington, D.C. He feared it would lead the church into apostasy.

It troubled many of the sincere veterans that our Adventist colleges sought accreditation from "worldly" organizations. B. G. Wilkinson, an educational leader in the church, saw that it would be a necessary step for our schools and urged such accreditation. Others were fearful. Richards listened sympathetically and asked himself, "Where does the truth of this movement rest? I say with the rank and file."

In 1939, when Reuben Nightingale brought news from the SDA seminary where he had been attending, he shared that even old stalwart M. L. Andreasen sensed that we would have to take a second look at some of the positions we had formerly held on Bible prophecy. Nightingale reported that Andreasen "says he's 'afraid of prophecy.'"

Several years later, on March 9, 1942, Richards' associate from Pennsylvania days, Howard Detwiler, was elected president of the Potomac Conference. He told H.M.S. that the attitude of some of the seminary teachers on the nature of Christ disturbed him. H.M.S. worried that this conflict had the possible proportions of the battle that shook the church in the early centuries as it struggled with Arianism.

While such questions caused unrest among church leaders, Richards kept his cool. Though he himself had views on the various issues, he had common sense enough not to let himself get seriously upset. He had confidence in the Lord and in the good sense of the common people who sit in the church pews.

Even when he disagreed with another Adventist over the interpretation of a Bible passage, he never allowed it to mar their relationship as Christian friends. He loved to tell the story of John Wesley and George Whitefield. Both were strong-minded leaders in the new group of young men who composed "the Holy Club," and who became the founders of the great Methodist Church. During their later years they allowed a disagreement in theology to cause them to drift apart. True to human nature, others exploited the differences, choosing up sides, polarizing the Methodist movement.

When Whitefield died, one woman in a malicious little dig came to John Wesley and asked him, "Do you think you'll see George Whitefield in heaven?"

"No, sister, I don't think I will."

"I knew it! I knew it! You think Whitefield won't be in heaven!"

"No, sister, I didn't say that. I think when I get to heaven, Whitefield will be so close to the throne of God in all its glory, that I won't even be able to get close enough to see him."

Also Richards often told the story of one of America's great preachers, De Witt Talmage. As Talmage lay near death, his son asked him, "Father, you have preached the great teachings of the church all your life. What do you believe now?"

"Son," he answered, "when I started in the ministry I had 100 doctrines, when I was 30 years old I had 50 doctrines, when I was 50 I had 10 doctrines. Now as I come to the end of my life, I have just one." When his eager family gathered around his bed and urged him to name it, he answered, "Now in the valley of the shadow, I have only one doctrine—the doctrine that I am a great sinner, and Jesus is a great Saviour."

That also characterized the gradual change in emphasis in the preaching of H.M.S. Richards.

All his life he had delighted to listen to the great preachers of other denominations. He had followed the counsel of Ellen White who said, "Our ministers should seek to come near to the ministers of other denominations. Pray for and with these men, for whom Christ is interceding" (*Evangelism,* p. 562).

Early in 1957 he wholeheartedly supported the efforts of some of the leaders of the Seventh-day Adventist Church to invite Dr. Donald Barnhouse, Dr. Walter Martin, and others to visit our headquarters in Washington, D.C., and dialogue about the great points of the Christian faith.

When Barnhouse, editor of *Eternity* magazine, was on the West Coast in February of that year, Richards and Orville Iversen went to hear him preach at the Los Angeles Mesa Presbyterian Church. After the meeting Richards invited Barnhouse to visit the Voice of Prophecy office and speak to the staff the next day, to which he graciously agreed.

"It was a good talk," Richards wrote in his diary of that morning, "plain and clear. He said he was in disagreement with Seventh-day Adventists on the Sabbath, on the state of the dead, and especially the Investigative Judgment, but the area of agreement was most important—God, the Deity of Jesus Christ, Redemption in Him and His atonement—not of works, but producing works."

Later that year when Dr. Barnhouse published a series of articles in his *Eternity* magazine defending Seventh-day Adventists as orthodox Christians, he encountered bitter criticism from many evangelical ministers, and suffered a substantial loss in subscribers. He paid heavily for his honesty and sincere Christian brotherliness, but to my knowledge never regretted taking that position.

Dr. Walter Martin, author of *The Kingdom of the Cults,* also came to the Voice of Prophecy offices and spoke in our assembly. He published an appendix of 92 pages on Seventh-day Adventist doctrines in this book. In the appendix he endorsed Adventists as true Christians, not to be classed among the cults, all the while disagreeing with some principle teachings—most notably, the Sabbath, the state of the dead, and the investigative judgment.

As an outgrowth of the dialogue with Barnhouse, Martin, and others, the denomination printed the book *Questions on Doctrine*. It caused and still causes considerable debate among some Adventists. During July 1957 Elder Roy Anderson confided to Richards that Andreasen opposed the consultations he and Froom and others in the General Conference had been having with Barnhouse and Martin. Richards could not understand this.

Late in 1957 and again in January 1958 Elder R. R. Figuhr, president of the General Conference, spoke to Richards about Elder Andreasen's opposition to *Questions on Doctrine*, asking if he had heard of much criticism of the book. H.M.S. advised that he had heard some discussion among some ministers in southern California, but not many of them.

During 1958 Richards wrote a series of 15 radio talks based on the book. In the May 30, 1958, entry of his diary he wrote: "The natural reaction against any new way of stating our truth for today and the added strong opposition of Elder Andreasen, is causing a lot of opposition to the book *Questions on Doctrine*—proving that some of the criticisms of us by other churches is true of some of our workers. So many have a fuzzy idea of the gospel and this colors all their message."

It even infected at least one of our own Voice of Prophecy employees. In his diary for February 12, 1960, Richards reported: "Yesterday I was not at the 8:00 a.m. meeting [at the Voice of Prophecy] and I am glad of it. I hear Brother Waldemar Jesskie made a strong attack on Dr. Barnhouse whom he heard at Covina a day or two ago. Too bad!"

When Dr. Barnhouse died in November of 1960, Richards wrote a warm letter of comfort to his widow:

> *"My dear friend in Christ:*
>
> *"This letter to you is late because of my absence from headquarters for a number of weeks. It was only when I returned home two or three days ago that I heard of your great loss. Mrs. Richards and I are grieved more than we can tell you. We just wish we could see you and clasp your hand and assure you of our deepest sympathy and prayers in your time of special grief.*
>
> *"Now we are face to face with the fact that one of the great preachers and Christian workers of this age has been taken from us.*
>
> *"Mrs. Richards joins me in the prayer that God will be very near to*

*you. If you should come to the coast at any time, we wish very much
that you would let us know. We would like to see you again.*

"Most sincerely yours in the faith of Christ,

"H.M.S. Richards"

Morris Venden, a young minister friend, patterned his life and theology after H.M.S. Richards. Here are a few H.M.S. quotes he remembers that give a little insight into Richards' theology.

"Question: What is the Adventist message?

"Answer: Jesus only.

"Question: What do you think about righteousness by faith?

"Answer: That's the only kind there is.

"Question: [asked of Richards in the 1960s] What do you think of the Jesus freaks?

"Answer: Sounds like a good idea. I've been one all my life.

"Question: How do you feel about makeup?

"Answer: If the barn needs painting, paint it."

Richards never did lose his love of books. He couldn't pass a used-book store without going in, and once in, couldn't leave without buying something. It was a disease. When he was 70 he still pursued his vice as feverishly as he did when he was 20, but not without a few thoughts about his mortality. Early in 1964 he wrote in his diary: "When I buy books I look at them and wonder whether I will get to read them carefully, or read them at all! And I wonder how my children and Mabel will divide them. It would be nice to keep them together. Whatever is done, I desire my children will never have hard feelings one with another concerning the books I have enjoyed and loved so much!"

In 1970 at the age of 76 Richards experimented with a new field of service. He received an invitation to teach a course on preaching at the California Graduate School of Theology in Glendale. It was a private, conservative, nondenominational school for ministers. He settled on "Preaching From the Life of Christ" as his theme, using *Crises of the Christ* by G. Campbell Morgan as the textbook. He had

59 preachers in his class. They loved him, and the class never had a better role model as a teacher and preacher. After almost every class period, the class, ministers of various denominations, would spontaneously rise and give him an ovation.

He regularly kept a diary. We still have them from 1922 to 1981. In that last diary, when he was 87 years of age, Richards continued to eagerly drink in ideas from his books. Some may not be interested in what he read in that last recorded year. If so, skip on past this, but in that last year for which we have diary entries, he went through the New Testament 15 times. In addition, he read *The Road to Khartoum* by Charles Chenevix Trench; *The Land's End* by W. H. Hudson; *History of Christian Doctrines,* Volumes I and II, by William G. T. Shedd; *Adventism Vindicated* by Russell and Colin Standish; *Feathers in the Wind* by Westphal; *The Openness of God* by Richard Rice; *Sister Mary Lou* by Wilma Ross and Chester E. Westphal; *Seeing Fingers* by Etta Degering; *Dutchman Bound for Paradise* by Albertino K. Tilstra; *Book of Leviticus* by G. J. Wenham; *The Antichrist, 666* by Teitan; *The King James Version Debate* by D. A. Carson; *Tin Miner's Son,* a biography of Harry Tippet, by Wilma Ross Westphal; *Italy and Her Invaders,* Volumes I through VIII, by Hodgkin; *Scotland Forever Home* by Geddes MacGreggor; *J. Gresham Machen* by Henry W. Coray. In his last-recorded entry, December 11, 1981, he stated he had finished the New Testament for the fifteenth time that year. Not bad for an 87-year-old.

We finished his library, and 137 visitors came to an open house on April 1, 1956. It wasn't a big building, only about 20' x 20', but it became a sanctuary for him. He had his own little nest in the corner where he could write sermons, compose letters, or just read for enjoyment. As he had often recommended to young preachers, Mabel was his "lioness," answering the many phone calls, guarding his study and prayer and writing time. Hundreds of sermons would issue from that little "sermon factory" during the next 30 years. It would, fittingly, be in that little sanctuary that he would suffer a stroke nearly 30 years later that would end his ministry, but he still had much of life left to be lived before that would happen.

"BE FRUITFUL AND MULTIPLY"

H.M.S. Richards loved his sons and daughter. Though he buried himself in his work, he had a deep sense of pride in their accomplishments. When son Harold, Jr., graduated on June 8, 1952, Dad was home from the first camp meeting trip of the summer to witness the big event with the rest of the family. "It seemed long when we looked ahead to this day," he wrote in his diary, "but it is here, and now seems a short time since he was a little boy! It was a thrill to us as to him when he marched by and received his degree—a five year course in theology. We thank God for him and pray for his success as a soul winner and our son!"

The next spring he took a plane to Dallas to spend a few days with Harold, Jr. "Harold and Mary and half the church met us with a special Texas welcome," he wrote. That night he spoke in the new church where Harold was associate pastor. "Had a terrible headache, but a good sweat while preaching cured it."

On Tuesday he recorded: "What a joy to work with my own son this week. We visited today. Several old people were filled with joy to see us. They all love Harold and Mary. I am so happy he has such a sweet wife. They hope for a baby and think it may be coming."

As Kenneth's graduation approached, Richards was overjoyed to find that the Colorado Conference, his own early proving ground, had expressed an interest in his son joining them as a new young minister. The leadership had him scheduled to work in Salida with Elder Alexander Snyman, a minister of Boer descent from South Africa.

In the spring of 1953 Father and Mother Richards celebrated their sixtieth anniversary in their little home on Eleanor Drive in Glendale. A number of Voice of Prophecy employees joined them in the festivities. Wayne Hooper took photographs.

On June 7, 1953, the family witnessed Kenneth's graduation. Elder Arthur Bietz gave the commencement address on "The Challenge of Freedom." H.M.J. Richards and Grandma Bertie were there, but the ceremonies were tarnished when the elder Richards fell down the steps of the church and cut his eye and nose. He had just the month before turned 84. Kenneth celebrated his own graduation by having his tonsils out five days later.

"What a fine handsome boy he is," the proud father wrote, "and how proud we are of him! I begin to know why sons and daughters mean so much to parents. Did not Homer say 3,000 years ago 'Happy is the man who has sons, and whose sons have sons, and who is privileged to die in battle!'?"

A few days later Kenneth and his wife, Jackie, had their first plane ride to Kenneth's new place of employment in Colorado. Within a week they had begun evangelistic meetings with Snyman in the Isis Theater in Salida.

The next month, as Richards and the quartet headed home from one of the summer camp meeting trips, we drove from Jamestown, North Dakota, to Salida to see Ken and Jackie. We sang and the Chief made a few remarks at the Isis Theater meetings.

The year 1953 brought two new grandchildren to Mabel and H.M.S. In March daughter, GeGe, presented them with Elizabeth Rae. Grandma and Grandpa proudly went to visit mother and new baby, their third grandchild, at the White Memorial Hospital.

In August the Chief and Mabel started their five-month world trip of Voice of Prophecy meetings mentioned in chapter 20. For H.M.S. it was a heart-wrenching experience. "How I love my growing boy, Jan," he wrote. "I feel sometimes that I am not doing my duty—that I am deserting him! He is growing into young manhood. I am so proud of him! I love him as I think Jacob loved Joseph! May God keep him safe! And dear Father and Mother, too. GeGe will live in our house while we are gone. Father fears he will not live to my return, but has never even suggested that I not go. It is God's work."

The trip took them to Europe, Africa, the Middle East, India, Pakistan, Indonesia, ending up in Australia, New Zealand, and some of the South Pacific islands, then landing them again in Los Angeles on January 17, 1954.

While Richards was away, the fourth grandchild, and the second one in 1953, made his appearance in the world on November 14. Harold Marshall Sylvester Richards III was born to Harold and Mary. The grandfather would not see his little namesake grandson until February, and by that time little "Three," as the family has come to call him, was three months old.

For a man who was recovering from what he had thought was a life-threatening illness, Richards was exceedingly busy and active all during 1955. He and the quartet crisscrossed the country several times, including several forays into both eastern and western Canada, performing at dozens of camp meetings, a youth congress in Cleveland, a laymen's congress in Kansas City, and a week-long evangelistic revival in Spokane, Washington.

Early in the year Mabel's Grandmother Eastman died at Mabel's sister's home. She would have been 102 years old if she had lived a couple more months. Always having a lot of verve and vitality for one her age, she didn't often speak of dying. Instead, she would say, "I want to live and see what's going to happen in the world."

While we were visiting the camp meeting in Texas, H.M.S. was able to spend some time with Harold and Mary. At the airport 19-month-old "Three" seemed to know his grandpa and jumped into his arms. It was also Richards' first time to see grandson Jon, who had been born the previous November. Bites from hungry Texas mosquitoes covered the 7-month-old child.

On Sabbath, June 9, the proud father preached the ordination sermon for his oldest son and three other candidates: Ralph Peuchel, William Hancock, and Henry Barron. His subject was "The Call of God." After the ordination service H.M.S. went down to the front row and escorted daughter-in-law Mary up for the first congratulations.

In early 1956 H.M.S., Mabel, and Jan visited Kenneth and Jackie in Cortez, Colorado. For the first time, Kenneth shared with his father the feeling that he was uncertain that he had been called to the ministry. Later in his diary, H.M.S. confided, "I think of Kenneth and of words to say to him and then when I try to write, it seems they do not sound right! Oh, I do not know what to say and can only pray, 'Lead him, O Lord, each step in his decision as to his work. If he is not called to the ministry, do not let him remain in it. If he is, don't let him forsake it!'" A few days later he wrote: "Phoned Kenneth to cheer him up."

In March of 1956 H.M.S. held a week-long series of evangelistic meetings in the Fresno, California, Civic Auditorium. Twenty-eight years before, Richards had held two big meetings in Fresno in one of the big tabernacles built by Grauer. The first series had lasted nine months, every night of the week, with 120 baptisms. A few months later they opened again in Fresno, this time for a four-and-a-half month campaign resulting in 60 more baptisms. For Richards to return to Fresno was a reawakening of happy memories.

The next month Richards and the quartet left on a one-month trip. It was a memorable, but not especially delightful, trip to me. As we left home, several of the children of quartet members had been ill with the mumps. As we approached Wichita, Kansas, I needled Orville Iversen. "Orville, you don't look well. I notice you have a little swelling there on your neck. I think you're coming down with the mumps!"

Orville looked obligingly worried, but the next morning, as I glanced in the mirror, it was abundantly clear that it was not Orville who had succumbed to the mumps. It was me!

A woman in the Wichita church, Mrs. Hayes, the mother-in-law of our good friend Charles Keymer, took me in and nursed me in her home the whole following week. I was miserable, but 10 days later I was able to catch up with the troupe in Denver.

"Bob Edwards returned to the fold again today," Richards wrote in his diary, "and we were all happy to hear his silver notes in the quartet again."

This trip was memorable for Wayne, too. A few days later he flew home to be with his wife, Harriet, for the birth of their son, David. Kenneth, still a minister in Colorado, sang baritone in Wayne's place for our remaining appointments in Colorado.

On May 25, 1956, Halbert Richards died at 4:40 p.m. on Friday afternoon. He had been ill for some time, and during his last months especially cantankerous. "Father won't take his medicine," Richards wrote. "I wish I could learn to be patient with him and yet help him."

The funeral took place at the Glendale Seventh-day Adventist Church on May 28. I had already left town by car with my family to meet the Voice of Prophecy team in North Carolina on June 1. Del Delker sang first tenor with the quartet in my place for the funeral.

In August of that same year Frances Eastman, Mabel's step-mother, died. Frances had married Mabel's father about 25 years before, after the death of Mabel's mother. Frances was the daughter of Governor Steunenburg of Idaho, who had been murdered by Harry Orchard. Orchard later became a Seventh-day Adventist, and H.M.S. and the quartet from time to time visited him in his little house on the grounds of the Idaho state prison, where he served a life sentence.

In September Richards got word from both of his sons that brought mixed feelings of joy and concern. Harold phoned from Wichita Falls, Texas, that he had baptized 10 converts from his meetings in Clayton, a nearby town. They were the firstfruits of his ministry since his ordination.

Jackie wrote from Colorado that Kenneth was still having a discouraging time in the ministry and had decided, because of health problems, to take a year's leave of absence from his work, beginning in November. It was a time for Kenneth to put into practice some of Dad's words of wisdom he had given to all his children. He had quoted from Paul's counsel to Timothy: "Thou therefore endure hardness, as a good soldier of Jesus Christ" (2 Tim. 2:3).

He told Kenneth there would be good times and bad, but that the words of Paul to Timothy would always help him get through his down times. Then he added a little poem that Kenneth had occasion to remember in his time of discouragement.

> *"Two frogs fell into a can of cream,*
> *Or so I've heard it told;*
> *The sides of the can were shiny and steep,*
> *The cream was deep and cold.*
> *'Oh, what's the use?' croaked number one.*
> *''Tis fate, no help's around.*
> *Good-bye, my friend! Good-bye, sad world!'*
> *And weeping still, he drowned.*

> *"But number two, of sterner stuff,*
> *Dog-paddled in surprise.*
> *The while he wiped his creamy face,*
> *And dried his creamy eyes.*
> *'I'll swim awhile at least,' he said,*
> *Or so I've heard he said;*
> *'It really wouldn't help the world,*
> *If one more frog were dead.'*
> *An hour or two he kicked and swam,*
> *Not once he stopped to mutter,*
> *But kicked and swam, and swam and kicked,*
> *Then hopped out, via butter!"*

I don't know who wrote this bit of doggerel, but it sounds very much like something the Chief himself might have composed. The little jingle helped Ken get through his troubled period. Yes, he had some up and down times. After only three months into his year's leave of absence, he accepted an invitation to pastor the little Adventist church in Azusa, California. He performed as a successful pastor in several churches through the years, earned his doctorate in Old Testament Studies, taught Bible at Newbold College in England and at La Sierra University in California, and finally "hopped out, via the butter" to join his brother Harold at the Voice of Prophecy as a researcher and writer for the broadcast. He had at last found his true niche in life and his dad had plenty of reason to be proud.

Richards shared in the excitement of our family when the television program *This Is Your Life* brought my Black "sister" from Africa. Alice Princess Siwundhla, and her husband and children, came to America in late 1956. Ralph Edwards put their life story on American TV, and made it possible for them to begin schooling at Oakwood College in Alabama.

As I sifted through his diaries during this time period, I came across a comical little episode that gives a glimpse of the kind of man H.M.S. was. It was an entry for February 13, 1957. "Mr. Thompson's dog is growing out of puppyhood and last eve and this a.m. came up under my north study window and had a hard attack of loud and troublesome barking. I did not want the habit to be permanent so went and took a hamburger—old and forsaken—and gave it to him judiciously. He now comes as a friend and has expectation in his eyes!"

Glendale Adventist Academy invited H.M.S. in June of 1957 to give the baccalaureate address for his youngest son's graduation. Teenage Jan had a compulsive desire to rent a sports car for graduation weekend to show off to his classmates. With Mother Mabel's help he rented a Ford Thunderbird, but amazed at all the red tape and big bucks it cost him, he vowed he would never do anything like that again.

Two weeks later Father participated in Kenneth's ordination at the Southern California camp meeting at Lynwood. The subject of his ordination sermon was "Ordained to Preach." The service ordained 11 ministers, but when the officiating ministers laid their hands on the candidates, the Chief made sure he was near Kenneth so he could lay his right hand on his son's head.

In May Richards had a sixth grandchild, Mary Patricia, born to Walt and GeGe. Grandma and Grandpa sandwiched a little vacation trip between our camp meeting appointments to visit Gold Beach, Oregon, to see the new baby in late June. Walt was doing family practice medicine in Gold Beach at the time. It was a great opportunity for Grandpa to get acquainted with 7-year-old Marshall, 6-year-old Lolo, and 4-year-old Betty Rae, as well as have his first look at Mary Patricia.

A few days later he was back on the road, traveling with the quartet to camp meetings again. Once in a while we would get stopped by the traffic police. Jerry Dill had the misfortune to be driving one August day in 1957. He was just cresting a hill in Kansas when he ran into a speed trap. The Kansas Highway Patrol caught him doing 40 mph in a 30 mph zone. At the bottom of the hill the old justice of the peace, dressed in bib overalls and with a power mower in the trunk of his car, was waiting to collect the money.

In late 1957 the Voice of Prophecy radio team attended a youth congress in Havana, Cuba. On the way, while we were in the Caribbean, we visited Puerto Rico, the Dominican Republic, Jamaica, and Haiti. Richards, ever the history enthusiast, was delighted that we were able to visit Cap Haitian and climb the mountain on donkey back to Black Emperor Henri Cristophe's Citadel fortress.

In Kingston, Jamaica, we met crowds of a size that we had never experienced before. At a big Saturday night meeting at the King George V racetrack, we were unable to get from our car to the large raised platform in the middle of the racetrack without the help of the police. It was quite a sight to see a couple big policemen grab 200+ lb. Bob Seamount and carry him on their shoulders out to the center of the track.

On December 16 we landed at the Havana airport. Our stay there was a delight. The people of Havana were warm and friendly, always ready to help the linguistically challenged North Americans of our group find their way around town.

One night I decided to take the streetcar home to the hotel from the Teatro Blanquita, the site of our youth congress. Instead of stopping at the hotel, I decided to go on around the loop and see the town. The conductor and motorman were kind and helpful, offering me coffee and doughnuts when they made their refreshment stops.

For a Friday evening meeting, the Chief preached and his old friend Henry Westphal translated for him. Westphal delighted us and the crowd by mimicking every gesture and inflection as he translated Richards' sermon into Spanish.

After the meetings in Havana, most of the group flew home so they could get there in time for Christmas. The last meeting in Havana had been on Saturday night, December 21.

Wayne Hooper had purchased a used Volkswagen in Miami, and asked me if I would drive with him back to California. Even though we figured it would mean we'd get home after Christmas, I agreed. We flew from Havana to Miami on December 22, then went from Miami to Tallahassee, Florida, on Sunday. Early Monday morning, at 4:00 a.m., we started out from Tallahassee, driving that little VW bug night and day. It would go only about 68 miles an hour, but it's amazing how many miles you can chew up if you keep driving and make your rest and refueling stops short. We reached my house in Glendale, California, at about 7:00 p.m. on Christmas Eve the next night—2,287 miles in 42 hours. I still have a hard time believing it, but we did it.

In June of 1958 the Voice of Prophecy attended the General Conference session at Cleveland, Ohio. It touched Richards' heart when he witnessed 20 individuals left without jobs when the nominating committee made their report. "Poor men!" he wrote in his diary. "I do hope Kenneth or Harold Junior can take over the *Voice of Prophecy* speaking when I have to step out. How soon the years have brought me to the 60s." He was already beginning to experience the withdrawal pains he would have when he would face his own retirement.

On the last day of the General Conference session, Harold, Jr., who was attending the meetings, received word that his wife had given birth to a daughter, Mary Margaret Elizabeth Richards.

After that General Conference session, H.M.S. was able for the first time to take Mabel, Jan, and Harold on a sightseeing trip to Valley Forge, Gettysburg, Philadelphia, New York, and other sites of national historic interest.

On the way west Harold couldn't wait any longer to see his wife and new little daughter, so he left the family at Hannibal, Missouri, and took a flight to Albuquerque. A few days later, Grandma and Grandpa arrived at Albuquerque to see little Mary Margaret Elizabeth, grandchild number seven on the Richards' family tree.

In September Ken's wife, Jackie, wrote that they were making a contribution to the family line of descendants, but it wouldn't be until March of the next year that she would inform the grandparents that she was having twins. They were born on March 31 while H.M.S. and Mabel were on a trip to England. They wouldn't see their eighth and ninth grandchildren, the only twins in the family, until May when they returned.

During the 1950s the Richards' sons and daughter had presented Grandpa and Grandma with eight grandchildren. Only Marshall had been born in the previous decade. The Chief was always happy when he was presiding like an Oriental monarch over his children and grandchildren.

On January 28, 1959, H.M.S. and Mabel left Los Angeles for London, England. He had been invited to hold a three-month series of meetings in the New Gallery Theater just off Piccadilly Circus. The flight from Los Angeles to London was his first time in a jet.

"What a thrilling experience," he wrote of the trip. "Safer than other planes. Don't have to warm up a jet engine. When someone asked the president of American Airlines about these jets, 'Are they silent?' he answered, 'Not exactly. The engines speak with authority!' "

Toward the end of that trip H.M.S. and his wife took a drive up to Scotland. Mabel soon learned the knack of driving on the left side of the road. While there they visited the Collins Bible Press that had printed the Bible with the H.M.S. Richards Bible Helps bound in the back. At Glasgow they stayed with an old Scottish friend named Logan, who lived just out of town. As they were getting ready to leave, Logan urged them to visit his son, who was a pastor in Blackburn. He phoned ahead to his son to expect H.M.S. and Mabel that evening.

All day they drove in rain and fog through the lake country of Scotland and northern England. They finally got to Blackburn, but as they looked for the address of Logan's son, they soon found that English street names frequently change without warning. Back and forth in the rain they searched for 70 Brownhill Road, stopping, making inquiries. Someone suggested, "Go to the pub. They'll be able to give you directions."

Soon they found the pub—it was a big one. They went in and met the wife of the publican. "Why yes," she said. "I can tell you where that street is. That street is named after me."

They started out again and figured they were just about there. A light streamed from the front door of a house just as though the occupants were waiting for them to arrive. But let Richards tell his own story as he related it to the Voice of Prophecy family later.

"We drove up and this young man came out. He looked exactly like this man as I remembered him. I hadn't seen him for 10 years I guess. I thought he was the son but I don't know who he thought we were, lost relatives maybe.

"I got out and introduced him to Mabel and we went in. We were in the house admiring the baby and everything, but after a while we began to sense that we didn't know these people and they didn't know us.

"I mentioned that we'd seen their in-laws that morning, how the mother was getting better, and I saw a blank look. Then I definitely knew something was wrong. He said something to the effect that his mother had died two years ago.

"Well, we soon figured out we didn't know each other and had a big laugh over it. But we made friends with those people. We found that the woman has a sister who lives in southern California and told them to come see us when they visited California.

"They helped us find Brother Logan's house which was just a few blocks away."

In August 1959 Richards passed his sixty-fifth-year milestone, and persuaded our Voice of Prophecy board to invite son Harold to the Voice of Prophecy to help with the heavy load of correspondence. The board reluctantly agreed. Some didn't think it would work to build what they called a "Richards dynasty," so they ended up extending an invitation to Harold for one year.

He arrived February 24, 1960, and took over much of the correspondence that had been such a heavy load for the Chief. Instead of one year, Harold's "temporary" visit to the Voice of Prophecy stretched to two years, then a lifetime. Harold, Jr., stayed on in full-time active service with the Voice of Prophecy for 30 more years before passing the torch as speaker-director to Lonnie Melashenko, and just as his father had done, continued actively assisting Lonnie even after retirement.

The next year would bring sorrow to Richards. The quartet that he had struggled so hard to put together 11 years before now began to come apart at the seams. It would bring him great grief, because he loved "his boys" almost as much as he did his own sons.

"HE MUST INCREASE, I MUST DECREASE"

In March the broadcast team went to Union College in Lincoln, Nebraska, to conduct a Week of Prayer. Harold, Jr., was with us there, and while his father preached twice a day to the college students, Harold held a Week of Prayer for the academy. It was the son's baptism into the Voice of Prophecy work.

In April of that year H.M.S. gave the sermon at Ventura Estates, a Seventh-day Adventist retirement home where his mother was living. As he preached, his mother sat in the audience, eagerly listening to her son's words. In his diary for that day, he tells that "in the middle of the sermon, Mother called out once, 'Not so fast.'" "Bless her dear heart," he said. In a week she would be 90 years old.

By 1960 our quartet had been singing together more than 11 years. It's not hard to figure out that after that long a time we started to get restive. We loved our work, but it was no longer the same challenge that it had been. Bob Seamount was beginning to devote more of his time and interest to flying, electronics, and other things. Wayne was having increasing trouble with his voice and had been hinting that he would like to retire from quartet work. Some young fellows who had sung in a good male quartet at Southern Missionary College had come to southern California, and I began to harmonize with them just for fun. Our old faithful quartet was imperceptibly drifting apart. The drift began to cause tensions among us that in time caused us to split up. It was a time bomb waiting to go off.

That summer, while on a camp meeting trip, we received a phone call in our motel in Pocatello, Idaho. It was from Andrews University, inviting H.M.S. Richards to give the commencement address on August 18, and also to receive an honorary doctoral degree from Andrews. He was gratified to be thus honored.

They say an honorary degree is not an "earned degree." In the case of H.M.S. Richards, that old saw couldn't have been further from the truth. His reading, his study, and his achievements had earned him a hundred degrees. In my view, no "earned degree" candidate in the history of the world had ever done nearly as much to merit an "earned" doctoral degree.

On August 18 at the Andrews University commencement and the occasion of receiving his own honorary degree, Richards spoke on the same topic he had used in his very first commencement address at Campion Academy, "The Worth of a Man."

On the way home from Michigan, the Chief and Mabel made a detour through Miami, Florida, to attend a week of radio/television meetings in a hotel at Miami Beach. When Richards reached California he recorded in his diary a bit of insignificant trivia that will help explain what kind of things fueled his imagination. The morning before boarding the plane in Miami, Richards took a dip in the Atlantic Ocean in front of the hotel.

"Six a.m. Went swimming in the Atlantic Ocean and took a drink of it. At 6:30 Mabel and I left for the airport. At 2:20 p.m. I waded in the Pacific Ocean and took a little drink from it. Coast to coast in half a day!"

In June of that year we attended a big youth congress in Atlantic

City, New Jersey. After it we drove to another appointment in New York City, and Richards tells in his diary of an incident that occurred on the road. He didn't often comment on our quartet conflicts, but this one must have been a dandy.

"The boys had a hard argument in the car on the way here. All seemed to blame Bob Edwards (Wayne not much), then Wayne and Bob Seamount and Dill. They have never done better for God and the devil can't stand it. I prayed as they talked and they slowly cooled and we met at 5:00 p.m. in my room and prayed and had a good service that evening."

I have tried to probe into my memory to figure out what we were arguing about, but I can't bring it back. I know some of us had stayed up all night with Milt Carlson of the advertising agency at the Atlantic City Auditorium, editing the program we had put on in the big hall the night before. The finished and edited tape of the program had to be on the airplane early in the morning to get it back to Los Angeles in time to air on the network Sunday. Our argument was probably an outgrowth of the stress and tension of preparing that program. Though I can't remember why their anger focused on me, I have no doubt that I had done or said something to merit it.

In itself that conflict in the car wasn't that important, but it was symptomatic of what had already begun to happen to us. It signaled the beginning of the end for a quartet that had been together for 12 long years. Many more years than we had thought we would sing together. We tried to weather the storm and capture the old magic, but nothing seemed to work. Instead we continued to drift apart and lost the old camaraderie we had enjoyed for so many years.

A few months later, in January of 1961, Richards wrote in his diary that the quartet had decided to make a change, bringing in John Thurber as second tenor. Bob Seamount stayed on as recording technician in our studios. Later he would become a pastor in the state of Washington, then Texas, and finally received a call to the Peruvian jungles of South America. He was able, during his mission service, to indulge his love for flying by ferrying a number of airplanes from the United States to mission fields in Asia and Africa.

Thus an era came to an end. No King's Heralds quartet has come close to equaling our record of longevity.

On the first day we sang with John Thurber, the Chief wrote in his diary: "Quartet and I to San Diego to take part in a banquet for chaplains of the armed forces. Quartet sang for the first time in public with the new man, John Thurber, as 2nd Tenor. They did well, of course, but I missed dear Bob—the years cannot be brushed away."

But even that change in the quartet didn't give us the infusion of new life we had hoped for. By the end of 1961, after a seven-week singing tour to visit our Portuguese and Spanish *Voice of Prophecy* programs in South America, we made an even more drastic change in the quartet. Wayne, by his own choice, retired from singing, but stayed on with the Voice of Prophecy as arranger and music director. Jerry accepted an invitation to go to Hawaii as a pastor. Jack Veazey and Jim McClintock joined John and me in the quartet.

Musically, it was a great combination. The three other singers, Jim, John, and Jack, had sung together for years in a college quartet at Southern Missionary College in Tennessee. Even though I was the senior member of the King's Heralds, a veteran of 14 years, I was now the new member in this quartet. It was a combination that would last for five years until John decided to leave the quartet and begin to work as a youth leader in Texas.

Even though the Chief came to love the new fellows in the quartet, he mourned the loss of his "boys" from the old one, Jerry Dill and Bob Seamount. Richards hated to see Bob and Jerry go. "I love Jerry," he wrote. "He is more like a son to me than any of the others."

June 1961 Jan, Richards' youngest son, graduated from La Sierra College. Elder E. E. Beach, formerly president of the Southern European Division of Seventh-day Adventists, presented the commencement address. It disappointed Richards that Beach read his sermon. "He does much better when he is a 'free' speaker," he commented. "How will it be without a boy at La Sierra?" he mourned. It had been 14 years since Harold had enrolled as a freshman and 18 years since Virginia had left the nest for college. Now the last of the flock had finished college.

As we traveled, Richards was not only our team minister, but our tutor and historical tour guide. That summer, on the way back west from the New York camp meeting, he guided us to Hill Cumorah in New York, where Mormon founder Joseph Smith claimed to have seen the vision of the golden plates and the angel Moroni. As I mentioned before, Richards loved to read about the history of the Mormon Church and had one of the most extensive libraries of Mormon literature in the United States. From Hill Cumorah we drove by Joseph Smith's old homestead where the "sacred spectacles" were on display. Joseph Smith claimed the golden tablets had been written in Egyptian hieroglyphics, and he could read and translate them only when he was wearing the "sacred spectacles."

That summer of 1961 several of the families of the quartet met them at the conclusion of camp meeting at Lacombe, Alberta, in Canada, intending to vacation in beautiful Banff and Jasper National parks, leaving the Chief and me to "bach it" alone for a few days. At that time he introduced me to a "bachelor's special" breakfast he and A. E. Milner, his old minister buddy from Canada days, had invented to sustain themselves during the days when Mabel was away taking care of her mother in Colorado. Here's his recipe in his own words: "Start with one quart of milk in a pan. When it starts to boil put in six shredded wheat biscuits and break into it four eggs, adding butter and salt to taste. Cook slowly. Eat with gusto." We did.

In the fall H.M.S. and Mabel Richards sent Jan off to Andrews University. It was a poignant moment for the Chief to see his youngest son sail off into the blue. "Mabel, Marcia [Jan's girlfriend], and I were there when the plane rose into the air. I felt desolate. He and I are so close—all the other children have been away with their own homes for years and he is the last. Our love and prayers go with them all, and now with him."

Richards was excited when Colonel John Glenn circled the

earth in a space capsule three times early in 1962. He was always interested in the latest advances in science.

On April 4, 1962, Harold and Mabel saw the youngest of the Richards clan married. Jan and Marcia Miracle had the ceremony at the Little Church of the Hills in Forest Lawn, Hollywood Hills. The Chief performed the ceremony; Kenneth was best man. "Mabel looked beautiful in her new green dress and shoes," Richards confided that evening in his diary. The only flaw in the day was that neither Harold, Jr., nor his wife, Mary, could attend. Harold had left the week before to hold three weeks of meetings in Seattle and Portland, and Mary had the measles.

No biography about Richards would be complete without acknowledging his impatience with committee meetings. Here are a few examples of references to such committees in his diary:

"January 17, 1963 Thursday. Publicity committees are always a trial to me. We must have these committees, but I like to be somewhere else."

"May 19, 1963 Sunday. Another Public Relations committee that lasted till nearly 6 p.m. How utterly tiresome to me! A lot of drudgery which must be done, but wearies me beyond words."

"April 28, 1964 Tuesday. All afternoon at PR Committee. How I do weary of the endless talk—but without it we could not do the work."

"September 23, 1964 Wednesday. From 2 p.m. to 5:30 p.m. in our tedious publicity committee. Of course it's necessary, like lots of other tedious jobs. Lots of talk, talk, talk, but a consensus usually slowly appears!"

When he was bored, Richards usually doodled, drawing fortifications, military battlefields, lines of advance for the army units. In some ways he seems to have been a frustrated general. But he was also an armchair poet. After one such committee meeting Wayne Hooper picked up a slip of paper Richards had dropped to the floor. On it were these words:

"No man is modern till he's fit
In some committee room to sit,
And sit and sit and sit and sit,
And toss things back and forth a bit.

"With clock hands moving round and round
As notes and arguments abound,
The weary chairman stands his ground,
But disappears in waves of sound.

"Tick tock! Honk Honk! Ding dong bell!
Scraps of agenda chewed up well!
Wise and otherwise things to tell,
Sonorous, dolorous, or pell mell!

"Tempus fugit! Let him fly!
Day is dying! Let him die!
Ah! We're rolling now in high!
Au revoir! Farewell! Good-bye!"

April of 1964 Kenneth phoned that Dr. Hirsch of Columbia Union College had invited him to teach at Newbold College in England. Kenneth left for London in August for a two-year term, with Jackie and the boys following in October.

In May of 1965 the two mother/grandmothers, Mabel and Goldie Hitron (Jackie's mother), flew to London to see Kenneth, Jackie, and the twins. That July Kenneth was scheduled to attend some education meetings in Norway, and H.M.S. couldn't stand it when Mabel was seeing his children and grandchildren without him, so he arranged himself a little vacation. Kenneth met him in Oslo, Norway, where the son was attending the educational conference. From Oslo they drove out to the Eyrefjord school, the site of the meetings. The fresh Scandinavian air must have had a beneficial effect on Richards' health. He reported that he slept till nearly noon.

"Best sleep I have had in a long time," he reported.

Earlier the Northern European Division had invited him to attend a youth congress in Helsinki, Finland, but the General Conference travel planning committee had disapproved of it. The committee acted as a watchdog to keep General Conference employees from overexuberance in making travel plans. But since Richards was already in Norway, he decided to be naughty and attend the congress in Helsinki despite the frown of the General Conference. In his diary he betrayed some feelings of guilt. "What will the men say? The president of the General Conference and Elder Murray wrote that I was not to go there, even though I had been repeatedly invited by Northern Europe. But since I am here on my own and on vacation, they may not mind—I hope!"

Mabel was able to go with him there, and after they returned to England, the Chief flew on home to California, while Mabel spread her own wings for a change and flew off to Australia and New Guinea and other points east. It must have been a strange feeling for both of them. Their roles had now reversed. Instead of her seeing him off on some far-flung trek, she would go and leave him standing at the gate.

At midnight, December 31, 1965, H.M.S. launched one of our Voice of Prophecy Bible reading marathons. He began the marathon by reading in Genesis at the stroke of 12:00. We continued reading the Bible aloud nonstop, with volunteers taking turns night and day for the next 84 hours and 35 minutes. At 12:35 p.m., Tuesday, the Chief finished the last verse of the last chapter of Revelation.

All of us who worked with him would say that the Chief was even-tempered and courteous. On rare occasions, he slipped, however. He never requested an unlisted telephone number, and since he was such a high-profile figure in the church, he sometimes received calls from thoughtless people. At 3:30 one morning (no doubt from someone in an Eastern time zone) he answered the insistent ringing of the telephone only to hear a woman's voice ask him, "What do you think of Medicare?"

"I think it's just fine," he said, hung up, and took the phone off the hook.

I think he might be forgiven for that.

An example of how Richards responded to a young man with a problem we can illustrate by another incident that happened in 1966.

Ed Khanoyan was an Adventist soldier recently transferred from Fort Sam Houston in San Antonio to Frederick, Maryland. At Fort Sam the top sergeant had given him a hard time every time he requested release from duty on Sabbath. Apparently another "Adventist" young man stationed in Fort Sam had caved in to pressure from his officers, and Ed's sergeant wanted to find out if the soldier was sincere or just goldbricking. Ed finally convinced his sergeant he was on the level, and from that time on had no more trouble in the military.

When I say Ed was an Adventist, I mean he was one of those young men who had been born into an Adventist family, but had not yet had a personal experience with the Lord. His mother had urged and coaxed, but as a typical rebellious youth, he had resisted her pressure to be baptized.

Through the influence of his top sergeant at Fort Sam Houston (who had become his friend), Ed received a transfer to the White Coats program near Washington, D.C. Priscilla, his Baptist girlfriend, would often go to Adventist meetings with him in the Washington area, but she had decided that Ed should become a Baptist, and Ed was equally determined that he would not. They often had hot arguments about religion, especially about the Sabbath.

One night as Ed and Priscilla attended an Adventist evangelistic meeting in Baltimore, evangelist Dick Barron made a call for his hearers to accept the Lord. The Holy Spirit moved on the young man's heart that night. He could hardly wait for Dick to finish so he could go forward and give his heart to the Lord, but even then he held off on committing to baptism. He wanted his mother to be able to be there when he took that important step, since she had been so persistent in her appeals to him about it.

In the meantime a personal crisis had arisen. Ed and Priscilla had become engaged, but that raised problems with her parents who were committed Baptists. They knew Ed and respected him, but were not at all sure they wanted their daughter to be married to an Adventist, a religious group they considered to be a cult. This created tension between Ed and Priscilla, between Priscilla and her parents, and between Ed and Priscilla's parents.

The stress finally became so great that he sought and obtained an eight-day pass from his top sergeant so he could try to resolve things. He flew to Southern California, thinking some time with his parents might give him some temporary relief from his problem, and some insight on how to solve it. That's where H.M.S. Richards entered the picture.

One day, as Ed was walking by the Voice of Prophecy office on Chevy Chase in Glendale, on an impulse he walked in, went up the stairs, and presented himself to Darlene, H.M.S. Richards' secretary.

"Do you have an appointment?" she asked.

"No, I'm a soldier on a short leave. I thought I might be able to take a few minutes of Elder Richards' time. Maybe he can help me with a personal problem."

The sincere young soldier standing patiently before her in his military uniform aroused Darlene's sympathy. "Elder Richards isn't here right now, but you might catch him up at the Glendale Adventist Hospital cafeteria. He's meeting there with a committee of ministers over lunch."

Ed found him just as he was walking through the cafeteria line, picking up his food. He briefly stated why he was there and asked Richards if he could give him just a few minutes of his time. H.M.S. could have told the young soldier that he was busy and to return later, but that wasn't his style. Instead he asked Ed to walk along with him as he passed through line and tell him his problem.

As they got to the end of the line, Richards put down his tray and turned to face Ed. "Why can't those Baptists realize that we Adventists read our Bibles, too?" he said. Then he called the group of fellow ministers over to the middle of the cafeteria. There they

290

joined hands, forming a circle around the troubled young soldier. While Richards prayed, everything and everyone came to a standstill in the hospital cafeteria. The people bustling through line, the servers behind the serving deck, the checkers at the cash registers—all stopped and bowed their heads and listened as Elder Richards asked the Lord to help Ed with his problems, softening the hearts of all concerned.

It was with a light heart that Ed flew back to Washington. Miraculously, everything and everyone seemed changed from that moment on. Ed was less militant and prickly in his religious attitude toward Priscilla and her parents, and this seemed to affect everyone in a positive way. They all came to sense that though they disagreed on some points of doctrine, they all loved the same Lord. You can never convince Ed or Priscilla that Richards' prayer didn't have a lot to do with that.

Priscilla was baptized soon after that, and she and Ed were married. When Priscilla's father died a few years later, her dedicated Baptist mother lived happily in the home of her daughter and son-in-law until her own death 17 years later.

Early in June of 1966 Richards received word from Washington, D.C., that his old friend Francis D. Nichol had died suddenly of a heart attack. "We need him so much! 'How are the mighty fallen, and the weapons of war perished!'"

On the way south from camp meeting in South Dakota that same month we stopped in Iowa at "The Little Brown Church" that had inspired the popular gospel song. The quartet, in a crowd of tourists, sang the song from the platform.

Later in the month, while our radio group was in Detroit, Michigan, attending the General Conference session, Richards received news from home that was not unexpected, but was saddening nevertheless. That evening he wrote in his diary:

"Today my dearest mother died. She fell asleep in Christ early today. What can I say, but that I feel a loneliness I cannot explain. For over 71 years she has prayed for me. Few have a mother's prayers that long. How wonderful when she and father will be reunited in a land where all our heavenly dreams come true!"

Five years before he had gone out to Ventura Estates to visit his mother. At that time she thought she had had a dream that she would die that day. "A white-robed lovely-faced person last evening told me I would pass away within 24 hours," she reported to her son. A few days later she told him she thought she might have 10 days to live. God gave her five more years.

On Friday, June 17, he flew home to his mother's funeral. Elder David Olsen preached the funeral sermon in a little funeral chapel in Thousand Oaks, California. Son Jan read Psalms 90 and 91. Mother Richards was buried next to her husband in Montecito, the little memorial park in Loma Linda.

A few days later Richards wrote a letter to friends and relatives announcing his mother's death.

> *"Dear Ones—relatives and friends:*
>
> *"I am writing this to bring you the sad news that my dear Mother, Berta Sylvester Richards, died on Wednesday morning, June 15, about 7 o'clock. She had reached her 96th birthday on April 25. Although she had been confined to her bed most of the time for the past several years, she had been happy, full of smiles and joy all the time. She was the light of Ventura Estates. She loved everybody. She was able to read most of the time until the last two or three weeks.*
>
> *"About seven weeks ago she had a light stroke. She was not paralyzed, but could not think quickly and it was hard for her to speak. The last two or three days of her life it was difficult and finally impossible to eat or drink.*
>
> *"We all prayed that she would not have any pain, and this prayer was answered. Every time we asked her if she had any pain, she said, 'No.' I said good-bye to her a little over a week before and went to attend camp meetings and our world General Conference Session in Detroit, Michigan. My wife, Mabel, had visited her the night before her death. She did not believe that Mother knew her. Mabel rubbed her back to relax her, and she said her body was in fine condition, no bed sores.*

The nurses had done their work perfectly. Her room was across the hall from the nurses' desk, so they could watch her all the time. She loved the nurses and they loved her. They tried to feed her with a tube, but she said, 'Just let me sleep.' They obeyed her will, and she went to sleep. When the nurse came back half an hour later, she was still asleep—not to waken until the morning of the glorious resurrection, when all God's people will meet and greet one another again.

"She loved all her relatives and dear friends so much. I know she received many letters that were not answered. We do appreciate so much the kind letters that were sent to her and the many prayers offered in her behalf.

"The funeral service was held at the Griffin Mortuary at Thousand Oaks, California, which is about three miles from Ventura Estates where she had made her home, so that those living at Ventura Estates could attend. Then we had a short service at the grave side at Loma Linda, California, in Montecito Memorial Park. Many friends who have known Mother for years attended. She sleeps by Father's side there. They had been married over 62 years at the time of his death.

"Anything I have been able to do in the ministry and my world radio work, Mother should get most of the credit, for she encouraged me, prayed for me daily and sometimes almost hourly. In her sweet and gracious life I saw acted out in this world the very wonderful love of the Saviour who came to this world to seek and to save the lost. I knew it must be true, for I saw it in my mother's life. And my prayer today is, 'Thank You, Lord, for giving me such a mother.'

"God bless all you dear ones. May we all meet again some day in that land where dreams come true.

> *"With love,*
> *"H.M.S. Richards"*

Anyone who knew H.M.S. Richards was keenly aware of his strong devotion to his mother. He wrote the long-time favorite poem about his memories of "When Mother Tucks Me In," which we quoted earlier in this book. Another eight-line poem expresses the reverence he held for her.

"Besides those names of Sacred Writ,
    Immortalized in hymn and prayer,
Whose solemn syllables resound
    In holy places everywhere,
There is a human name I know,
    And love it as we love no other
From cradle days to latest breath,
    For that blessed name is Mother."

That summer when we visited the camp meeting in Lacombe, Alberta, we had an unusual experience. A woman attending the camp meeting, the wife of a church member, had as a young girl been raised in London by parents who were devil worshipers. The coven met regularly in a building near Piccadilly Circus at 3:00 a.m. four floors underground. The father had given the girl to Satan when she was a child. During all the succeeding years demons had troubled the woman.

The night before we arrived, a group of the ministers had met at the invitation of the family to pray for the woman's freedom from the evil spirits. During their prayer a strange guttural voice came from the throat of the woman, ordering, "Leave us alone. We're comfortable here!" The woman tried at the ministers' urging to say, "Dear Jesus, help me." She would try, but all she could say was, "Dear _____, help me! Dear _____, help me." She couldn't get the name of Jesus to come from her lips.

Finally, after 30 minutes of prayer and encouragement, those with her at last heard her whisper, "Lord Jesus, help me!" She found relief instantly.

In September Richards received news that his physician friend Clifford Anderson had cancer of the brain. Clifford was the brother of Elder Roy Allen Anderson. Even though Dr. Anderson went to the Mayo Clinic in Rochester, Minnesota, he lived only a few more months, dying June 2, 1967.

On Christmas Day, 1966, a crowd of 12,000 helped us celebrate the twenty-fifth anniversary of the *Voice of Prophecy* as a national broadcast in the Long Beach, California, Arena. The original Lone Star Quartet was there, even though first tenor Louis Crane had to come by ambulance. The quartet tremulously sang a few bars to the acclaim and admiration of the audience. Every member and former member of the King's Heralds quartet attended except for Elwyn Ardourel, a dentist in Denver, and Ralph Simpson, who had recently died.

In 1967 John Thurber decided to leave the quartet to begin working with young people in Texas. Jerry Patton, from Lincoln, Nebraska, took his place.

During July of the same year physicians diagnosed my wife, Irene, with lymphosarcoma. None of the doctors gave us any hope of a cure. I explained to the Chief that I thought I should probably leave the quartet because I knew I would need to spend more time at home with my family. The Chief urged that I postpone any decision for the time being. He felt I should not make such an important decision while under such pressure.

My wife died on September 25, 1967. Richards was in London, finishing up a trip he had led to the Holy Land. When he got word of Irene's death, he took the next flight to Los Angeles so that he might honor my request to preach her funeral sermon in the Eagle Rock Seventh-day Adventist Church. He took his theme from the last chapter of the book of Ruth, "They Two Did Build the House of Israel."

Richards loved his children and grandchildren, even when they seemed to be spiritually confused. In late November he was at La Sierra College to speak. Afterward a little Asian-American girl came to him and asked, "Is Marshall Cason your grandson?" When he acknowledged that he was, she started to tell something that was a great trouble to her. He answered that he knew something of Marshall's problem. She smiled and left.

"Poor Marshall," Richards wrote in his diary. "What can we do for him but pray? He is very young—knows very little of the Bible or Christianity or church history or comparative religion. Like most boys his age he is confused and at sea."

Actually Marshall was an avid scholar and very knowledgeable about Christianity, as well as several Oriental religions. What Richards and the family did not know at the time was that Marshall was gay, and because of that he had been a troubled and confused young man all during his growing up years. He suffered greatly from feelings of guilt, unworthiness, and rejection. When baptized at the age of 14, he thought this would change things for him, but of course it didn't. Although he had gone to his academy principal for help, the sincere minister didn't know how to deal with the problem and simply told Marshall how wicked and sinful he was.

Finally Marshall gave up on Christianity, but Christ hadn't given up on him. Like Francis Thompson's "The Hound of Heaven," Jesus pursued the young man wherever he went "with unhurrying chase . . . And unperturbed pace . . . Deliberate speed, majestic instancy."

After graduating from college, Marshall wandered around the world and visited all the places he had heard about when sitting on his grandfather's lap as a little boy. Among other places he went to England, Europe, the Middle East, and Southeast Asia, and he worked in Indonesia and Australia. After several years he returned home and worked in the United States, periodically returning to Australia for special jobs.

His mother, Virginia, confided to her father of her months and years of care and sorrow over Marshall. Finally, in desperation, she had prayed alone and then put her burden in the Lord's hands. When she did this, a mighty peace came over her heart, even while she watched him live a lifestyle that brought sorrow to her heart.

About 10 years after the death of his grandfather, Marshall became ill with the last stages of AIDS. During his final months of life his mother remained at his side night and day, almost 24 hours a day.

He had often talked almost flippantly of his death, but in the final stage he called his father on the phone and said, "Dad, they tell me I'm dying, and I don't want to die." "Marshall," his father said, "we can all be together again, you, and Betty Rae, and Grandpa and the whole family. You don't have to do anything. All you have to do is want it."

"I want it, Dad."

Virginia then came on the line and said, "Marshall, some day we'll all gather around the big tree together."

"What tree, Mom?"

"Oh, I mean the big tree that will spread over the river of life in the New Jerusalem, Marshall, right next to the throne of God. Betty Rae will be there. Grandpa will be there and will be so happy to see you."

"I'll be there, Mom."

Just a few days later Marshall went to sleep peacefully, with the assurance that when Jesus comes, He'll call out, "Wake up, Marshall. It's time to get up. All your family is waiting for you, and Jesus is here, too."

As the 1960s drew to a close, new things began to appear on the Voice of Prophecy's horizon. In January 1969 the local Voice of Prophecy board voted to recommend to the general board that H.M.S. Richards, Jr., take over as *Voice of Prophecy* speaker, and his father would be his helper as he was able. What a joy it was to Father to see his son step into his footsteps.

On April 2, 1969, the vote came. Not only was Harold to take over as speaker-director, but Gillis would retire and a new manager of the Voice of Prophecy elected. The board voted Al Munson in by a majority vote. Though Richards was apprehensive, Munson proved himself an able leader. The Voice of Prophecy prospered under his direction. The April 2 board meeting introduced one note of discord, though. Both Richards' name and the name of I. E. Gillis, the Voice of Prophecy manager, appeared on the list to be retired. As father and son sat side by side in the Voice of Prophecy board meeting, Harold pointed out the item on the agenda:

"SUSTENTATION [retirement] REQUEST—H.M.S. RICHARDS.

"The board recognized the outstanding contribution of Elder Richards, not only to The Voice of Prophecy, but also to the church as a whole. His preaching, his fine example of Christian living, his dedication and his untiring efforts to advance the message of truth helped to build The Voice of Prophecy into a worldwide program of soul winning. It was voted that a statement of appreciation be made part of the minutes. (RRB [R. R. Bietz]).

"The Chairman indicated that H.M.S. Richards desires to go on sustentation as of July 1, 1969."

"Did you know about this?" Harold, Jr., asked.

"No."

The son started to get up and object to the item, but his father pulled him down, not wanting to make waves.

Later he would say, "Who gave him this information? Not I. I had no intimation in the least that this 'request' was to be presented. The whole proceeding was a shock to me."

For some reason, probably by accident rather than design, no one had mentioned it to Richards. Even though he was delighted to see his son step into his role, and even though he was almost 75 years old, he felt a little hurt to be unceremoniously put on the shelf without anyone advising him ahead of time that it would be on the agenda. In his diary for the day Richards noted, "Brother Gillis and my name on agenda for sustentation. He moved his name and I moved mine. Who put my name there? Not a word to me before I saw it."

By the next night the feelings of pain seemed to have seeped away. He was in Lodi with his son for a big revival meeting. In his diary he said: "I made a call and Harold Jr. took up when I left off. How wonderful to be with him. My son, our first boy! Just a few days ago he was little and loved stories in the story chair! And now he is a mighty preacher of the glorious gospel of the blessed God! What greater joy could I have on earth!"

Many things had happened in the previous 15 years, some happy, some sad. Sons had graduated from college. He had seen all three sons married. All his grandchildren had been born. His beloved mother and father had gone to sleep in Jesus. The quartet that had become extended family to him had split up, old members like sons going off to other work, new members adopted into his family.

He had seen the *Voice of Prophecy,* the beloved work of his life, expand around the world.

Toward the end of the 1960s Richards quoted a poem sent to him that had touched his heart:

> "Dear Master, as the old year dieth soon,
>   Take Thou my harp;
> And prove if any strings be out of tune,
>   Or flat or sharp.
>
> "Correct Thou, Lord, for me
>   What ringeth hard to Thee,
> That heart and life may sing
>   The new year long."

"This poem was sent to the Voice of Prophecy by someone with initials D. C., but who is D. C.?" he wrote. It so impressed him that he copied it on December 31 several years in a row.

Then on January 1, he copied this verse, author unknown:

> "A little while for patient vigil keeping,
>   To face the stern, to wrestle with the strong;
> A little while to sow the seed with weeping,
>   Then bind the sheaves and sing the harvest song."

But as the 1960s came grinding to a close, a cloud appeared on the horizon that would trouble his declining years. A problem that he called the "amalgamation" of media ministries. Was it a sign of progress or a step that would lead his beloved Voice of Prophecy into oblivion? Only time would tell.

AMALGAMATION

From the first, when the Voice of Prophecy became a General Conference institution, it had a split organization. The ministry, which included sermon selection, preparation, and delivery, was headed by Richards. Director and speaker of the program, he was appointed by the General Conference Fall Council in session. Since the quartet was also hired by the Voice of Prophecy general board under the direction of the General Conference, we were coworkers with Richards, functioning under General Conference rules and policy and subject to his leadership and direction.

The manager, also appointed by the General Conference Fall Council in session, headed the business end of the Voice of Prophecy. He had charge of personnel management, hiring and firing, fund-raising and other business matters and expenses, the Bible School, the care and handling of the mail, public relations, and promotion and advertising. A house board or house committee assisted the manager in the mechanics of keeping his finger on the pulse of the business operation.

A committee under the direction of the

Voice of Prophecy local board and general board purchased radio time on networks and independent stations. The hired advertising agency took care of the mechanics of such time buying.

This two-headed management team might not seem to be a workable arrangement, but during all the years between 1942 and 1969, with a few exceptions, it functioned without a hitch. Richards did his job of preparing and delivering sermons for the broadcast. The quartet, under Richards' beneficent oversight, selected and prepared music for the broadcast, and with Richards and the associate speaker, made public appearances to promote the ministry. The manager, with consultation and suggestions from Richards, did his part in raising the funds to keep the broadcast and the office running smoothly.

Before Gillis retired as manager and Richards retired as speaker-director, Gillis drew up an organizational chart that modified the arrangement. Since Harold, Jr., the new speaker-director was young and with less experience and clout than his father, Gillis placed the speaker-director under the manager, rather than under the General Conference Radio Department. When Richards noticed this in the minutes of the meetings, he objected.

"I do not accept the outline of our Voice of Prophecy organization as drawn up by Brother Gillis," he wrote. "I was Director and Speaker from the first and was elected or appointed by the Fall Council of General Conference in session the same as he. Therefore, I am not under or less in authority than the manager. If Harold accepts the suggested subservience to the manager, he will soon not be able to work as we have in the past. This should be cleared up soon."

A few days later he had a one-and-a-half-hour talk with Al Munson, the incoming Voice of Prophecy manager. It seems to have cleared up some of the misunderstanding, but it presaged a new set of operating rules that would drastically change the way the Voice of Prophecy would be able to operate in future years. But that was a problem yet to come.

In May of 1969 Richards preached at the funeral of Waldo Crane, second tenor of the Lone Star Four quartet. Waldo had been ill for some time. A few days later Cal Gepford, a nephew of Waldo and an employee in the Voice of Prophecy press, died of a brain tumor. For years Cal had suffered terrible headaches, but the doctors he consulted could find nothing. Every Voice of Prophecy employee held a special place in the Chief's heart.

Even though Richards was relieved to have Harold take over as director and speaker for the broadcast, yet when the day actually came it was stressful. In his diary he wrote on June 30, 1969: "My last day as Director of the Voice of Prophecy. This day is a heavy one for me. The years since we started the Voice of Prophecy seem a dream over all too soon, and I feel that I should work now the same as ever."

And he did work, assisting his son, just as his son had assisted him during the past nine years. But at 75 he was more frail and subject to accidents than when he was younger. That summer, when we were visiting the Florida camp meeting, Richards walked across the parking lot of the motel to get a few things at the supermarket when it began to rain. In his hurry to keep from getting wet, he tripped over a concrete parking block and hit his head. Jim McClintock, Jack Veazey, and I drove him to the emergency room to get him patched up. Fortunately, he hadn't broken anything, not even his glasses. It would have been a great tragedy if he had damaged his only good eye in the accident.

That same day he got a Father's Day card from Harold that said, "If you hear strange sounds behind you, it is me trying to follow in your footsteps."

He was beginning to sense his own frailty. Just before his birthday he had his hearing tested, and discovered to his shock that he had lost 80 percent of his hearing.

That summer I was trying to be a father, mother, and a quartet member all at the same time. My two younger children, Chuck and Connie, ages 13 and 11, were out of school, so we packed our little blue VW bug with luggage and camping gear and did our best to follow along behind the Voice of Prophecy and keep up with them as they visited camp meetings and other appointments.

Even though Richards was almost 75 years old, he still had a keen interest in what was happening in the world around him. On July 16 he recorded in his diary: "Apollo moon flight started. They hope to land on the moon. What a fantastic time to live. Daniel 12:4."

And on Sunday: "Man on the moon today. 'A small step for man, a great leap for mankind.'"

Richards always maintained close touch with his old evangelistic team members. In August he and Mabel drove down to visit old Uncle Henry de Fluiter. Uncle Henry had worked with him since Canada days, nearly 50 years in all. He had even been around Campion when Richards was a boy in school. When Richards visited Uncle Henry in the hospital, he asked why De Fluiter wasn't using a cane. "If I use a cane, people will think I'm old," Uncle Henry retorted. "I'm not old. I'm only 97."

Although Uncle Henry may have been trying to show the world he wasn't old, he didn't live much longer. He fell asleep in Jesus a few months later in March of 1970. On the day of De Fluiter's funeral Richards wrote: "A gloomy day for me. Dear Uncle Henry de Fluiter, my comrade in so many evangelistic campaigns and in my memory from boyhood in Colorado."

In November of 1969 I requested a six-month sabbatical from the quartet. The stress of traveling and trying to take care of my teenagers at home was causing a lot of turmoil in my life. Richards agreed to my time off. I didn't know until later when I researched his diary that Richards didn't think it would solve the problem, and he was right. The day before I began my sabbatical, he graciously wrote, "No one ever can take his place. How he needs a good, loving wife in his home!" A couple years later God brought Sharon Bullard into my life. She became a loving wife and a compassionate mother to my four children.

On April 14, 1970, H.M.S. and Mabel celebrated their fiftieth anniversary in Athens, Greece. Virginia and Walt Cason had been organizing and conducting tours of Bible lands with him as the mentor and leader of the group. They always had a waiting list of H.M.S.

Richards fans who were eager to follow him in the footsteps of Jesus and the apostle Paul on such Bible land tours.

In his diary for that day he wrote: "It seems only a little while ago. What has happened to the years! Thank the Lord for the wonderful gift of the right wife! And thank you, sweetheart, for your love since April 14, 1920, at 8 p.m. at Harmony Corners. The good friends of our tour group gave us a big party in Athens."

The next month he assisted in two funerals on successive days. On May 11 Lon Metcalfe, our former quartet coach, was buried. The next day Richards grieved with his old comrade at arms, as Reuben Nightingale laid his wife, Pauline, to rest. Richards had married Reuben and Pauline in his evangelistic tabernacle in South Gate in 1933. The entire evangelistic audience had enthusiastically brought them gifts. When I was working with Nightingale in evangelism in Florida 14 years later, Reuben was still commenting about the mountain of wedding gifts he and Pauline had received in the tabernacle wedding.

As Richards grew older, funerals of old friends and family seemed to come with increasing frequency. In November the wife of Harold Schultz, our Voice of Prophecy printshop manager, died. A few days later Richards received word that his minister friend Arthur S. Maxwell had gone to his rest. "Sad, sad, sad news," he wrote. "A. S. Maxwell died last night. He is younger than I." He was becoming more aware of his own mortality.

In December he attended the funeral of Roy F. Cottrell, co-worker in the early days of evangelism in southern California, and a few days later that of Martha Lovell, sister of John Turner, his co-worker from Colorado days. For many years Martha had been supervisor of the Voice of Prophecy Junior Bible School.

But the heaviest blow came when his own brother, Kenneth, died in late 1971. "A phone call from David in Silver Spring informed me that my only brother, Kenneth, had just died. Now I am alone. Father, Mother, and all before them have died and the sweep of the days moves over us, the relentless advancing of eternity envelops all."

Kenneth's service took place in the Sligo Seventh-day Adventist

Church in Takoma Park, Maryland, on November 29, 1971, a little more than 25 years after he had returned to Jesus in that very place.

The most troubling event of Richards' later years was the move of the Voice of Prophecy from Glendale to Thousand Oaks. In the fall of 1970 Elders Robert Pierson and Neal Wilson began to urge the merger of the Voice of Prophecy, Faith for Today, and It Is Written into one big Adventist Media Center complex located on a single campus. Richards began to hear the first rumblings of it in September.

For years the General Conference had wrestled with the problems of keeping the three media organizations going. The Voice of Prophecy at the time was healthy financially, needing only about a 10 percent subsidy to keep broadcasts and Bible school going and advancing. The television media were more costly and required more General Conference support. The argument given initially was that such a move would save money. The church leadership promised each ministry that it could operate its own program just as before, but the Media Center would provide support services for all—printing, computer, treasury, and administration. In his diary for September 11, 1970, Richards prophesied what he thought would actually happen: 1. The finances would drop. 2. Freedom for all would end. 3. No administrator can lead one, much less three evangelistic approaches. A few days later he added: "I fear such an eggnog. It will lead to confused and hard feelings and partial or complete failure as a soul winning venture, and in the long run will cost more than all three cost now. O, Lord, deliver us from this latest attack by good and well meaning brethren on the Voice of Prophecy and others."

In October H.M.S. Richards, Jr., went to Washington, D.C., for the meeting on the proposed "amalgamation," as he had begun to label it. "May the Lord defend us!" Richards wrote. "We must be torn up, sell out to provide money for this strange three-headed thing to eat money and cause endless problems."

The consultations and plans continued. In March 1971 the Chief attended a meeting that discussed the planned consolidation. "They said it will save money. I urged them not to do so. We all kept our cool and parted with prayer."

The following April Richards received a letter from Robert Pierson, president of the General Conference, advising him that the plan was now settled to consolidate the Voice of Prophecy, Faith for Today, and It Is Written. Richards' response to his diary was still optimistic and hopeful: "Even yet, God may order otherwise."

Undoubtedly the planned consolidation was a sincerely held concept, and Richards' continued opposition troubled the leadership. In May they put him on a committee to raise $130,000 to build a new Seventh-day Adventist 250,000-watt radio station in Lisbon, Portugal. It was something they knew he had been urging for years, and perhaps felt this would soothe what they considered were his ruffled feelings. "Why have they waited all these years?" he lamented in his diary. "Now when I am old and sorrowful in soul about the planned execution of the Voice of Prophecy, why am I asked to do anything like this!"

The same day he received another letter, listing his name with another group to choose a site for the new Adventist Media Center. "Why am I put on this committee for this coming complex for the non-descript three-headed arrangement. . . . All I can say is, 'Behold there come three woes more hereafter.'"

As the days and months passed, it became increasingly clear that the Adventist Media Center was a fait accompli. Richards never reconciled himself to the idea. He foresaw that as problems and expenses increased, the church leadership would recommend and institute tighter consolidation and less autonomy for each ministry in a futile attempt to save more money. Recognizing that each of the television and radio ministries had separate and distinct needs and goals, he feared that each ministry would little by little lose all control over their own destiny.

Richards' views were prophetic. The time came, after his death, when financial times became so critical that the church eliminated the manager and treasurer positions and operating boards of each ministry and created a central Adventist Media Center Board.

Strange as it seems, not one of the media ministers, H.M.S. Richards, Jr.; Dan Matthews; or George Vandeman belonged to the board, and thus they had virtually nothing to say about the plans and operations of their own ministries.

In his diary for June 6, 1978, you will find this bittersweet note: "This is the first of three days to be devoted to move the Voice of Prophecy, body and soul, body mainly. Big vans—Bekins. It's a sad day for me in spite of my desire not to be sad! However, we are of one mind to do our little best to work with the Lord for all the success His blessing will bring to us and all others. It is our prayer to do the will of the Lord faithfully and with His joy!"

Years later, at Richards' funeral, Graham Maxwell remembered a story he had heard Wilbur Alexander tell of those troubling days. Maxwell reminded us that "it's no secret that he wasn't very enthusiastic about the move to Thousand Oaks, to say the least. But did that make him disloyal to his church? Not for a moment. Yesterday at the graveside, Wilbur Alexander told the story of the Fall Council meeting when the arguments were presented to move to Thousand Oaks, Elder Richards did his best to present the other side, but the vote didn't go his way. When it was all over they asked if he would pronounce the benediction. 'Oh,' he said, 'I cannot benedict something I don't think is entirely right.' There was no hypocrisy in him. But you didn't see him pack up and leave, did you?

"I like to think that some day Elder Richards will bring this up to the Lord in heaven. 'Tell me, Lord, did You really want us to move the Voice from Chevy Chase to Thousand Oaks?' I can imagine the Lord saying, 'Well, to tell you the truth, We really would have preferred that you move the whole thing to Geneva. Or maybe if you'd moved the whole thing to Guam, you could have kept an eye on that powerful transmitter to make sure they tell the truth to the billions over there.' And I can see Elder Richards smiling back and saying, 'Lord, You always were far ahead of us, and we were always trying to catch up.'"

Maxwell was right. Richards never had small plans. He kept in close touch with the Lord, and I think through his ministry, the Lord kept in close touch with him.

Was he wrong to resist the consolidation of the media ministries? Who knows? In Glendale the Voice of Prophecy had a comfortable, though modest, place to work. It was paid for. On the other hand, the campus of the Adventist Media Center in Thousand Oaks was beautiful and the offices were spacious. It was the pride of the denomination. No one needed to be ashamed of the three magnificent buildings set on 14 acres of land along Rancho Conejo a few blocks from the freeway. It was a delightful place to work.

But as the years went by, at least for a time, every one of the media ministries went into decline. Eventually, after some 20 years at that location, the Adventist Media Center sold all its buildings to the Amgen Pharmaceutical Company, and the center moved to smaller offices a few miles away in Simi Valley.

Some have argued that the ministries might very well have gone into decline even if left to themselves. That is possibly true. No one knows what would have happened had we continued to run our own show. But it would have been our own plans or lack of the same that would have brought us down. Richards thought that we each should have been allowed to succeed or fail on our own. He had a good point.

By the same token, we don't know the future. At the moment of writing, things are looking brighter at the Adventist Media Center. What will happen in the future? Only God knows.

God works with human beings, and human beings make mistakes. Anyone who suffers from the hallucination that every committee decision has heaven's endorsement is extremely naive. But I will never forget the wise words of Elder W. A. Spicer. A group of us dormitory boys were standing in the halls of Maplewood Academy in Minnesota, talking to the old pioneer. He had been conducting a Week of Prayer at our school, and we confided in him that we weren't happy with some of the decisions the faculty had imposed on us. Elder Spicer at that time was retired and in his late seventies.

"Well, boys," he said with a twinkle in his eye, "through the years I've seen the brethren make some terrible mistakes. Terrible mistakes. But I've also been surprised at how often the mistakes of the brethren have seemed to work out."

Through the succeeding years those words of advice from a wise old man have stuck with me. I always remember them in connection with the passage in Romans 8:28, in which the apostle reminds us that "all things work together for good to them that love God, to them who are the called according to his purpose."

Paul doesn't say that all things that happen are good, but that God can take our mistakes, our fumbling efforts to do the right thing, and even when we make serious errors in judgment, God can work things out to fit His eternal purposes.

Elder Richards would have subscribed to that bit of theology, too.

FADING IN BODY, STRONG IN FAITH

In the years following the election of Harold, Jr., as speaker-director of the Voice of Prophecy, father and son worked in close harmony.

Harold, Jr., was eager to begin a radio program to reach the world's youth, but his idea hit a snag when the committee tried to determine what kind of music it should use. One group urged contemporary music in order to appeal to youth. Those opposed to it felt strongly that the conservative donor base that supported the Voice of Prophecy would not accept such music. Eventually the VOP decided that instead of a youth radio program, the Voice of Prophecy would prepare youth Bible lessons that it called WAYOUT. Young Paul Johnson wrote the lessons, and the VOP printed them with colorful layouts. It was an immediate success.

Paul used language that was common among the youth culture that had just come out of the troubled 1960s. Though H.M.S. was past 75 years of age, he saw the value of appealing to youth. His chronological age did not blind him to what Harold was trying to do for youth through the WAYOUT ministry.

As we mentioned before, during the years following Richards' retirement, daughter, Virginia, and son-in-law, Walt Cason, arranged to have him lead a number of tours to Europe through the cities of the Reformation—Germany, Scotland, Ireland, England, France, Switzerland; and to Bible lands—Israel, Egypt, Turkey, Syria, Lebanon, Greece, Italy. Between 1967 and 1978 H.M.S. would direct 20 such tours, with Walt and Virginia carrying the entire load of planning and managing, allowing H.M.S. to do what he did best—provide spiritual inspiration and historical background to what the traveling group was seeing. It was a wonderful shot in the arm for H.M.S., and it also blessed the hundreds of people who eagerly lined up year after year to travel with him, to soak up his wisdom about the Bible and history.

My wife Sharon and I were privileged to tag along on a Bible lands tour in 1976. As we were visiting the pyramids in Egypt I was amused to see how Richards handled the sometimes overly aggressive camel drivers.

I had to admire those young men who over the course of years had developed a technique to get more "baksheesh," extra money in tips from those who rented the camels. They could carry on a modest conversation in a variety of languages. As they strode along beside you while you teetered precariously atop those ungainly ships of the desert, they would size you up and venture a few words in different languages. If you were fair-skinned, they would try out a variety of European languages on you until they found one that got a response.

Richards invariably stumped them, however. Whenever they would speak a few words in some language to him, he would respond in a gibberish that sounded like a language, but wasn't. I would see them cock their heads and try out another language on him, only to get the same response. Finally they would give up in bewilderment.

I had seen him use the same technique on panhandlers in Manhattan. When some drifter would approach him for "a dime for a cup of coffee" as he sat in our car waiting for the quartet to take some pictures or see some sights, he'd look intently at them and go through his gibberish routine. The beggars invariably would retire in confusion and not bother him further.

In the middle of July 1971 I started out on my last trip with the Voice of Prophecy radio group. For me it was a time of sorrow. I had been traveling with Richards on such trips for 24 years. It had been the joy of my life to be associated with such a man. He had changed my life. Every person who ever worked with H.M.S. Richards will confess to the same thing. Now this unique blessing was coming to a close. On that trip we attended camp meetings in Arizona, Oklahoma, Michigan, and Wisconsin, finally ending up in Soquel, California, on August 7, 1971. He graciously gave me a wonderful tribute at that last meeting. "The King's Heralds will never be the same again!" he said. "No one can imitate his voice and personality! Thank God for him!" How could I not help but love such a man? Incidentally, the media center hired John Ramsey to take my place, and to my chagrin the quartet didn't miss me at all. They sang on without missing a beat.

When I dropped out of the quartet, the Voice of Prophecy asked me to stay on as a writer and producer of a new daily 15-minute broadcast, and also help H.M.S. answer letters from radio listeners. I continued in that role until I retired 19 years later.

In December of 1971, when Al Munson became president of the "Tripartite Conflation of *Faith for Today, It Is Written,* and *Voice of Prophecy,*" as Richards sometimes called it, Elder Daniel Guild became manager of the VOP. He and Richards—both father and son—got on beautifully. Guild had a wonderful knack for organization. This took a great load from Harold's back, and was a source of relief to H.M.S. to have someone in the saddle in whom he had confidence.

It broke Richards' heart when his young evangelist protégé, Dick Barron, died in a tragic plane crash in April of 1972. He had seen Dick recover several years before from what everyone thought would be a fatal cancer of the back that had put him out of any active service for years. Young Dick, after he was miraculously healed, had gone with Richards, father and son, on a world trip to Adventist mission stations. It was incomprehensible to Richards that death should take Dick, in the prime of life, from his work for the Lord.

On June 1, 1972, his own 19-year-old granddaughter, "sweet Betty Rae," received fatal injuries in an automobile accident. She died in spite of all that the skilled physicians of Loma Linda Medical Center could do to save her. "Why is one so sweet, so young, so beautiful, suddenly taken away from life, and the old and decayed left in a form of life?" he asked his diary. "Our own dearest GeGe has her first great loss of her own beautiful child. May our loving Christ and Saviour comfort her tonight." It was also his first loss of a child or grandchild.

On July 9, 1972, Richards agreed to perform the wedding ceremony for me and Sharon Bullard, my bride. It had been almost five years since I had lost my wife Irene to cancer. Now the Chief rejoiced with me that I had found a companion to share my life and help me care for my children. He married us in the Chapel of the Roses in Pasadena.

The next month Al Munson, who had accepted the responsibility as president of the new Adventist Media Center, suffered a mild heart attack. It should have been a warning to Al, but for the next four years he would throw all his energy and talents into building the magnificent Adventist Media Center buildings in Thousand Oaks. It was no small task trying to find funds to construct the $7,000,000 project. He would not live to see the components move into their new headquarters. Another massive heart attack claimed his life in late 1976. The Voice of Prophecy would not move into their new building until June 1978. Elder Robert Frame from Australia now became president of the Adventist Media Center in Al's place.

In September 1972 Richards' youngest son Jan phoned to say he had been offered a teaching position in the California State University system. "May God use him greatly there or in one of our schools," he wrote in his diary. He had long been hoping Jan would find a place either as a pastor or as a teacher in the Seventh-day

Adventist work force, but recognized that God could use his youngest son wherever he was.

A month later (October), as H.M.S. concluded one of his Bible lands tours, he flew directly from Rome to Mexico City to attend the Adventist Autumn Council meetings. At that time he was still hoping that something would abort the proposed amalgamation of the Adventist radio and TV organizations.

The next month (November) Virginia informed him she was planning to write a book about him. He expressed his view that it would be inappropriate to have such "an elitist type book on him as a servant of Christ," but when *Man Alive* finally came off the press, he was gratified that his only daughter thought so highly of him that she put many hours of love in such a beautiful tribute to her dad.

As he approached 80 years of age he continued to experience what we all do when we reach that stage of life. He saw his peers begin to drop in quick succession. In March of 1972 he had attended the funeral of his old friend and classmate, Bill Scharffenberg. Bill had been sick only a week and died quickly of a massive heart attack.

The following January Aletha Detamore, wife of Fordyce, his old companion at arms, died.

In April he visited Martha Bietz in the hospital. Martha was the wife of his fellow minister, R. R. Bietz. Suffering from terminal cancer, she would live only a short while longer.

The next month he visited fellow minister Robert Thomas, also suffering from cancer. Thomas was the young man who had swaggered into his meetings in Santa Barbara more than 40 years before, smoking his cigarette, ready to fight the usher who asked him to take off his hat and put out his cigarette.

In March 1973 Braulio Perez, the speaker-director of the Spanish language *La Voz de la Esperanza,* died of a heart attack in his sleep.

On February 14 of the next year he was stunned to hear of the tragic death of Jerry Pettis, his pastor friend from Phoenix days. Jerry was a U. S. Congressman from the San Bernardino district. He had been flying his Beech Bonanza from Palm Springs to Loma Linda in marginal weather and had struck the top of a cloud-shrouded mountain in Banning Pass. Richards would preach Jerry's funeral service on February 18 at Loma Linda with 80 of Jerry's fellow congresspersons present. His text for Jerry's funeral sermon was from 2 Samuel 1: "My Brother Jonathan."

The next month he conducted the funeral sermon for Reuben Nightingale. He had held Pauline's funeral service three years before. Reuben had been a teenager singing in the choir for Richards' meetings in Bakersfield almost 50 years before, and later as a young minister he and Pauline had worked with Richards in many of his Los Angeles evangelistic campaigns.

In October he preached the funeral sermon for Thomas Jefferson Hooper, father of Wayne, longtime member of the King's Heralds quartet.

A few days later he received news that Bob Seamount was in surgery in Orlando, Florida. The physicians found an inoperable brain tumor.

Several times in late 1973 and early 1974 he visited my daughter-in-law, Lee, who was in the Glendale Adventist Hospital suffering from acute granulacitic leukemia. The physicians had discovered the disease when she had entered the hospital to have her baby. On Valentine's Day, 1974, he wrote in his diary: "I met Bob Edwards' son in the hall—three seconds later met Bob who told me his son's wife had just died. She leaves an eight-month-old baby, and a seven-year-old girl. What sorrow and pain in this world!"

In March of 1976 he preached the funeral sermon of John W. Osborn, his fellow minister. John and his brother Calvin had been little boys sitting on the front row of Sabbath school and church when Richards was a student pastor at the Capitol Hill church in Washington, D.C., in 1918 and 1919.

That June his old "ape man" friend, Manuel Mancuso, died. Manny had performed in his ape suit for many of Richards' evangelistic meetings when he preached on evolution.

In January of 1977 he was asked to preach the funeral sermon for

Doctor Harry Miller, the "China Doctor," at Loma Linda. Dr. Miller was 97 when he died.

The next month he attended the memorial service for Walter E. Atkin, manager of the Voice of Prophecy during the traumatic days when Richards' beloved King's Heralds quartet had been uprooted.

Later the same year he attended the funeral of Chester Turner, brother of Ray Turner, bass for years in the King's Heralds.

On November 20, 1977, he preached the funeral service for Elder G. A. Roberts. Roberts was "a very fine man and good friend," Richards wrote in his diary. "Elder Roberts was my president in Southern California years ago when I was in evangelism when I started radio. He was very kind to me, utterly sincere and faithful to God. He started the trust work for our whole denomination and world field. He gathered material to start the index of the writings of Ellen White. . . . In some ways he started more activities than any worker, including a General Conference president, except James White. That's my view."

On the last day of the Adventist General Conference session in Vienna in 1975, at the age of 80, he wrote, "It impressed me deeply that at least I would never again see most of the old friends here today in this world. So goodbye till we meet by the Big River at last."

As he attended that General Conference he was reading a book by D. A. Delafield about Ellen G. White in Europe. Delafield's book reprinted a letter from Louis R. Conradi to Ellen White. Conradi was a prominent Adventist leader until he separated from the church in 1932, because he couldn't fully accept Ellen White's ministry in her role as a special messenger of the Lord. Conradi joined the Seventh Day Baptists. Richards remembered that Conradi had approached him during his early days in the ministry in Canada, inviting him to help develop the Adventist Church in Europe. "Whatever would have become of me had I done so?" he asked his diary. "God delivered me."

As his generation fell asleep in Jesus in quick succession, it brought his own mortality into sharper focus, but it didn't stop his enthusiasm, even though his vital energies had begun to flag.

In October 1974 he performed the first marriage ceremony of a grandchild, that of Laura Dale Cason.

Mabel and H.M.S. were in Jerusalem on one of the Bible lands trips for their own fifty-fifth wedding anniversary. On the evening of April 13 she had asked him if he would write her a poem in honor of their anniversary the next day. He didn't tell her that he had already composed one several days before and had been keeping it in his pocket until the 14th as a surprise to her.

"Our special day has come again,
And we are still alive—
My sweetheart bride of twenty years
When I was twenty-five.

"The fleeting hours have touched our lives,
Have left their marks and fled;
But still our hearts are just the same
As on the day we wed.

"When April 14 comes around
Your cheeks are rosy still,
And when I share your loving kiss
I find the same old thrill.

"Our married years are fifty-five,
And more to come, I pray;
Just like the ones already past
Since our blest wedding day.

"And may the love I now renew
Be ever as alive
As when my bride was twenty years,
And I was twenty-five."

In 1977 when someone began to print a small "yellow rag" publication attacking some of the leaders in the church, Richards resented it. "When I see the caricatures of some of our leading brethren going the rounds—and can agree that some of the things criticized do need to be changed—yet when critics descend to this mudslinging I deeply resent it. It's crude, heathen, and wicked in my view. Typical of this age! Which knows not the Lord nor loves Him or His followers. As it was said of old, 'We shall all eventually go to our own place.' Have mercy upon us, O Lord."

In August 1978 Mabel and H.M.S. went to the Glendale Adventist Hospital to visit their old friend Dan Kaplan who many years before had loaned them their first car—the old Starr coupe. The Starr was the car in which Mabel learned to drive. Kaplan was near death's door.

I unearthed from his correspondence file a letter he wrote to a hotel in Tokyo when he was 86 years of age. It is notable only because it shows his sensitive conscience. In it he enclosed a check for $170.

"Sirs:

"I write this letter for a personal reason. Many years ago, between 1960 and 1966 I believe, my son and I stayed for one night in your very fine hotel. In the morning, when we paid up our bill at the desk, the clerk was very busy as several people were in a hurry and leaving at the same time.

"After leaving the desk and starting on our way, I felt in my pocket, and it seemed to me that I had more money than I should have as change from the clerk, and I felt that he had made a mistake. I do not know to this day whether he did or did not, or how much he gave me.

"Whether I made a mistake, he made a mistake, I want to be sure that everything is right. In case the clerk made a mistake and gave me too much money in the amount of $20 or $30, I propose to pay the hotel with some interest. You will find in this letter a bank draft with $170, which I believe will about cover it at this time.

"Whether there has been a mistake or not, it is only right for me to do my best as a Christian to clear everything up that could possibly be *wrong. I am 86 years old and know that I will not be in this world too much longer. Some day all men must meet the great judge of eternity. I am a disciple of Jesus Christ, who instructed all men to live peaceably and honestly with one another. This we must all do to please Him, the Saviour of the world.*

"The teachings of the Lord Jesus Christ, which it is my greatest desire to follow, are found in the Holy Bible, especially the New Testament section. Jesus taught that men and women on this earth should seek to have an honest and good heart. (See Saint Luke 8:15.) And His great apostle, Saint Paul, declared that the disciples of Jesus should seek to owe no man anything but to love one another (Romans 13:8).

"God bless all of you there at the hotel, and all the kind people who live in beautiful Japan.

"Most sincerely,
"H.M.S. Richards."

On August 22, 1982, in a flower garden at the new Voice of Prophecy headquarters in Thousand Oaks, H.M.S. Richards with Harold, Jr., conducted the wedding ceremony of longtime Voice of Prophecy staff member, Joe Santos, to his bride, Mary Lou Cote. My 4-year-old son, David, was the Bible boy. It was the Chief's last public appearance.

One week later a magnificent eighty-eighth birthday tribute had been scheduled for him in the Glendale Civic Auditorium, but he would not be present. On August 25, in his library in back of the home on Bywood Drive, Richards suffered a stroke from which he never recovered. The great mind would never again be the same.

THE LAST CHAPTER HASN'T BEEN WRITTEN

On Sunday evening, August 29, 1982, the surprise birthday testimonial convened in the Glendale, California, Civic Auditorium. Richards would have been embarrassed to be there and hear the tributes paid to him from friends across the country and around the world. But four days before the testimonial dinner he had suffered a severe stroke while working in his library study at home.

United States Congressman Moorhead from the 27th Congressional District, in which Richards resided, was there in person to read a letter from the president of the United States, Ronald Reagan, and his wife Nancy.

A letter came from California Senator S. I. Hayakawa, and from Governor Edmund G. Brown, Jr., of California.

Participants read letters from California Attorney General George Deukmajian and Los Angeles Mayor Tom Bradley.

Oswald C. J. Hoffman, speaker of the *Lutheran Hour* broadcast and an old friend of Richards, sent his personal greetings, and taped greetings came from General Conference President, Neal Wilson.

Elder Charles Bradford was at the dinner in person to bring his tribute to Elder Richards. He reminded us of the time he was scheduled to preach while H.M.S. Richards was on the platform. "Elder Richards," he said to him, "you should be preaching tonight."

Richards just laughed and said, "Brad, rare back on your hind legs and preach."

Elmer Walde was there, as was Harold Young, who had been one of the four young men who at times would go with Richards for a weekend retreat in the mountains above Los Angeles. Harold Young recounted the time he had shamed Richards into starting to preach on radio.

Louis Venden, master of ceremonies for the evening, reminded us that in the early days many good and sincere people believed radio to be a tool of the devil that Adventists shouldn't use, but that didn't stop Richards.

Pastor Morris Venden gave the keynote address. Morry remembered when the Voice of Prophecy radio group had come to town in their big black Cadillac—the one once owned by a movie star. He described how he and the other little children had pressed around that Cadillac to see the people inside. All they could think of was the Mafia or John Dillinger riding in such a big, long black car. Then they saw a tall preacher with horn-rimmed glasses get out, along with another big man and some singers. It had been one little boy's first introduction to the Voice of Prophecy and H.M.S. Richards.

Later, as a teenager in high school, Morry heard Richards speak in a tremendous camp-meeting auditorium in Soquel, California. His teenage heart had strangely warmed as Richards preached on "The Three Circles of God's Love," and on "Who Broke the Sacred Heart of Jesus?" Venden noted that no matter what Richards' sermon subject, he always seemed to get around to preaching about Jesus—always Jesus.

When Morry went to college God led him to study to become a preacher himself. During his college years his class attended a great Bible conference in Washington, D.C. Highly educated Bible scholars read scholarly papers all week, but the preacher in the horn-rimmed glasses gave a devotional at the Bible conference. He had talked about Barnabas, an early Christian leader, and took his text from Acts 11:24: "For he was a good man, full of the Holy Ghost and of faith: and much people was added unto the Lord."

For the next 40 minutes Morry presented tribute to the modern Barnabas who was "a good man, full of the Holy Ghost and of faith: and much people was added unto the Lord."

Venden remembered Richards and the quartet coming to camp meeting after he had become a young minister. After the meeting he had sought Richards out.

"Elder Richards," Morry said, "I'd like to talk to you about righteousness by faith."

"Is there any other kind?" Richards replied.

Later Morry and some fellow ministers visited Richards' study-library behind his home on Bywood Drive in Glendale. Someone pointed up the hill to the place where Richards often went—that spot on the mountain where he could see the great city of Los Angeles fading out into the smog. "That's where Richards goes to pray for the city of Los Angeles," the others told Venden.

Morry was present at Pacific Union College when a student interviewed Richards. "What is the central part of the Adventist message?" the student asked.

"Jesus only," Richards replied. "Jesus only."

As we went home from that testimonial dinner that night, those words continued to burn into our own hearts: "For he was a good man, full of the Holy Ghost and of faith: and much people was added unto the Lord."

Richards was a good man. He was a kind man. Sometimes, though, he would become provoked, usually at himself for forgetting his hat in a restaurant or some other such trivial thing. The strongest expletive I ever heard him utter was, "Oh, pshaw!" No profanity or near profanity. Just "Oh, pshaw!" spoken with vehemence.

After his stroke his great mind was never the same. One Sabbath afternoon the King's Men male chorus, a group of men who sang from time to time for the *Voice of Prophecy* broadcast, decided to visit the Chief at the Ventura Estates rehabilitation center near Thousand Oaks. We wheeled him in his chair to the big lobby and gathering around him sang several songs as friends and visitors watched and listened. As we closed we decided to sing our familiar *Voice of Prophecy* prayer theme: "Near to the Heart of God."

> *"There is a place of quiet rest,*
> *Near to the heart of God;*
> *A place where sin cannot molest,*
> *Near to the heart of God."*

Then we began to hum the chorus—the place where for 40 years he had come in speaking the words—

> *"Oh, Jesus blest Redeemer,*
> *Sent from the heart of God;*
> *Hold us who bow before Thee,*
> *Near to the heart of God."*

But this time as we hummed there was only silence. Tears came to our eyes as his broken mind reached for the familiar words, but could no longer make the connection.

Elmer Walde remembers the time in late 1983 or early 1984 when he went out to Ventura Estates to visit the Chief. It was the last time he was to see him alive. As Walde wheeled the thin figure out onto the lawn, Richards' eyes darted back and forth from tree to tree. He told Elmer he was watching "the birds," but Walde couldn't see any birds.

All of a sudden Richards turned and said, "Elmer, are you going to General Conference?"

Walde, who had retired by this time, answered, "No, Chief, I'm just going to trust the brethren."

Richards leaned over with a mischievously wicked smile on his face. "Elmer, do you think we can really trust the brethren?" Then he turned and began to watch "the birds" again.

His son Kenneth faithfully went to see Father nearly every day. Knowing how much he had always loved to read, Kenneth would read to him from the Bible, or from some of the great books Dad had always treasured. His father would sit silently, sometimes registering comprehension, sometimes not.

Del Delker remembers the time she visited. For a few minutes they talked about the Lord, his favorite subject. He was most lucid when he was talking and thinking about God.

"Do you still talk to Him, Chief?" she asked.

"Every day," he answered with solemn, wide-open gaze. "Every day."

The great heart continued to beat for 32 months after the great mind could no longer track as it had done so faithfully for 88 years; then on April 24, 1985, it stopped.

On Friday, April 26, the family and a few close friends gathered for a final goodbye at Montecito Memorial Park in Loma Linda, California, but the next day, on Sabbath, friends who had loved him packed the Loma Linda Seventh-day Adventist Church.

As I sat there on the platform that day, remembering, I thought about how the Chief had loved to preach about the soon coming of Jesus. One of those sermons he called "The Christmas Yet to Come." Jesus came as a baby to Bethlehem 2,000 years ago, but He's coming yet again. There's "A Christmas Yet to Come."

Thousands of Richards' friends and fellow workers crowded into the church that Sabbath afternoon in honor of his memory. One of the most beautiful poems the Chief ever wrote was about the resurrection. Wayne Hooper set the words of "It's Always Morning" to music. I was asked to sing it to open the memorial service:

> *"When it is night, with shadows deep and still,*
> *And all the cloudy flags of day are furled;*

However dark the hour, remember, friend,
  It's always morning somewhere in the world.

"In the soul's night, when every star is gone,
  And love's bright chalice into fragments hurled;
Ah, heart know this, the sun will shine again;
  It's morning always somewhere in the world.

"Long, long ago, within a garden close,
  A stone was moved before the dawn had pearled;
And One arose victorious over death;
  So now it's always morning in the world;
So now it's always morning in the world."

Daniel Guild, Louis Venden, Robert Frame, J. L. Tucker, Walter Blehm, Graham Maxwell, Wayne Hooper—all had their own personal memories of Richards. Just before Charles E. Bradford's sermon, the surviving members of his old King's Heralds quartet sang what H.M.S. had often called his favorite song, "Still, Still With Thee." He loved the words of the poem by Harriet Beecher Stowe. We always urged him to introduce that song before we sang.

"Harriet Beecher Stowe was a mother," he would begin. "She was the sister of the great preacher, Henry Ward Beecher, and the wife of another preacher. Sometimes, as it is with mothers, when the pressures would seem to get more than she could bear, she would go into a little room and close the door. The children knew that was mother's prayer room, and they would whisper as they played around the house while Mother was in her prayer room. There Mother would find comfort and restoration of mind and heart.

"One morning, early, she went into that little prayer room and wrote the words of the song the King's Heralds sing now, 'Still, still with Thee, when purple morning breaketh.'"

Then we would sing—

"Still, still with thee, when purple morning breaketh,
  When the bird waketh, and the shadows flee;
Fairer than morning, lovelier than the daylight,
  Dawns the sweet consciousness, I am with Thee.

"Alone with Thee, amid the mystic shadows,
  The solemn hush of nature newly born;
Alone with Thee in breathless adoration,
  In the calm dew and freshness of the morn.

"So shall it be at last, in that bright morning,
  When the soul waketh and life's shadows flee;
O in that hour, fairer than daylight dawning,
  Shall rise the glorious thought, I am with Thee."

Charles E. Bradford in his memorial sermon reminded us that Dwight L. Moody was said to have depopulated hell by one million souls. "H.M.S. Richards is responsible under God for adding multiplied thousands to the Lamb's Book of Life.

"H.M.S. Richards was a man of the future," Bradford said. "In fact, his future orientation was so strong that his whole life was bent that way. That tall frame always was bending toward the future. His whole life, his face was turned toward the city, 'the city that hath foundations, whose builder and maker is God.' He looked for a new heavens and a new earth.

"In the words of the song the King's Heralds sang, 'So, shall it be at last, in that bright morning, . . . when the soul waketh and life's shadows flee. . . . O, in that hour, fairer than daylight dawning, . . . shall rise the glorious thought, I am with Thee.'

"And Harold Marshall Sylvester Richards shall awake clothed in his new equipment. His new eyes will blink for the first time, his new heart will beat, new life will thrill through his body, every nerve will be atingle. And he shall see Him in whom his soul has delighted, Him whom he has placarded before the world, pictured

327

Him dying, buried, risen, ascended, and coming again. And Harold Marshall Sylvester Richards shall be satisfied."

To conclude the memorial service, Del Delker sang the song that builds on the words of Jesus in John 14:1-3—"Let Not Your Heart Be Troubled."

As family and close friends had gathered around his casket on the previous day, just before it was lowered into its resting place beside his father and mother, near his granddaughter Betty Rae, the attendant was asked to open the casket so that we might have one last view through our tears at Richards' face resting peacefully.

The story of a person's life must come to an end. The final chapter must be written, but the last chapter of the life of H.M.S. Richards has not yet been written.

Richards loved to preach about the second coming of Christ: "When God Writes 'Thirty' for Tonight," "Yesterday Is Tomorrow," "Five Minutes to Twelve," "The Last Prayer in the Bible," "The Christmas Yet to Come." He would often conclude with this story:

"In the days before the discovery of the New World, the Spanish minted a gold coin. On its face was the picture of the Pillars of Hercules, that gateway to the Atlantic Ocean from the Mediterranean. Etched on the coin were the words 'Ne Plus Ultra,' 'No more beyond.' Then Christopher Columbus and his men sailed out through those giant gates. His men were fearful that their ships would fall off the edge of the world, but by great vision and daring they reached a new world. The new gold coins that came from the Spanish mints now read 'Plus Ultra,' 'More Beyond.'

"When Jesus came from the tomb, He gave us the eternal hope of 'More Beyond.' This life isn't the end of the story. There's 'More Beyond.'"

As we said our goodbyes to our "Chief" that Friday afternoon, we remembered the words he had uttered so many times in his sermons to remind listeners that Jesus was coming soon.

"I want to be living when Jesus comes," he said, "but it may be in the providence of God that I'll go to sleep for a little while. People may tell you, 'Richards has gone to his final resting place,' but if you ever hear that, don't you believe it! They're never going to get me in any *final* resting place. Oh, I may go to sleep for a while. I may take a little nap until Jesus comes, but when the voice of the Lifegiver shouts His command, I'm going to look in His blessed face."

The poem Richards wrote about his mother, "When Mother Tucks Me In," is a fitting benediction to the life of H.M.S. Richards:

> *"How the changing years have borne me*
>   *Far away from days of home!*
> *Now no Mother bends above me*
>   *When the time for sleep has come.*
> *But it gives my poor heart comfort,*
>   *And it brings me rest within,*
> *Just to dream that I am little*
>   *And my Mother tucks me in.*
>
> *"As I kneel there with my brother*
>   *By the bed above the stairs,*
> *And I hear my gentle Mother*
>   *Whisper, 'Boys, remember prayers!'*
> *Then she comes and prays beside us,*
>   *'Father, keep them from all sin.'*
> *Oh! her kiss is tender, loving,*
>   *When my Mother tucks me in.*
>
> *"When at last the evening finds me*
>   *And life's busy day is done,*
> *All the bands of earth that bind me*
>   *Shall be broken one by one.*
> *Then, O Lord, be Thou my comfort,*
>   *Calm my soul Thy peace to win;*
> *Let me fall asleep as gently*
>   *As when Mother tucked me in."*